A DISCERNING CHURCH

A Discerning Church

Pope Francis, Lonergan, and a Theological Method for the Future

---

THEOLOGY AT THE FRONTIERS

Gerard Whelan, SJ

Foreword by Robert M. Doran, SJ

Paulist Press
New York / Mahwah, NJ

Cover image by DavidZydd/iStock.com
Cover design by Dawn Massa, Lightly Salted Graphics
Book design by Lynn Else

Library of Congress Cataloging-in-Publication Data
Names: Whelan, Gerard, 1959– author.
Title: A discerning church : Pope Francis, Lonergan, and a theological method for the future / Gerard Whelan, SJ.
Description: New York : Paulist Press, 2019. | Series: Theology at the frontiers series | Includes bibliographical references and index.
Identifiers: LCCN 2018042428 (print) | LCCN 2018048469 (ebook) | ISBN 9781587688386 (ebook) | ISBN 9780809154463 (pbk. : alk. paper)
Subjects: LCSH: Francis, Pope, 1936- | Lonergan, Bernard J. F. | Theology–Methodology. | Vatican Council (2nd : 1962–1965 : Basilica di San Pietro in Vaticano) | Lonergan, Bernard J. F. Method in theology.
Classification: LCC BX1378.7 (ebook) | LCC BX1378.7 .W44 2019 (print) | DDC 230/.2092—dc23
LC record available at https://lccn.loc.gov/2018042428

ISBN 978-0-8091-5446-3 (paperback)
ISBN 978-1-58768-838-6 (e-book)

Published by Paulist Press
997 Macarthur Boulevard
Mahwah, New Jersey 07430
www.paulistpress.com

Printed and bound in the
United States of America

Contents

Foreword

MY EARLIEST ACQUAINTANCE with Jorge Mario Bergoglio occurred in 2007, when I read what has come to be referred to as the Aparecida document, the concluding document of the General Conference of the Episcopal Council of Latin American Bishops held in Aparecida, Brazil, in 2007. It is well known that the then Cardinal Bergoglio was the principal author of this document, and it can easily be shown how often he has returned to it in his pontificate as Pope Francis.

To say that I was very positively impressed by the document would be an understatement. Its effect on me was deeper than that, and for at least two reasons.

First, I sensed the presence of grace in the very framing of the document. As Bernard Lonergan has emphasized in his overlooked thesis on actual grace in his 1946 work "De Ente Supernaturali," actual grace is partly a matter of insights that are more than the product of human ingenuity and intelligence.[1] I had the sense that this document was the result of a complex series of such insights, of human collaboration with divine guidance, of a very profound exercise of the ministry of the word in cooperation with the Divine Word. I thought the document was a treasure that we could not afford to lose. This evaluation was part of the reason I was overjoyed by the election of Cardinal Bergoglio to the Chair of Peter in 2013.

Second, and more self-referentially, the document is very *simpatico* with emphases that I had absorbed from the work of Bernard Lonergan and had developed in my own work, especially in *Theology and the Dialectics of History*.[2] It is very interesting that the Aparecida document (and its author!) have drawn reactions from left and right in the church that are very similar to those that Lonergan's work has sparked. For years, I have maintained that some of the resistance to Lonergan's work from the ecclesial left is due simply to the fact that, for all his creativity, which most acknowledge, he remains orthodox, while some on the ecclesial right, wary of the radical implications of his work for ecclesial reform, might perhaps wish that he were not orthodox, so that they could more effectively take issue with him. Again, for some on the social and political left, Lonergan's suspicion of some forms of social activism smacks of intellectual elitism, while neoliberals are offended by his insistence on such things as a social dividend on profit that morally must be reinvested in the economic process rather than accumulated in the pockets of the 1 percent. In 2007, I began to suspect that if the framers of the Aparecida document were to become familiar with Lonergan's work, their response to it might be like that of Carlo Maria Cardinal Martini, who seems to have adopted Lonergan as the principal theological figure influencing his exercise of episcopal ministry.

In this very fine book, Gerard Kevin Whelan, SJ, has developed several ways in which the philosophical, theological, economic, and methodological work of Lonergan and the thoughtful, profound, deeply spiritual resonances of Pope Francis's pontificate lend themselves to a convergence that would promote and advance the most authentic emphases of each. Whelan has emphasized especially (and correctly) the resistance of both Lonergan and the pope to what Lonergan has dubbed classicism. Even before reading this book, I had been saying in casual conversations that Pope Francis is probably the first nonclassicist pope, the first who does not take a particular set of cultural meanings and values, however noble they may have been in their origins, as normative for genuine humanity. Whelan has also correctly suggested that the main source of resistance within the church to Pope Francis's agenda and style comes from the *stylus curiae* that infects a large segment of the church's hierarchy and that is classicist to the core, even when the hierarchs cannot trace their cultural lineage to European roots. Let me draw attention to two comments made by Lonergan that would seem to anticipate Pope Francis's criticism of that form of classicism rampant in the Catholic Church that we know as clericalism.

The first is found in notes that Lonergan wrote for a course titled "De Systemate et Historia" (System and History) taught at the Gregorian University in the fall of 1959. The significance of this course is clear from its title: Lonergan is attempting to work his way toward a systematic theology where the system is provided not by a set of objects, but by the normative Christian subject achieving an appropriation of his or her cognitive and existential operations. The system breaks from classicism and takes historical mindedness seriously, thus generating a sequence of systematic positions that continues to develop over time, that adapts to changing circumstances, and that is prepared to tackle new questions, all without abandoning the "rock" that establishes continuity. This rock is the Christian subject in love with God and performing his or her tasks attentively, intelligently, reasonably, and responsibly. Among the obstacles in the way of such a goal is what Lonergan calls "premature systematization," and among the "isms" that Lonergan accuses of premature systematization are "feudalism, liberalism, capitalism, socialism, nationalism, *clericalism*, and anticlericalism."[3]

A second, similar comment is found in Lonergan's lecture notes for the course he taught titled, *"De Methodo Theologiae"* (The Method of Theology), in the spring of 1962. Here, Lonergan is interested in the differentiation and integration of "worlds," where "world" refers to "determinate combinations" of objects generated from "a group of combinations of differentiated operations." In this course, Lonergan differentiated worlds into sacred and profane, interior and exterior, visible and intelligible. Once these worlds have been differentiated, there remains the task of integrating them anew. But specific sets of cultural meanings and values can obscure the task of differentiation and so prevent mature integration, and one of the sources of such obscuring is named "clerical culture," where, says Lonergan, "the only branches of knowledge cultivated are philosophy and theology, and these very often in an easy-going and nonscientific way."[4]

This is just by way of illustration of common stances, horizons, basic options, especially in the form of mutually compatible identifications of obstacles on the part of Lonergan and Pope Francis. More positively, let me suggest two areas of actual convergence. I will use Lonergan's language to specify these areas because it helps to provide a conceptual framework that can clarify the significance of the pope's preferences. The first is the emphasis on what Lonergan calls a hierarchy or, better, scale of values, and the second has to do with meaning as mediating and constituting the real human world.

First, then, the scale of values. At some point during the decade when I was writing *Theology and the Dialectics of History* (basically, the decade of the 1980s), I commented to a fellow Jesuit that one of the problems with some variations of both liberation theology and the Jesuits' commitment to the integration of faith and justice was that faith is a matter of what Lonergan calls "religious values" and justice a matter of what he calls "social values." However, these two "levels" of value are joined to each other in Lonergan's scale of values through both personal authenticity and the entire realm of culture, where culture means the sets of meanings and values informing ways of living. I was concerned that some liberation theologies and some Jesuit governance and apostolic planning might easily neglect these realms of personal integrity and cultural values. My Jesuit interlocutor commented that what I was proposing was similar to Pope John Paul II's suspicions about both liberation theology and the Jesuits! I was a bit surprised to hear this, since my evolving work really *did* take seriously the liberation and Jesuit emphasis on the preferential option for the poor, and I did not want my critique to be interpreted as opposed to that option. Since then, of course, Pope John Paul II expressed his own variation on the preferential option, and I realized that we were probably coming at the issues from compatible standpoints. The scale of values that I learned from Lonergan—from "below," vital, social, cultural, personal, religious—subsequently became the central conceptual framework of my efforts in *Theology and the Dialectics of History*, and I am hopeful that it represents what Lonergan has to contribute to a number of efforts, including the integration of faith and justice through personal authenticity and a commitment to world-cultural meanings and values for a global community.

I mention all of this here because a similar approach to these issues is found in both the Aparecida document and the subsequent writings of Pope Francis. If I may use my own language to express this, "faith" becomes *social grace* through culture, through the change of cultural meanings and values that sometimes is possible only because of cumulative conversion of heart and mind on the part of individual subjects. As the late Daniel Berrigan, himself hardly an individualist, in effect insisted in a letter he wrote to Jesuits in 1970, until the individual changes, nothing changes.[5] The way forward to the development of the reign of God in human affairs is through conversion, not through violent revolution.

But personal conversion is not enough. It is and must be oriented to cultural transformation, to the establishment of the common meanings and values that would support and encourage the further transformation of the structures of polity and economy that would guarantee an equitable distribution of vital goods to the entire human community. Without the formal effects of habitual and actual grace moving into the cultural domain and becoming social grace, personal conversion is shortchanged. Yes, until the individual changes, nothing changes, but when individuals change, many other things change as well. And the only stable guarantee of a change in the social structures that deliver vital goods to the human community lies in the radical transformation of the cultural meanings and values that inform the various ways we live our lives.

This is what is often missed in those attempts at integrating faith and justice that would not pass through personal and cultural conversion. It was not missed, though, in the Aparecida document, and it is not missed in the subsequent reflections of Pope Francis. If I may come full circle on my initial observations here, I'm sure that among the reasons that the Aparecida document drew my attention in a special way was the fact that its principal author saw this and emphasized it. In fact, I suspect that he emphasized it against some great opposition among his confreres and Latin American associates. I would not be surprised if this integration of faith and justice *through personal conversion and cultural transformation* will be recognized as defining the ministry of Jorge Mario Bergoglio/Pope Francis. And if this is the case, then I have no doubt that the emphases of Bernard Lonergan and Pope Francis are already well on their way to convergence.

May the present book hasten the arrival of that day.

Robert M. Doran

Introduction

FROM THE TIME of his election in 2013, Pope Francis has caught the imagination of the world. His message offers hope at a moment of anxiety and tension in world affairs. This popularity has been reflected among most Catholics, although a remarkable phenomenon of resistance to him has also emerged within certain Catholic circles. There are diverse explanations for this resistance, but one of specific interest is that of Cardinal Walter Kasper. Kasper explains that Pope Francis represents a shift in emphasis from previous pontificates and the beginning of a "new reception of Vatican II." He suggests that the shift is not one of a change of doctrine, but rather of a change of theological method. He adds that those people who do not understand—or wish to accept—this shift are likely to dismiss the preaching and actions of this pope as "merely pastoral" and thus lacking in "theological substance." He states that such critics form a "party" within the Catholic Church that "has alienated itself from the faith and the life of the People of God." He suggests that there remains a task for theologians who do not suffer from this alienation to understand and to explain to others how the "new perspectives that are emerging" in this pontificate have merit.[1]

This book takes up the challenge of explaining the significance of Pope Francis to a theological audience. Important support for this challenge can be found by relating the thought of Pope Francis to that of the Jesuit philosopher and theologian Bernard Lonergan. This Canadian Jesuit lived from 1904 to 1984 and is considered by some to be one of the great Catholic theologians of the twentieth century. One of his achievements was to produce a book, *Method in Theology*, published in 1972. I do not pretend that Pope Francis has read Lonergan, but I suggest that his thought converges with that of Lonergan, who can provide explanatory depth to it. Essentially, this book attempts to identify the "sign of the times" that Pope Francis represents, both for theology and for the manner of proceeding of the church. Hopefully, theology, with the support of future popes, will recognize the full significance of the call of Pope Francis for a "discerning church."

Outline

This book covers much ground across nine chapters. Chapter 1 presents a brief outline, in parallel, of the notions of theological method found in both Pope Francis and in Lonergan. Chapter 2 employs Lonergan's thought to offer a broad panorama of world cultural history, suggesting that the central challenge to culture today is the shift from classical mindedness to an authentic historical consciousness. Chapter 3 builds on Lonergan's conviction that religion can play a key role in mediating redemption to history, and, consequently, helping world culture negotiate a transition to historical consciousness. However, it notes that negotiating such a transition is complex and that, in recent centuries, the Catholic Church has tended to be so alert to negative aspects of modernization that it resisted even its positive aspects. Chapter 4 offers an account of the Second Vatican Council. It stresses the significance of the call by Pope John XXIII at the beginning of the council for members to avoid being "prophets of doom" with respect to modernity and to be willing to employ "modern methods of study" in theology. It traces the subsequent events of the four-year council and suggests that the council represents an emphatic decision to embrace historical consciousness and to become, as stated in the subtitle of the document *Gaudium et Spes*, "The Church in the Modern World." Nevertheless, chapter 4 retains a notion, rooted in the thought of Lonergan, about just what historical consciousness should mean and identifies considerable ambiguity in the statements of the council regarding what it means to undertake the epochal shift for which it was implicitly calling.

Chapter 5 traces the implementation of the council in the fifty years since it was held. I identify a "battle for meaning" that occurred at many levels.[2] Again, employing a Lonergan-based perspective, we consider many of the issues debated that could have been better addressed on the basis of what Lonergan calls "intellectual conversion" and the kind of method that flows from this. Chapters 6, 7, 8, and 9 locate the thought of Pope Francis within postconciliar Catholic theology. In these chapters, we explore the Argentine tradition of interpreting Vatican II, how this influenced the young Jorge Bergoglio, and how Bergoglio remained loyal to this perspective—while also developing his distinct approach to it—throughout his life. Furthermore, we observe that Pope Francis's theological positions are, in fact, close to those that would have been proposed by Lonergan. In chapter 9, we note the opposition to Pope Francis and its focus on criticism of his apostolic exhortation *Amoris Laetitia*. An examination of this criticism suggests, on the one hand, that it represents a classicist worldview that resembles the one expressed by what was known as the "council minority" at Vatican II; and that, on the other hand, those defending *Amoris Laetitia* would benefit from the thought of Lonergan in explaining how it is an example of authentic historical consciousness at work in theology.

The conclusion offers a reflection on how a theological method such as that called for by Pope Francis might unfold after his pontificate.

For the Reader

Writing this book required judgment calls about what issues to address and at what depth to do so. The book is ambitious in scope, and yet it is intended for an audience that, while theologically informed, is not composed of professional theologians. It covers a wide swathe of issues ranging from world cultural history, to Vatican II, to the history of Latin American liberation theology. Similarly, it touches upon foundational questions of epistemology and theological method. Rather than communicating a host of details, the goal is to communicate the overarching insight that Pope Francis is a key figure in helping the church move toward a historical consciousness, and that Lonergan's thought can help with this project. Hopefully, the reader recognizes that covering so much ground justifies the central insight that the book communicates. There are suggestions for further reading in footnotes for readers interested in pursuing topics in greater detail.

In addition to being extensive in what it covers, this book also invites readers to the intensive and highly personal task of attempting intellectual conversion. In fact, Lonergan's thought does not primarily involve a set of ideas but is an invitation to self-knowledge. It is on this basis of his epistemology that his discussion of method rests. Unfortunately, there is something in human nature that resists such an attentiveness to interiority. Many of us are happier to remain at a more extroverted level of activity. For those who are academically inclined, this can include a delight in the understanding and comparing of complex concepts. Such readers may be interested only in Lonergan's system of ideas in comparison with the systems of other thinkers. The challenge, then, is how to invite readers to undertake the journey of self-knowledge. In my teaching, I have the good fortune to engage with students who have a committed life of prayer. Intellectual conversion can often relate to the discernment in one's prayer life with which they are already familiar. In this book, readers are invited to make similar connections.

There is another dimension of the book that may surprise some readers; it passes sharp judgments on certain theological positions. This is what Lonergan calls *dialectic method*. He encourages those who have undergone intellectual conversion to proceed to evaluate the foundational presuppositions that lie behind the arguments of others. This involves passing judgment on how authentic or inauthentic the process of reasoning of an author is. Lonergan stresses that almost every thinker includes "positions" that deserve to be "advanced"— because they are based on valid presuppositions—and "counter positions" that deserve to be reversed. In the following chapters, we apply such a method, and the limits of space require that, at times, we focus more on counterpositions than positions. For example, we criticize some of the theologies that emerged in the 1970s in the name of Vatican II as part of what Lonergan calls a "scattered left." Similarly, we identify considerable counter position in neo-Augustinian approaches to theology that emerged in the late Middle Ages. This leads us to criticize aspects of the teaching and decision-making of both Popes St. John Paul II and Benedict XVI, inasmuch as they were influenced by neo-Augustinianism. On the contrary, Pope Francis has been influenced by a form of liberation theology that is more Thomist in origins. This is what Lonergan explains as a "position," and furthermore as in keeping with the spirit of Vatican II. In passing such judgments on popes, I recall the statement of Kasper, who points out that to suggest that a pope was employing an imperfect theological method is not to dispute his authority or orthodoxy.[3]

Personal History

The editorial board of this series of books encourages contributors to offer some autobiographical details and to explain how these relate to the books that contributors have written. In truth, the thought of both Lonergan and Pope Francis fascinate me and exercise what I would describe as a vocational pull. A result of this is that the project of promoting the thought of each of them has become part of my sense of direction in life. The fact that they, too, are both Jesuits, provides an interpretation that may assist others.

After attending a Jesuit secondary school, I studied for a university degree in social science with a major in economics. Broadly speaking, I am grateful for these studies, which helped form a mentality to understand the social context in which I live, with the hope of being able to make a positive contribution to it. At the same time, I felt frustration with these studies. In sociology, I learned much from some Marxist professors but could never identify with the set of categories through which they studied the world. In my study of economics, I encountered an alternative system using a similarly rigid set of instruments that professors claimed could explain events, but were not open to question. This was the era when Margaret Thatcher was in power in Britain and Ronald Reagan in the United States. For many of my economics professors, economics presented a degree of scientific objectivity where ethical questions were not welcome. The dictum of Margaret Thatcher was sometimes quoted: "There is no alternative." Only later would I be able to articulate that I had ethical questions that were not being met either by Marxism or neoliberal economics.

More personally, during my university years, I undertook activities working with the poor and underwent some deep religious experiences. These helped me move from being something of a drifter and a nominal Catholic to a committed one. As soon as I had completed my degree in 1982, I decided to join the Jesuit novitiate. From there, I continued with my Jesuit formation until I was ordained a priest in 1992.

Many of my experiences helped me to identify with the similar process undergone by Jorge Bergoglio, thirty years earlier. Like him, I resonated deeply with the statement of the mission of the Jesuits that they had articulated in 1975 in a General Congregation of the religious order: "The service of faith and the promotion of justice." However, also like him, I felt uneasy about some aspects of the ways that Jesuits were interpreting and implementing this mission. I often felt that there was a left-leaning ideology at work in the way that some Jesuits of the "social apostolate" operated. This, in fact, led me to study Lonergan. In this methodological thinker, I found someone who could help me integrate faith and justice in a more profound way than was being done by some of my fellow Jesuits.

In truth, I came to an interest in Lonergan studies relatively late — primarily during doctoral studies. However, in retrospect, I recognize that my interest in him resonated with the spiritual formation I had received, beginning in the Jesuit novitiate. As a novice, in addition to undergoing the *Spiritual Exercises of St. Ignatius*, we were all invited to undergo some psychotherapy. During therapy, I learned something of the complex and often hidden world of my own motivations. For example, I recognized how easy it was to confuse a righteous anger at social inequality with anger emanating from my own psychological woundedness. This helped me embark on the first steps of a humble practice of discernment of spirits, where I had to distinguish between merely apparent good and the real good to which God was calling me. In many respects, the thought of Lonergan is an extension in the academic realm of the Ignatian principle of the discernment of spirits. Similarly, I resonate with the thought of Pope Francis and employ one of his terms, "A discerning church," as the title for this book.

Further Comments

In these introductory comments, I would like to add a point about ecumenism. Encountering fellow Christians of different denominations has been a joy for me, and working for church unity is one of my central commitments. However, in this book I say little about this. A reason is that I primarily address an issue that is internal to Roman Catholic theology — how Pope Francis poses a challenge to Catholic theological method, and how this relates to the thought of Lonergan. However, various friends of other ecclesial communities have assured me that issues currently being debated within Roman Catholic theology are of intense interest to them. They also assure me that Pope Francis is a positive figure for those interested in church unity.

Finally, I offer words of gratitude. For ten years, I have been a professor at the Pontifical Gregorian University in Rome where Lonergan studied and taught. I am grateful to my superiors, who have encouraged me to build "a little school of Lonergan" here. Because of this support, the ideas presented in this book are in fact the product of years of work with students, fellow professors, and academics from other institutions whom we have invited to the Gregorian.[4] On a related point, the enthusiasm for Pope Francis expressed in this book is echoed by other Jesuit professors at the Gregorian. Together we are contributors to this series of books, Theology at the Frontiers. In this project, authors—not only from the Gregorian, and not only Jesuit—draw on broadly Ignatian resources to explore issues in theology that converge with the concerns of Pope Francis. I thank these confreres, as well as the staff of Paulist Press—especially the ever-patient Mark-David Janus—for the opportunity to pursue this project.

1

The Question of Method

MOST OBSERVERS NOTE that Pope Francis represents a shift in style from his two predecessors, Pope St. John Paul II and Pope Benedict XVI. However, perceptive commentators note that Pope Francis also represents a shift in theological method. This chapter provides a first introduction to this broad theme. It offers a brief outline of the theological method of Pope Francis and an introduction to how Lonergan's notion of theological method resembles and deepens this.

The Method of Pope Francis

The theological method of Pope Francis has three major characteristics: it is rooted in a notion of discernment drawn from the *Spiritual Exercises of St. Ignatius*; it adopts the inductive style of the "See-Judge-Act" method; and it employs a preferential option for the poor.[1]

DISCERNMENT

Early in his pontificate, Pope Francis gave an interview to a Jesuit journal where he stated clearly that the notion of discernment, as understood in the *Spiritual Exercises of St. Ignatius*, is central to his approach to life.[2] The best way to understand the meaning of the term *discernment* in Ignatian spirituality is to undergo the experience of the

Spiritual Exercises, which is offered in the form of a thirty-day silent retreat. In this experience, one meets a spiritual director each day. In fact, the *Spiritual Exercises of St. Ignatius* is not meant to be read by the retreatant but to be employed as a manual to guide the director in his or her guidance of a retreatant. In short, learning the skill of discernment of spirits involves learning to differentiate between interior states of consolation and desolation and to become confident that decisions made in times of consolation are likely to be consistent with the will of God. The *Spiritual Exercises* help to school individuals in practicing this method of self-awareness in a way that is intense, subtle, and can form the habit of a lifetime. They prompt individuals to take a process-oriented approach to life, something Ignatius describes as being "a contemplative in action."

Those familiar with an Ignatian notion of discernment recognize how deeply the interview Pope Francis gave in November 2013 reveals him to be a contemplative in action. He describes how "the wisdom of discernment redeems the necessary ambiguity of life," and adds that it is a humbling experience and helps one adopt a method for decision-making that "does not always coincide with what looks great and strong." With remarkable honesty, he speaks about mistakes he made in his life, indicating that, in fact, becoming a discerning person is the achievement of a lifetime. He states that he was required to carry responsibility in Jesuit governance when he was too young to do so. He describes how he behaved in "an authoritarian and quick manner" that led him to encounter serious problems, and from this experience he learned to be more consultative in his style of governance. He quips that, having learned his lesson, "I am wary of the first decision, that is the first thing that comes into my mind when I make a decision. This is usually the wrong thing."[3]

Francis also explains that Ignatian spirituality expands naturally to a philosophy of knowing that, in turn, influences one's approach to a world of pastoral concerns. When offering advice to his fellow Jesuits, he states, "The Jesuit must be a person whose thought is incomplete, in the sense of open-ended thinking." He adds, "Discernment is always done in the presence of the Lord, looking at the signs, listening to the things that happen, the feeling of the people, especially the poor."[4] Reference to issues such as the signs of the times and the importance of listening to the poor brings Francis beyond questions that appertain strictly to Ignatian discernment and on to broader questions of a method for pastoral decision-making.[5]

INDUCTIVE METHOD

Jorge Bergoglio was ordained a priest in 1968, and so was still pursuing his studies in theology during the years of Vatican II. His teachers took care to be updated with developments at the council, and Bergoglio shared in their sense of excitement that major changes were afoot in Catholic theology.[6] During this time, he learned the significance of the call by Pope John XXIII, in the opening speech of the council, for the event to be "pastoral" and not primarily doctrinal. Bergoglio's teachers explained that such a pastoral attitude implied adopting an inductive and historically conscious approach to theology, one that contrasted with the primarily deductive approach of the neo-Scholastic theology in which they themselves had mostly been trained. As pope, he would note that one of the main problems with neo-Scholasticism was that it operated at a level of abstraction that created a "divorce between theology and pastoral care, between faith and life." He would add that "one of the main contributions of the Second Vatican Council was precisely seeking a way to overcome this divorce."[7]

Bergoglio learned that key examples of an inductive method at work in the council were found in two of its four major documents, or constitutions. In the first, the Dogmatic Constitution on the Church, *Lumen Gentium*, the church is described as the people of God. By using this image, the church is understood as an actor in history, a fellow traveler with the rest of humanity. The second document is *Gaudium et Spes*, the Pastoral Constitution on the Church in the Modern World, where use of inductive method is most evident. In this document, two characteristics demonstrate its inductive approach: the use of a method popularly described as "See-Judge-Act" and reference to "the signs of the times."

The notion of what an inductive method is will be the focus of subsequent chapters. For now, we note that Bergoglio opted for this approach to theology. When he was ordained a priest, he was appointed to a series of positions of authority in quick succession: novice master, provincial superior, and rector of the Colegio Máximo of philosophy and theology. While he did not remain long as novice master, it influenced his thinking. He would always bring the resources of Ignatian spirituality to bear on an inductive approach to theology. This became evident when he was provincial and began to formulate his theological vision in speeches and articles in terms of four pastoral principles.[8] He has been consistent in referring to these principles throughout his life, and they are evident in *Evangelii Gaudium*.

The first of the pastoral principles of Bergoglio is *time is greater than space*. Here he speaks of the importance of patience in trying to address the "processes of people-building" and adds that those who "opt for space," instead of time, try to short-circuit this process and impose solutions on situations that are not the fruit of the insight that comes from dialogue and deliberation. He suggests that those who opt for space usually do so for selfish reasons. His second principle is *unity prevails over conflict*. Here, he discusses the appropriate manner of engaging with conflict, insisting, "conflict cannot be ignored or concealed" when it arises. He suggests that we commit ourselves to "face conflict head on, to resolve it and to make it a link in the chain of a new process." His third principle, *realities are more important than ideas*, expresses his distrust of abstract ideologies. His fourth and final principle is *the whole is greater than the parts*. Here he rings a note of realism about not overemphasizing the importance of the specific processes of which one might be part. He suggests that "an innate tension also exists between globalization and localization" and proposes that we pay attention to both. He recommends paying attention to the global "so as to avoid narrowness and banality," and to the local, "which keeps our feet on the ground."[9]

A PREFERENTIAL OPTION FOR THE POOR

Bergoglio's enthusiasm for Vatican II was further stimulated by witnessing how it was being interpreted in Latin America. He was aware that theologians across the continent were developing a school of theology called liberation theology. A position shared by these theologians was that, in Latin America, the fundamental sign of the times was that of poverty and oppression. Theologians such as Gustavo Gutiérrez were employing a biblical term to capture this problem: "the cry of the poor."[10] Staying loyal to an inductive approach to theology, these theologians held that a "preferential option for the poor" should imbue all three stages of the See-Judge-Act process. In the first of these steps, they suggested that resources such as social science should be employed to study the current social and cultural context with special attention to the situation of the poor. Next, they invoked principles from hermeneutical philosophy to insist that insights deriving from the first step should influence the way one conducts subsequent steps. Concerning the moment—Judge—they proposed that the way resources of Scripture and Tradition are retrieved should be guided by questions arising from the first step—See. For example, the term *liberation theology* was derived from the preference of theologians to invoke the liberating acts of Moses as he led the people of Israel across the desert to the promised land. When they arrived at the third step of an inductive process, Act, they stressed pastoral action that would assist social transformation in favor of the poor.

As pope, Francis reveals the influence of liberation theology on him as follows. He states that a key starting point for theology is "contemplating the face of God, revealed in Jesus Christ as a Father rich in mercy." He then adds that such contemplation is "also the source of the imperative to allow our hearts and minds to heed the cry of the earth's poor and to give concrete expression to the social dimension of evangelization." Invoking the hermeneutical principle beloved of liberation theologians, he adds, "This option must pervade the presentation and study of Christian truth" (*Veritatis Gaudium* 4a).

In addition to accepting the broad principle of a preferential option for the poor, Bergoglio adopts a specific way his Argentine professors had chosen to interpret this principle. In fact, this way had placed Argentine theologians at odds with their colleagues in other Latin American countries. In 1967, the Episcopal Conference of Argentina had convoked a commission of theologians, philosophers, and social scientists to develop a pastoral plan for the church of Argentina in the light of the council. In 1972, this commission produced a proposal and continued afterward as an informal network that constituted a distinctive school of liberation theology. Above all, this group eschewed the use of Marxist categories in conducting theology. This resulted in an understanding of a preferential option for the poor that was subtly but significantly different from other liberation theologians. The Argentine thinkers drew on traditions of European romantic philosophy to stress the value of the culture of the poor, not least as expressed in popular devotions such as processions honoring the Blessed Virgin. They suggested that the poor have a wisdom to which theologians must carefully attend as they seek to proceed from the stage of seeing, to those of judging and acting. They related the wisdom of the poor to a traditional category in theology: "a sense of the faith" (*sensus fidei*) among ordinary people that operates as a source for theological reflection.

Argentine theologians were clear that their understanding of a preferential option for the poor differed markedly from some liberation theologians more influenced by Marx. They noted that such thinkers considered the culture of the poor to be merely "the false consciousness of the ruling class" and thus not to be respected.[11] Consequently, there is a distinctively non-Marxist tone in the following statement of Pope Francis from *Evangelii Gaudium*:

> This is why I want a Church which is poor and for the poor. They have much to teach us. Not only do they share in the *sensus fidei*, but in their difficulties they know the suffering Christ. We need to let ourselves be evangelized by them.... We are called to find Christ in them, to lend our voice to their causes, but also to be their friends, to listen to them, to speak for them and to embrace the mysterious wisdom which God wishes to share with us through them. (no. 198)

Let us now compare these three characteristics of the theological method of Pope Francis that we have just outlined with the approach of Bernard Lonergan, one of whose most important works was entitled *Method in Theology*.

Lonergan's Method

For much of this book, we will be exploring how the thought of Pope Francis can be illuminated by that of Bernard Lonergan. In this first exercise of comparison, we consider the thought of Lonergan in two steps: first we offer a general biographical account of this Canadian; second, we focus on his intellectual biography, highlighting how his thought mirrors the three characteristics of the theological method of Pope Francis.

BIOGRAPHICAL DETAILS

Lonergan was born in 1904 near Montreal, Canada. He was the eldest of three brothers and would later describe his childhood as happy. His father was an engineer, and his mother was a woman of cultivated tastes in music and other arts. After attending a Jesuit high school in Montreal, he joined the Jesuits at the age of seventeen. He was one of those geniuses who do not always shine early in life. His exam results from school and the reports on him by his superiors did not speak of anything exceptional. He was an introvert by personality, with a tendency to make cutting comments about others. However, at an early stage in his training, it was recognized that he was academically gifted. At the time, it was the custom for Canadian scholastics (the term used for Jesuit seminarians) to be sent to England for philosophy. There, he showed talent and his superiors began to consider him as a potential teacher of philosophy or theology. On his return to Canada, he spent four years in Montreal teaching in the high school he himself had attended. There, he lived under the authority of a superior who took a dislike to him, and the future of his Jesuit vocation seemed at risk, not to mention his assignment to an academic career. However, a change of superior brought a change of fortunes. He was told that he could expect to be assigned as a lecturer in the Pontifical Gregorian University in Rome, and for this reason, he was sent to that institution to complete his theological studies leading up to priesthood. This came as a relief and a joy to him.

He was ordained a priest in Rome in 1938 and completed a doctoral dissertation in theology there in 1940. Because of the outbreak of World War II, he was not able to continue immediately in the Gregorian as a professor but returned to Canada—first to Montreal and then Toronto—where he taught theology for the next fourteen years. It was during these years that he composed the first of his two masterworks: *Insight: A Study in Human Understanding*.[12] Finally, in 1954, he returned to the Gregorian and taught there until 1965. He witnessed at close hand the developments of Vatican II. He was registered as a *peritus* for the council but was not actively involved in debates or the drafting of texts. Significantly, a reason he offered for this was that the council did not explicitly address questions of theological method, which was his specialty. However, he does seem to have exercised an influence on some of the other *periti*. At least one of these would quote him explicitly as suggesting that, in fact, questions of method were a key underlying theme of the council, even though the council fathers were not always expressly aware of this.[13]

Lonergan missed the final session of the council because, in the spring of 1965, he was diagnosed with lung cancer and had to stay in Canada for treatment. He underwent two operations and had one of his lungs removed. He survived this treatment but did not return to Rome. The years leading up to 1965 had been a phase of immense intellectual creativity for him and this had culminated in his receiving key insights that he would express in *Method in Theology*. However, after his cancer operations, he had less energy and his creative output was reduced. He did succeed in publishing his book on method in 1972. He lived for his remaining years in semiretirement between Boston College and Regis College, Toronto. He died in 1984.

Lonergan considered *Method in Theology*[14] to be his masterwork, but most commentators place *Insight* on a par with this and suggest that, to understand the later book, it is necessary to understand the former. This makes Lonergan's thought difficult to explain. For the remainder of this chapter, we examine in more detail the intellectual biography of Lonergan, highlighting aspects of Lonergan's thought that overlap with the three characteristics of the theological method of Pope Francis.

THE EARLY INTELLECTUAL VISION

Lonergan's early intellectual development unfolded in four steps.[15] These early developments would give direction to the later works of Lonergan that he wrote primarily in his forties and fifties. His intellectual development over these years relates closely to what we described in Pope Francis as a concern for the inductive method and a preferential option for the poor.

A first characteristic of the early Lonergan is that he was not impressed by the manualist, neo-Scholastic thought presented to him during both his philosophy studies in Heythrop College, England, and his theology studies at the Gregorian University, Rome. This was the age of dogmatic theology framed in terms of conceptualist metaphysics. The Jesuits followed a tradition of interpreting Aquinas first articulated by Francisco Suarez (1548–1617). Little encouragement was given to speaking of personal experience, to cultivating one's own powers of inquiry, or to investigating questions that had not already been answered by authorities from the past. On this matter, Lonergan was wont to exercise his sardonic wit. Speaking of the philosophy and theology he was being taught at this time, he would later assert, "One entered the rationalist door of abstract right reason and came out in the all but palpable embrace of authoritarian religion."[16] He became convinced that his Jesuit training was encouraging him to defend the truth claims of Catholic religion without exercising much of one's own intelligence. During his time in England, he had a visit from his provincial superior, who asked him, "Are you orthodox?" He gave evidence of an attitude that would provoke suspicion among some authorities when he answered, "Yes I am orthodox, but I think a lot!"

Second, the early Lonergan developed an interest in empirical method. This interest was assisted by living in England and by the fact that, as well as undergoing his seminary studies in philosophy, he was given permission to study for a civil degree in mathematics and classics in the University of London. Through his study of mathematics, he was exposed to the English intellectual tradition of scientific thought, which seeks to discover the mathematical laws that govern natural phenomena (recall that he was the son of an engineer). He began to appreciate the significance of the modern Scientific Revolution and how dangerous it was for Catholic theology to be basing itself on outdated Aristotelian notions of scientific reasoning.

Third, Lonergan expanded his notion of empirical method to include attentiveness to questions of subjective interiority. He would come to speak of the importance not only of attending to the data of sense, but also to the data of consciousness. As well as studying mathematics in his university degree, he studied classics. This helped him to expand his notion of empirical method. During his university studies, he felt an increasing attraction to ancient philosophy, intuiting that reference to ancient sources would help current Catholic philosophy escape from the straitjacket of abstract and propositional Suarezianism. Given these interests, it was perhaps inevitable that he would be attracted to the thought of that eminent English churchman of the nineteenth century, John Henry Newman. In Newman, he encountered a mind that had engaged with the rapid modernization of Britain in the nineteenth century, trying to find a place in this new world for religion. He appreciated Newman's critique of those who tried to defend Christianity by making rationalistic and pseudoscientific arguments. He read Newman's *The Grammar of Assent* many times and noted how Newman explored the subtleties of how we think and decide. He appreciated Newman's conclusion that the mind that is so apt at developing natural science is equally apt at undertaking distinct but no less authentic acts, including artistic creativity, ethical decision-making, and, finally, an act of religious faith.

A fourth concern of Lonergan arrived later than his interest in cognitional theory but quickly gave direction to it. In the 1930s, he developed a deep concern to redress the lot of the poor. In 1929, the collapse of stock markets around the world led to the Great Depression of the 1930s. This was the time when Lonergan completed his philosophical studies in England and returned to his native area of Montreal to teach in a high school. There, he witnessed the effects of poverty on families he knew and became filled with a sense of scandal regarding this situation. He employed his competence in mathematics to begin studying economics and became convinced that the economic depression he was witnessing could have been avoided. His sense that Western civilization was in crisis deepened. He was subsequently sent to Italy for studies, and there he witnessed the rise of fascism and the outbreak of the Second World War. He became convinced that erroneous and biased forms of thinking had much to do with these disasters.

At this stage, Lonergan recalled that one of his lecturers at Heythrop College had spoken of the challenge for the Catholic Church of developing an approach to philosophy that could parallel the achievement of figures like Karl Marx and Hegel. This lecturer had pointed out that Marx had first developed a philosophy of history and then a theory of economics. Lonergan conceived the desire to devote his life to creating a parallel system of thought consistent with Catholic thought.[17] A focus for his attention was an effort to assure that that world economy would avoid another great depression. Twice during his theology studies in Rome, Lonergan wrote to his provincial superior in Canada asking that he be allowed to commit his life to the developing of a philosophy of history. He also devoted spare time to writing long essays on this topic.[18] His superior did not give him direct permission to do this, but rather instructed him to pursue a doctorate in theology so that he could teach at the Gregorian. He was at first disappointed by this, but quickly recognized that this was a blessing in disguise because he could integrate such theological studies into this broader concern for history. One biographer of Lonergan, Frederick Crowe, stresses how the concern for history—and the concern for the poor that lay behind it—became a guiding focus for the works of Lonergan's maturity:

> My claim then was that the need to understand history, basic history, the history that happens, is the chief dynamic element in his academic work: not insight, not method, not economics, not emergent probability, but history. I will call it the "essential" Lonergan, not in the sense of those books that collect the chief writings of an author…but in the sense of the key to all those writings, the principal of any collection of them, and the single idea or set of ideas that unlocks the secrets of someone's mind and life and works.[19]

THE MATURE LONERGAN

In studying Lonergan's thought in the years of his maturity, we recognize that, in a sense, his two masterworks, *Insight* and *Method in Theology*, can be understood as an effort to deepen that dimension of the threefold thought of Pope Francis that we have described as his commitment to inductive method.

In the late 1940s, Lonergan made a decision that would direct the work of the rest of his life: instead of trying to pursue many questions at a superficial level, he concentrated in depth on the most foundational questions. He decided to leave aside studies in fields such as economics and moral theology and to concentrate instead on questions of epistemology and theological method. Frederick Crowe employs a military metaphor to describe this strategic decision by Lonergan: "a massive withdrawal in anticipation of an equally massive return."[20] He points out that this decision led to him authoring *Insight: A Study of Human Understanding* and *Method in Theology*. He adds that Lonergan was so consistent in working at this foundational level that not all of those who became interested in his thought in subsequent years were aware of the social-ethical concern that guided it.

Insight is a work of eight hundred pages and is of such depth that it is impossible to do justice to it in these pages. The first half of the book is dedicated to inviting the reader to an act of self-affirmation that

Lonergan calls intellectual conversion. Lonergan explains that intellectual conversion confirms for a person that "I am a knower" and so answers the basic questions of any theory of knowledge, epistemology. Lonergan next explains how epistemology can extend into metaphysics:

> Thoroughly understand what it is to understand and not only will you understand the broad lines of all there is to be understood but also you will possess a fixed base, an invariant pattern, opening upon all further developments of understanding.[21]

The notion of finding an "invariant pattern, opening upon all further developments of understanding" is what Lonergan understands by moving beyond epistemology to metaphysics. He introduces the notion of a "heuristic category" to capture this insight. Such a category anticipates the broad structure of any act of knowing that is likely to follow. There is much to explain about the metaphysics that Lonergan explains in the second half of *Insight*. Here, it is sufficient to note that, at a certain stage, he turns his metaphysical abilities to develop a "metaphysics of human history." The phenomena of human intelligence and freedom, he explains, are creators of new instances of being. However, he adds that they can do so in ways that are either authentic or inauthentic. For this reason, he introduces two heuristic categories for history: "progress" and "decline." At the end of *Insight*, he introduces a notion of a third heuristic category of history: redemption. This involves a supernatural intervention of God in history to overcome the problem of evil and to make it possible for a process of reversing decline and promoting progress to begin.[22]

A major conclusion of *Insight* is Lonergan's suggestion that a community of those who are intellectually converted can form a presence within culture that can help to reverse decline and promote progress. He calls this community a cosmopolis:

> What is necessary is a cosmopolis that is neither class nor state that stands above all their claims, that cuts them down to size, that is founded on the native detachment and disinterestedness of every intelligence, that commands man's first allegiance.[23]

At the end of *Insight*, Lonergan explains that it is his intention to write a book on the theological method that can help religion play its appropriate role in a culture of cosmopolis. Eventually, he publishes *Method in Theology*, where he makes a permanent contribution to Christian thought on this matter.

In fact, *Method in Theology* does not represent merely an application of the philosophy of *Insight* to the question of theological method. In the years after authoring *Insight*, Lonergan made further discoveries into some key philosophical questions that he had left underdeveloped in the earlier book. Above all, he recognized that his account of ethics had been weak. After completing *Insight*, Lonergan began to read European philosophers that he liked to call the German historicists. He now began to employ the vocabulary of intentionality analysis (a term coined by Edmund Husserl) to explain his epistemology. This included expanding his account of how feelings are involved both in decision-making in general, and in "religious conversion" in particular.[24]

This reflection by Lonergan on the realms of affectivity and decision-making next led to perhaps the greatest insight of his life into theological method. He recognized that theological method should be conceived of with reference to the four levels of consciousness that he had now identified. These levels are constituted by *experience, insight, judgment,* and *decision.* He devotes his book *Method in Theology* to communicating this insight. Here, he proposes that theological method should involve a collaboration of experts operating in a series of eight steps, organized in two phases. The first phase involves retrieving a religious tradition, the second involves mediating this tradition to a cultural context. He defines the function of theology as follows: "A theology mediates between a cultural matrix and the significance and role of a religious tradition in that matrix."[25] He suggests that each phase is a process of cooperation between experts working in four functional specialties. He adds that the goal of each functional specialty is analogous to one of the four levels of consciousness. He speaks of a first phase of this method involving *research* (with an aim analogous to experiences), *interpretation* (insight), *history* (judgment), and *dialectic* (decision). Next, he speaks of a second phase as involving *foundations* (decision), *doctrines* (judgment), *systematics* (insight), and *communications* (experience).

In this vision of functional specialties, the final one, communications, takes on immense importance. Lonergan states that it is here that theology "bears fruit" in mediating redemptive meanings to history:

The message announces what Christians are to believe, what they are to become, what they are to do. Its meaning, then, is at once cognitive, constitutive, effective. It is cognitive inasmuch as the message tells what is to be believed. It is constitutive inasmuch as it crystallizes the hidden inner gift of love into overt Christian fellowship. It is effective inasmuch as it directs Christian service to human society to bring about the kingdom of God.[26]

In later chapters, we will examine how what Lonergan calls "empirical theology" can provide explanatory depth for the kind of inductive theology that is conducted by Pope Francis.

LONERGAN AND IGNATIAN SPIRITUALITY

Up to this point, we have yet to discuss how Ignatian spirituality — one of the three characteristics of the method of Pope Francis — is present in Lonergan's thought. In fact, the relationship of Lonergan to Ignatian spirituality needs careful explaining. For most of his life, it was more implicit than explicit.[27]

Three years after Lonergan published *Method in Theology*, he was listening to a talk given by a young Jesuit who was relating the thought of Karl Rahner to the notions of consolation without cause and the discernment of spirits in the writings of St. Ignatius of Loyola. He describes how he suddenly recognized that much of what this speaker was saying about Rahner could be said of his own work:

I had been hearing those words since 1922 at the annual retreats made by Jesuits preparing for the priesthood. They occur in St. Ignatius's "Rules for the Discernment of Spirits" in the Second Week of the *Exercises*. But now, after fifty-three years, I began for the first time to grasp what they meant.[28]

Lonergan began to recognize that terminology used by of St. Ignatius could be related to themes he had explored in *Method in Theology*. This point needs explaining.

From the above comments of Lonergan, the following question arises: If *Method in Theology* so resembles the *Spiritual Exercises* in certain respects, why was Lonergan not more aware of this while writing it? Lonergan was asked this question by an interviewer toward the end of his life and reveals that he had done some reflection on this matter. He states that, just as theology had fallen into decadence in the neo-Scholastic era, so had the Jesuit understanding of the *Spiritual Exercises*. He describes how his experience of doing the "long retreat" as a novice was not a positive one. Instead of benefitting from an individually directed retreat as would be the case for Jesuits younger than him, his novice master had preached principles from the *Exercises* to a large group of novices as if they were paragraphs of theology to be memorized. He describes this as "a reduction of St. Ignatius to decadent conceptualist scholasticism."[29]

Lonergan expresses no small resentment about the poverty of the spiritual formation he received. However, he also felt obliged to acknowledge that something of the real Ignatius had communicated itself to him in Jesuit formation. In retrospect, he recognized that his readiness to respond to figures who wrote about the importance of interiority—such as John Henry Newman—had been inspired in part by the fact that he had imbibed something of the spirit of St. Ignatius, despite the poverty of his formation personnel. Indeed, it is interesting to note that some commentators suggest that Lonergan had a tendency in later life to exaggerate the evils of his religious formation as a young Jesuit![30] One commentator notes that there exists in the Lonergan archives notes that Lonergan took during his long retreat as a novice. He identifies aspects of a prayer life of the young Canadian that run deeper than what Lonergan would describe later in life. He also suggests that themes from these retreat notes reemerge in the lecture notes that Lonergan would later teach on the themes of Christology and Trinity.[31]

Nevertheless, when one compares Lonergan's thinking about discernment to that of Pope Francis, two comments come to mind. First, one is struck by the difference of age between these two Jesuits and how this explains the more explicit and frequent reference to discernment of spirits by the younger man. Bergoglio, in fact, was among the first generation of novices who benefitted from the renewal of thinking about the *Spiritual Exercises* that was well underway by the 1950s. Lonergan, by contrast, was thirty-two years older than Bergoglio and was part of the pioneer generation that had to struggle for a renewal of Catholic thought and spirituality on a variety of fronts. Lonergan found his vocation more in philosophy and theology than in spirituality, but eventually recognized how these developments converged with each other.

Second, while Lonergan arrived late at using a vocabulary of Ignatian spirituality, his thought remains a rich source for reflection on how the individual practice of discernment of spirits can extend to more organizational and historical practices of religious organizations. He offers a uniquely differentiated account of how the person in spiritual consolation can engage in consistent self-transcendence. His work in *Insight* and *Method in Theology* helps students avoid any lazy substitution of religious enthusiasm for the challenging intellectual work of becoming members of the culture of cosmopolis that mediates redemption in history by reversing decline and promoting progress. At the same time, his account of conversion—religious, moral, and intellectual—is easily recognizable as being in continuity with the invitation to self-reflection made by St. Ignatius. Toward the end of his life, Lonergan addressed a group of young Jesuits soon to be ordained priests. While Jorge Bergoglio was not in this group, he was, in fact, ordained just one year later than those to whom Lonergan gave this address. What Lonergan states is so redolent of reference to Ignatian spirituality that it could have been written by the future Pope Francis:

> In personal living questions abstractly asked about the relations between nature and grace emerge concretely in one's concern, one's interests, one's hopes, one's plans, one's daring and timidity, one's taking risks and playing safe. And as they emerge concretely, so are they solved concretely.... Our time is a time for profound and far-reaching creativity. The Lord be with all of us—*ad maiorem Dei gloriam*—and as I have said, God's own glory, in part, is you.[32]

Conclusion: Lonergan and Pope Francis

Pope Francis is fully aware that his own reflection remains at a primarily pastoral level. In a document about ecclesiastical universities, he speaks of how a zeal to evangelize must translate into a "persevering commitment to a social and cultural meditation on the Gospel

16

undertaken by the People of God in different continental areas and in dialogue with diverse cultures." He adds, "The time has now come for it to be consolidated and to impart to ecclesiastical studies that wise and courageous renewal demanded by the missionary transformation of a Church that 'goes forth'" (*Veritatis Gaudium* 3).

For the rest of this book, Lonergan's notion of theological method will offer academic support for the project of Pope Francis to promote a "church that goes forth." However, in concluding this chapter, there is already some indication of how this service can work. In outlining the theological method of Pope Francis, we noted how he likes to summarize his approach in terms of four pastoral principles (*Evangelii Gaudium* 222–37). We now indicate how Lonergan's thought can help to deepen each of these principles.

When Francis states "time is greater than space," one can recognize that he is describing how social process should be constituted by the unfolding of the transcendental precepts—be attentive, be intelligent, be reasonable, be responsible—all of which take time. Conversely, one can recognize that the reference to opting for space by Francis is a description of bias and decline. The second pastoral principle of Pope Francis states that "unity prevails over conflict." Use of Lonergan's thought can help distinguish a key point: those seeking to promote progress must negotiate two different forms of conflict. The first kind is essentially healthy and involves, even within an "ideal line of pure progress," a tension between a principle of stability and a principle of change in all social and cultural situations. The second kind of conflict involves a tension between truth and falsity, good and evil, progress and decline. On this issue, one recalls what Lonergan explains as the way in which the divine solution to the problem of evil seeks to sublate evil by employing "the law of the cross." This is in continuity with Francis, who advises, "Face conflict head on, to resolve it and to make it a link in the chain of a new process."[33]

The third pastoral principle of Pope Francis states that "realities are more important than ideas." Here one can recognize both how Lonergan supports this point and how he would warn against a possible misinterpretation of it. On the one hand, Lonergan would recognize that this principle represents a critique of abstract, deductivist thinking that is not the product of authentic insight into situations. He would add that the criticism Pope Francis offers of systems of thought such as neo-Scholasticism, Marxism, and extreme forms of neoliberal capitalism explains that each of these provide faulty heuristic categories for a study of society. On the other hand, Lonergan can help prevent the expression of Francis from being interpreted in an anti-intellectual way. He would stress that good ideas, applied at the appropriate time, are the engine of progress. He would support the quip "there is nothing as practical as a good theory." Possibly, here, Lonergan's thought has most to contribute to the Pope Francis project.

Finally, when Francis speaks about how the "the whole is greater than the parts," Lonergan helps one recognize that one's own group is only part of a much wider set of groups and that progress involves a process of healthy negotiation and compromise (the task of politics) between the needs of separate groups.

2

Historical Consciousness

IN THE PREVIOUS chapter, we identified aspects of the theological methods of both Pope Francis and Lonergan that converge with each other. In this chapter, we begin a longer process of relating each thinker to the other. Both here and in subsequent chapters, Pope Francis represents an impressive example of a thinker who has shifted from what Lonergan calls classicism to historical consciousness. This shift locates the Argentine pope firmly within the tradition of Vatican II. In this chapter, we will define the terms *classicism* and *historical consciousness*, as Lonergan understood them.[1]

Note that, to find this account convincing, readers must work on their own process of intellectual conversion. In later chapters, we will discuss the phenomenon of resistance to the approach of Pope Francis within current Catholic theological circles. This often involves a reluctance to shift from classicism to historical consciousness that is related to a philosophical bias—perceptualism—that became prominent in classicist thought in the late Middle Ages and persists today. Consequently, in this chapter, we present a historical overview not only of an idealized notion of progress from classicism to historical consciousness, but also of a history of factors that have blocked or distorted such progress.

The Emergence of Classical Culture

Lonergan claims that a key way to interpret history is by recognizing that it passes through epochal changes in how cultures exercise control over meaning: "If social and cultural changes are, at root, changes in the meanings that are grasped and accepted, changes in the control of meaning mark off the great epochs in human history."[2] He draws on the philosopher Karl Jaspers to speak of an epoch-changing moment as an "axial period." With Jaspers, he suggests that world culture passed through one axial period around 600 BC and is on the threshold of another axial period. He explains that the first axial period involved a shift from undifferentiated consciousness to a theoretic differentiation of consciousness characterized by "classicism." He adds that the second shift is toward historical consciousness and is still underway in world culture.

Lonergan suggests that the first such epochal change occurred when cultures in the ancient world shifted from primal societies to civilizations characterized by the emergence of the major world religions. On this issue, Lonergan turns to the thought of Karl Jaspers and his book *The Origin and Goal of History*.[3] Jaspers describes the first axial period as broadly associated with the technological developments in the first millennium BCE that led to the establishment of city-states and early empires. These technological developments included the domestic use of the horse, and the use of iron in fashioning tools and weapons. The emergence of new political entities coincided with a shift in thinking at a cultural level. Now, instead of primarily associating human nature with the rhythms of nature, cultures began to make a series of new distinctions. This modification, while taking on different forms in various places, had some characteristics in common: a belief in a metaphysical realm of being in which humans as created beings participate; a confidence that truths concerning this metaphysical realm can be accessed by way of a self-reflective process, in meditation or philosophy; and a commitment to training citizens in the forming of virtuous habits.

Jaspers grounds this analysis in the empirical studies of historians and anthropologists. However, he stresses that the most significant shifts in culture were philosophical and religious in character. He describes how key axial figures such as Buddha, Confucius, and Zoroaster were founding figures for new religions and civilizations. He

20

also identifies axial shifts occurring within preexisting religions such as Hinduism and Judaism. Of such axial cultures, he states, "This overall modification of humanity may be termed spiritualization." He adds, "Man proved capable of contrasting himself inwardly with the entire universe. He discovered within himself the origin from which to raise himself above his own self and the world."[4] He next suggests that the axial thinkers of ancient Greece had strengths in the realm of philosophy that distinguished them from other axial cultures:

> Rationality and rationally clarified experience launched a struggle against the myth (logos against mythos); a further struggle developed for the transcendence of the One God against non-existent demons, and finally an ethical rebellion took place against the unreal figures of the gods. Religion was rendered ethical, and the majesty of the deity thereby increased.[5]

Jaspers understands Greek philosophy to have ushered in an era of classicist thinking that led to the formation of European culture.[6]

Lonergan next introduces his own vocabulary about the axial period outlined by Jaspers. He speaks of the emergence of a second stage of meaning from a first, with the former involving undifferentiated consciousness, and the latter a theoretic differentiation of consciousness. He describes the second stage of meaning as freeing human minds to pursue "systematic exigence" and suggests that this exigence prompted a sequence of shifts within an overall theoretic differentiation of consciousness. He notes two important shifts, with the first occurring in the era of the early councils of the Christian church. One scholar summarizes Lonergan's thought on this issue as follows:

> The first development [in theology] led to the differentiation or development of doctrine and creed from Sacred Scripture....The great Trinitarian and Christological councils, beginning with Nicea (AD 325), realized that to assure that the Word of God in Scripture was true, one had to invoke other than biblical terms.[7]

Lonergan suggests that, for all its strengths, Greek philosophy, not least Platonism, was ambiguous about questions of the objectivity of the claims we can make about metaphysical realities. He describes this as a tendency toward idealism. By contrast, in an article, "The Origins of Christian Realism," he claims that the Christian church began to develop new philosophical ideas so that it could support a notion of Christian doctrine. He notes that the Council of Nicea declared that anyone who says that there was a time when the Son of God was not, is to be separated from the Christian community. He points out that by taking this step, the church developed a decision-making structure whereby it declared that not all interesting ideas applied to God can be accepted as true. In this way, the church began a path, however implicitly, toward acknowledging the ability of the human mind to distinguish between insight and judgment.[8] Consequently, the Council of Nicea was not only significant for theological development but also for the development of philosophy in Western culture. According to Lonergan, it represented an important moment where Western thought matured, while still remaining within a classicist paradigm.

Lonergan then suggests that during the centuries after Nicea, Christian theology progressed as theologians such as Augustine of Hippo accepted the doctrines that were declared by the church but continued to explore the intelligibility of these doctrines. He traces the emergence of an increasingly systematic approach to these theological explorations, especially in the new universities—or schools—that were established in many cities of Europe in the late Middle Ages. One commentator notes that Lonergan suggests that the thought of Aquinas represents a step forward in "exigence of intelligence and system" in Christian theology, which, in turn, had an impact on European culture:

> As this doctrinal and creedal development continued there were questions that arose about the inner intelligibility of the many doctrines and creeds. These questions led to the second development, which differentiated theoretical *Summae* from collections of doctrines and creeds. An essential question was the extent to which this differentiation of theoretical theology would succeed in being faithful both to the scriptural and doctrinal, on the one hand, and to the exigencies of intelligence and system, on the other hand. Theology is both wisdom requiring holiness and goodness and a science, a scholarly discipline, requiring intelligence

22

and theory. The great figure representing this integration was Thomas Aquinas.[9]

Lonergan describes how the intellectual syntheses provided by Scholasticism contributed to a flourishing of European civilization in the century of Aquinas. He explains that in addition to applying the resources of Aristotelian philosophy to Christian thinking, Aquinas employed a distinction between natural and supernatural realms of inquiry. This allowed for the relatively autonomous functioning of natural philosophy from theology and suggests that this, in turn, would allow for classicist culture subsequently to undergo a revolutionary development. The discovery of modern science.

The Scientific Revolution

On the issue of the emergence of modern science, Lonergan makes a complex point. First, he claims that it occurred in two waves: the first wave lasted from about 1500 to 1700 and involved the emergence of natural science; the second wave emerged during the 1800s and involved the emergence of the human sciences. Second, Lonergan claims that while the first wave was enormously significant, it nevertheless represented only a further refinement within what remained a theoretic stage of meaning. By contrast, he describes the emergence of the human sciences as bringing culture to the threshold of a second axial period in human history. He claims that it is here that the transition is being made from a control of meaning based on a theoretic differentiation of consciousness to one based on interiorly differentiated consciousness. He describes this as the shift from classicism to historical consciousness.[10]

FIRST WAVE: NATURAL SCIENCES

Lonergan liked to quote historians of science who emphasized the continuity between the natural philosophers of the High Middle Ages and the natural scientists of early modernity. He suggests that once a confidence in the power of reasoning was established in the Scholastic era, it was only a matter of time before scholars would begin to question the adequacy of the tools for understanding the world offered by Aristotle. On this matter, he liked to employ the analysis of one historian of science, Herbert Butterfield.[11]

Butterfield acknowledges that modern science emerged out of the natural philosophy of late medieval times. However, it also represented a revolution in how people came to understand their powers of reason. He traces just how difficult it was for thinkers to advance beyond seeking to explain things by appealing to permanent causes to adopting a new—empirical—method. He describes the need for a "change of thinking cap" and notes that a figure like Copernicus could be considered only a transitionary figure in this process. Butterfield acknowledges that Copernicus was one of "the greatest geniuses who broke through the ancient views in some special field of study," but was also one of those who "would remain stranded in a species of medievalism when they went outside that chosen field."[12] He next points to the importance of Galileo, who, around 1610, articulated a breakthrough insight: that the universe is governed by mathematical laws and that a method of reasoning must be developed that bases itself on trying to discover these laws.

Butterfield traces how Galileo had grasped the insight that modern science would need a completely new thinking cap. He suggests that Galileo articulated the broad lines of the empirical method toward which reason must now turn. He adds that the image of Galileo dropping a weight from the Leaning Tower of Pisa, whether historically accurate or not, symbolizes this method. It involves a series of steps: first, one observes a situation; second, one guesses at what might be the law governing it; third, one formulates an experiment to test one's hypothesis; and finally, one judges whether one's hypothesis has been verified. Moving beyond Galileo, Butterfield suggests that the process of helping modern thinkers shift to a modern scientific paradigm culminates in the publication by Isaac Newton of his *Principia Mathematica* in 1687. He explains the significance of this:

> It is the "scientific revolution," popularly associated with the sixteenth and seventeenth centuries, but reaching back in an unmistakably continuous line to a period much earlier still. Since that revolution overturned the authority in science not only of the middle ages but also of the ancient world—since it ended not only in the eclipse of scholastic

philosophy but in the destruction of Aristotelian physics — it outshines everything since the rise of Christianity and reduces the Renaissance and Reformation to the rank of mere episodes, mere internal displacements, within the system of medieval Christendom. Since it changed the character of *men's habitual mental operations* even in the conduct of the non-material sciences, while transforming the whole diagram of the physical universe and the very texture of human life itself, it looms so large as the real origin both of the modern world and the modern mentality that our customary periodization of European history has become an anachronism and an encumbrance.[13]

Lonergan was impressed by Butterfield's analysis but qualifies it in one respect. He suggests that Butterfield's analysis needs to be developed to clarify how the Scientific Revolution included two distinct stages, or waves. He suggests that it is the second wave of the Scientific Revolution that represents a shift from the world of meaning based on theory to the world of meaning based on interiority. He suggests that this implies the arrival of a new epoch where a significantly new control of meaning would be employed.

SECOND WAVE: HUMAN SCIENCES

In describing the second wave of the Scientific Revolution, Lonergan liked to appeal to the account offered by Alan Richardson, who built his account on that of Butterfield.[14] Richardson suggests that "it is one and the same movement of critical enquiry" that first culminates in the achievement of Isaac Newton and then proceeds to the development of historical method in the nineteenth century. He notes that the first wave of the Scientific Revolution had provoked an interest in interiority by its focus on the mental operations involved in studying nature. He adds that once the critical faculty had been awakened in this way, "it was bound to go on from there to the critical investigation of the more intractable region of human nature." He suggests that key insights would emerge into "the idea of development." Development understood in this way begins with a study of how sciences such as biology emerged from physics. However, it soon extends beyond this to reflecting about what is distinctive about studying the human phenomenon.

Richardson explains that human studies attempt "to understand scientifically how, in fact, man and his institutions, have come to be what they are." He then adds,

> Since the nineteenth century it has been an axiom of Western thinking that men and their institutions cannot be understood apart from their history, or that to know what a thing is, it is necessary to give an account of its past. This is part, at least, and a very important part, of the meaning of the statement that we nowadays live in an historically-minded age. The historical revolution in human thinking, which was accomplished in the nineteenth century, is just as important as the scientific revolution of two centuries earlier. But they are not two separate revolutions; they are aspects of the one great transitional movement from the mediaeval to the modern way of looking at things.[15]

Richardson's account of the movement from the first to the second wave of the Scientific Revolution proceeds in four steps. First, perhaps inevitably, there had been a tendency in the realm of philosophy and politics to apply directly to thinking about human affairs those methods that were developed only for the study of the natural order. This tendency was expressed in philosophies of rationalism, which developed differently in the English-speaking world of Britain and North America and in continental Europe. Second, when rationalism was at its height, especially in countries like France and Germany, some prophetic voices began to challenge it. Even before the French Revolution, some thinkers identified an inherent violence in rationalism, which sought to impose universal concepts on specific situations. In contrast to such an approach, these thinkers began to stress notions such as cultural tradition as a bearer of wisdom; cultural solidarity and nationalism; the need to form citizens in virtue; and the importance of cultivating a sense of beauty in order to grow in wisdom and virtue. Such thinkers represented the emergence of a "romantic movement" in European culture in the late eighteenth and twentieth centuries. This movement first emerged in the world of literature and the arts but soon extended to realms of philosophy and political movements.[16]

Richardson's third point is to trace how, during the nineteenth and twentieth centuries, ideas that had been more vaguely stated within the romantic movement began to shape a new movement that emerged in two steps: first, the emergence of the human sciences in the nineteenth century; and second, a corresponding wave of "historicist" philosophy.

The emergence of the human sciences was closely associated with the establishment of faculties of history in universities in Germany and England in the 1800s. Here, a new group of academic experts began to emerge in the fields of archaeology, linguistics, and textual criticism. These brought to light a vast new realm of historical data that needed interpreting. However, many of these historians failed to develop skills in the art of interpreting, which left them open to manipulation by politicians. Richardson describes how one of the greatest historians of the nineteenth century, Leopold von Ranke, let himself become "the foremost myth-maker of the Bismarckian National State." Similarly, he notes how, decades later, many students of von Ranke became Nazis.[17] He suggests that part of the problem here was that historians had failed to consider questions of the authenticity of the individual who might be called to interpret the historical facts that were being uncovered. He considers this "positivist" approach to historical interpretation as an example of the naive application of the principles of Enlightenment rationalism to human affairs, not unlike what happened in the realm of political philosophy at the time of the French Revolution.

Next, Richardson traces how one important German thinker, Wilhelm Dilthey, began to chart a way forward. Dilthey was both a competent historian and a thinker of philosophical originality. He drew on aspects of the romantic tradition to reflect on how historians could not prescind from questions of what perspective they were employing as they interpreted events from the past. In this way, Dilthey helped historians embrace questions of philosophy:

> The historian, because he is himself an historical being can project himself into the experience of others and thus enlarge his own present experience through the understanding of the past. Historical understanding means to relive… the past experience of others and so to make it one's own; there is nothing that corresponds to this in the non-human sciences, and the latter can tell us nothing about mankind except the physical facts.[18]

Richardson then suggests that a generation of "German historicist" philosophers explored the questions that Dilthey had raised. Individuals such as Hans-Georg Gadamer would explore questions of how the authenticity of the horizon from which we operate as interpreters influences the authenticity of how we are able to interpret the past: "It is essential to [the historian's] calling that he should be seriously concerned to understand the moral, political and social issues of his own day; if he is not thus involved in his own age, he will not be able to bring a past age to life."[19]

In his use of Richardson, Lonergan suggests that what Richardson is calling for is best achieved by inviting intellectuals and cultural leaders to intellectual conversion. As described in chapter 1, Lonergan believes that this would help such intellectual leaders form a community of cosmopolis and help culture advance to a third stage of meaning, one based on an interior differentiation of consciousness.

Decline in the Stages of Meaning

So far, our account of the stages of meaning involves an explanation of what Lonergan called an ideal line of pure progress in culture. However, Lonergan was also clear that history is characterized at least as much by decline as by progress. Consequently, he explains that any account of the history of ideas should include an account of the persistence of bias.

BIAS

Lonergan assumes that individuals who live in cultures of the first stage of meaning include the same distribution of saints and sinners as those in later stages. However, rather than spending time discussing this, he concentrates on an analysis of how bias and decline have been present in cultures undergoing the second stages of meaning and are present also as world culture negotiates a transition to a third stage.[20] In the previous chapter, we noted how, in *Insight*, Lonergan speaks of bias in the cognitional process of individuals and how this is related to decline in history. We also noted how Lonergan identifies one key dimension of bias in the tendency of thinkers to adopt a *perceptualist* notion of knowing.

BIAS AND DECLINE IN THE SECOND STAGE OF MEANING

Lonergan suggest that the bias of perceptualism emerged as a shadow side of the positive developments occurring in the development of ideas during the Middle Ages.[21] He explains how a bias of perceptualism appeared in writings of various philosophers during this time. In fact, he begins his analysis of perceptualism by returning to a discussion of Plato. Plato invited his readers to examine their interiority and by this means, to recognize that they had the capacity to employ universal ideas by means of which they could understand the instances of being in the world that was revealed to them through their senses. Lonergan praises this position and suggests that his own call to intellectual conversion is in continuity with it. In *Insight*, he claims that what Plato really meant by appealing to eternal ideas can be explained in terms of notions of "heuristic categories" and "a notion of being." However, he acknowledges that Plato's meaning could only remain implicit until modern philosophy developed the tools of making it explicit. He notes that this lack of clarity in Plato contributed to an inadequate interpretation by some of his followers, thereby attributing to Plato the biased attitude of a perceptualist. Lonergan recalls that perceptualism is usually expressed by a belief that one can know things other than oneself by "taking a good look" at them. He then notes that some Platonists, especially the Neoplatonists of the late Roman Empire, applied such a perceptualism to Plato's notion of universal ideas. They believed that Plato was inviting us all to "take a good look" at our interiority and to recognize eternal truths there. These misinterpreters then claimed that Plato suggested that we should compare universal ideas with earthly realities and recognize that earthly realities are "mere shadows."[22] Lonergan suggests that this tendency to consider the act of knowing as analogous to taking a good look continued into the Middle Ages. He describes how a new form of perceptualism quickly emerged to oppose the Scholasticism of individuals like Aquinas. This was *nominalism*.

Before explaining nominalism, one needs to understand how so-called monastic theology came to oppose Scholastic theology. This tendency had already emerged in the eleventh century when Bernard of Clairvaux opposed Abelard and proposed "a non-dialectical type of reflection, contemplative, nurtured in prayer based on communion with the celebrated mysteries which have become part of one's life."[23] This approach received further support from the advent of St. Francis of Assisi and the emergence of a tradition of Franciscan theologians in his wake. Preeminent among these was Bonaventure (1221–74), who became a prominent opponent of Aquinas. As one scholar explains,

> [For Aquinas] theology is an intellectual wisdom, acquired by personal effort, which tries intellectually to comprehend and reconstruct the order of the works and the mysteries of God by tying them up with the mystery of God Himself. As for Bonaventure...[theology] is identical with the infused gift of the Holy Spirit.[24]

Lonergan stresses that there is an error in Bonaventure's account of theological knowledge. He speaks of it as a new example of the recurrent human bias of perceptualism. He suggests that Bonaventure's notion of theological knowledge as "infused gift" confuses heightened religious experience with knowledge. He adds that while this imbalance begins with Bonaventure, it becomes compounded in the decades that follow in the thought of other Franciscans, Duns Scotus (1265–1308) and William of Ockham (1285–1347/49). These thinkers often identified with Augustine of Hippo as opposed to Aquinas. Lonergan traces how a sophisticated form of perceptualism, called nominalism, emerged with the philosophy of Duns Scotus. He suggests that the problem of Scotism is that it represents an "oversight of insight":

> The Scotist rejection of insight into phantasm necessarily reduced the act of understanding to seeing a nexus between concepts; hence while for Aquinas understanding precedes conceptualization which is rational, for Scotus understanding is preceded by conceptualization which is a matter of metaphysical mechanics.[25]

Lonergan next explains a complicated point: while Scotism was profoundly different from Thomism, its oversight of insight came to be accepted, unwittingly, even by thinkers in following generations who thought that they were remaining loyal to the thought of Aquinas. One scholar summarizes Lonergan's view of this decadent Scholasticism:

> The synthesis of wisdom and science in Thomas Aquinas required intellectual, moral, and theological virtues that were not adequately practiced and deepened in subsequent theologians. Despite efforts to counteract it, nominalism spread, replacing wisdom with increasingly fragmented attention to particulars in isolation from their natures and ends within the universe of being. Metaphysics was increasingly dominated by a conceptualism that eclipsed the acts of judging and the knowledge of being.[26]

As noted in chapter 1, Lonergan vehemently criticized the abstract deductivism of neo-Scholastic theologians such as Suarez. We can now note that he identifies the origins of this decadent philosophy in the perceptualism of Bonaventure and Scotus.[27]

BIAS IN MODERN PHILOSOPHY

Lonergan next makes an ironic point: while modern philosophers prided themselves (mostly legitimately) on how they differed from their medieval predecessors, in fact, they directly imitated some of the most biased aspects of medieval philosophy.[28] While he admires the call of Descartes to perform a "turn to the subject" as a basis for philosophy, he suggests that Descartes failed to bring this turn to completion. Instead, Descartes adopted a perceptualist approach to studying interiority; Lonergan claims that the Frenchman failed to recognize that subjectivity is characterized by a "normative pattern of operations" that prompt us to pass from experience, through insight, to judgment. He notes that Descartes could only posit the existence of a *res cogitans* (a thinking thing) as constituting subjectivity, to distinguish this from a *res extensa* (an extended thing), which is the objective universe. He points out that this incomplete account of the subject resulted in Descartes implicitly believing that a gulf exists between subjectivity and objectivity. Lonergan concludes that this would create impossible difficulties for the realm of ethics, where one subject tries to persuade another that certain moral positions have objective validity.

Lonergan follows up his critique of Descartes with one of Kant. He suggests that the German tried to explore subjectivity in greater detail than Descartes but again failed to arrive at a point of intellectual conversion. Kant performs a deductive exercise of reasoning about what must be going on in the subject for it to be capable of knowing. Lonergan stresses that such a priori reasoning is deductivist and a far cry from a genuine empirical attentiveness to the operations of intentional consciousness. He notes, "Kant deduced, as well, a list of *a priori* categories of the understanding from a list of twelve types of propositions." He adds, "It is a fundamental Kantian assumption that what makes knowledge is experience, not a grasp of the unconditioned, not something that occurs in judgment." Consequently, he suggests that, like Descartes, the epistemology of Kant leaves a gulf between subjectivity and objectivity.[29]

BIAS IN POSTMODERN PHILOSOPHY

Earlier in this chapter, we noted the importance that Lonergan gives to the second wave of the Scientific Revolution, since it involves a transition to the third stage of meaning in culture. We also explained how so-called historicist philosophers, often from Germany, were particularly innovative in helping the transition to historical consciousness. It is now important to note that Lonergan believes that the German historicists included a good deal of perceptualist bias in their thinking.

Lonergan recalls that historicist philosophers stressed how different their thinking was from Enlightenment thinkers such as Descartes and Kant. Broadly speaking, these historicist philosophers can be understood as inaugurating the "postmodern philosophies" much referred to today. However, for all their differences, Lonergan suggests that a similar irony exists in this philosophical shift as did during the shift between medieval philosophy and the Enlightenment: despite the many differences, a *perceptualist* bias communicated itself from one philosophical approach to the next. Lonergan suggests that the perceptualist bias in historicist thinkers expresses itself in an inability to distinguish an act of insight from an act of judgment, with a resulting inability to resolve the problem of how subjectivity related to objectivity. Consequently, Lonergan identifies a tendency to relativism in thinkers that include Wilhelm Dilthey, Edmund Husserl, Hans-Georg Gadamer, and Martin Heidegger. Of these authors he states,

Experience and understanding taken together yield not knowledge but only thought. To advance from thinking to knowing there must be added a reflective grasp of the virtually unconditioned and its rational consequent, judgment. There is an insufficient awareness of this third level of cognitional activity in the authors we have been mentioning and a resultant failure to break away cleanly and coherently from both empiricism and idealism.[30]

Lonergan stresses that biased thinking always contributes to decline in history. Consequently, the persistence of perceptualism in postmodern thinking is deeply problematic.

Toward an Authentic Exercise of Historical Mindedness

This chapter has defined the terms that will be essential for understanding the argument of subsequent chapters. Diagram 1 provides a visual expression of basic terms introduced in this chapter, such as *stages of meaning, classicism, historical consciousness, perceptualist bias, progress,* and *decline.* The complex points outlined here are well captured in an article written by a student of Lonergan, Louis Roy, titled "Overcoming Classicism and Relativism."[31] He summarizes Lonergan's position as follows:

There is a subjectivity to be blamed because it fails to transcend itself, and there is a subjectivity to be praised because it does transcend itself. There is an objectivity to be repudiated because it is the objectivity of those that fail in self-transcendence, and there is an objectivity to be accepted and respected, and it is that achieved by the self-transcending subject.[32]

Hopefully, Christianity can contribute to a successful negotiating of the second axial period by world culture. In the next chapter, we begin a more concrete discussion of historical developments within Christian and Roman Catholic theology by tracing how both progress and decline were present in theological developments. This will form the basis for a discussion, in subsequent chapters, of the key developments in Vatican II and the significance of Pope Francis.

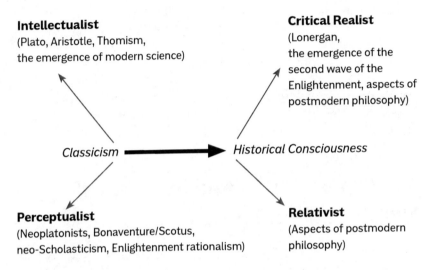

Diagram I: The Development from Classicism to Historical Consciousness

3

The Problem of Modernity
(1700–1962)

IN THIS CHAPTER, we examine how Catholic theology has been faring as the stages of meaning have been unfolding in history. Based on Lonergan's study, we observe how the church played a prominent role in the emergence of classicist culture in Europe, but then became sidelined during the period of Enlightenment. We then describe how the renewal of theology occurred as theologians of the nineteenth and twentieth centuries began to recognize that the second wave of the Enlightenment, characterized by historical consciousness, had the potential to enrich theology. We then trace the tension that arose between the Catholic magisterium and certain theologians on this matter, preparing for a discussion in the next chapter of how Vatican II took a decisive step in favor of a historically conscious theology.

Catholicism and Modernity

In his study of the stages of meaning in European history, Lonergan notes that the church never succeeded in engaging sufficiently with the culture of the Roman Empire to help arrest its decline and collapse.[1] By contrast, he praises the culture-building contribution of the church during the Middle Ages. With Herbert Butterfield, he suggests that it was the distinction between the supernatural and natural orders that allowed diverse faculties of theology and natural philosophy to emerge in universities, which would eventually enable the emergence of modern science. However, he also notes that, rather than embracing the innovations of modern science, church authorities tended to reject them.[2] As one Lonergan scholar stated, "The modern world and Catholicism had come to define themselves in opposition to each other for centuries."[3]

REASONS FOR RESISTANCE

Lonergan suggests that while it was regrettable that the Catholic Church demonstrated this resistance, it was understandable for three reasons. First, it was always going to be difficult for the church to accept the shift from an approach of reasoning based on Greco-Roman philosophy to one formed by modern science. Christianity had inherited this notion of reason at its founding and had not thought to question it for 1,400 years.[4] Also, after Thomas Aquinas's seminal contribution to theology had been recognized, it was always going to be difficult to acknowledge that Aquinas's thought would need to be subjected to major "transposition." Furthermore, Aristotelian approaches to reason seemed an excellent basis for Christian theology. Aristotle believed that science involved a search for the permanent causes of natural things, and this seemed compatible with a theology that was deeply concerned with questions of eternal truth. By contrast, modern science deals with the laws that govern contingent realities and never considers one theory to be the final word on a topic. It would be difficult for theologians at the beginning of the modern era to understand how such thinking could support a belief in the existence of God, let alone in supernatural revelation offered by an incarnate God.

A second reason that Lonergan offers for resistance is that Catholic theology had become subject to bias. In the previous chapter, we outlined Lonergan's description of this bias. He suggests that, during the fourteenth century, there emerged in Western Christian theology a version of Scholasticism—a neo-Scholasticism—that was understood to be following the thought of Thomas Aquinas, but was, in fact, more nominalist than Thomist. Lonergan suggests that there is a relativist approach to truth implicit in nominalism. He notes that a perceptualist expression of theology was produced in well-organized manuals used for the training of priests. Authors of such manuals included Carolus (ca. 1400), Cajetan (ca. 1500), Melchior Cano (ca. 1550), and Suarez (ca. 1600). He agrees with one commentator who identifies the following weaknesses in this theological system: "the excessive domination of a method too exclusively rational and logical; the danger of useless subtlety; and the danger of crystallization in to petrified systems."[5] Church authorities enforced adherence to the ideas outlined in seminary manuals:

> They seem to have thought of truth as so objective as to get along without minds...the same insistence on objective truth and the same neglect of its subjective conditions informed the old catechetics...and an old censorship, which insisted on true propositions and little understood the need to respect the dynamism of the advance toward truth.[6]

He adds that such a petrified system was never likely to be open to the modern challenge of radically rethinking its presuppositions.

A third reason that Lonergan offers to explain the resistance of Catholic theology to modernity has also been touched upon in chapter 2: the expressions of modern and postmodern philosophies with which the church was being confronted often themselves included much bias. Describing the failure of the Catholic Church to adapt to modernity, he states,

> To a great extent, this failure is to be explained by the fact that modern developments were covered over with a larger amount of wickedness. Since the beginning of the eighteenth-century Christianity has been under attack. Agnostic and atheistic philosophies have been developed and propagated. The development of the natural and of the human sciences was such that they appeared and often were said to support such movements. The emergence of the modern languages with their new literary forms was not easily acclaimed when they contributed so little to devotion and so much, it seemed, to worldliness and irreligion. The new industry spawned slums, the new politics revolutions, and the new discoveries unbelief.[7]

The three reasons outlined in this section offer what Lonergan called a critical and dialectical explanation of the philosophical motives for the early resistance of the Catholic Church to modernity. This analysis can be complemented by a study of the political history of modern Europe and the way the Catholic Church would become increasingly marginalized within it.

SOME DETAILS OF CATHOLIC REACTION

Commentators describe the eighteenth century as one of the most difficult that the Catholic Church had ever experienced. They recall that the pope had lost all influence over the Protestant states of Europe, and that the Catholic minorities that remained in those countries often suffered marginalization and persecution. At the same time, they note that, in the so-called Catholic states of Europe, governments were becoming increasingly nationalistic and resistant to the influence of the pope.[8] This sorry situation deepened as the French Revolution unfolded and when Napoleon Bonaparte came to power, conquering many states of Europe. In 1796, Napoleon invaded Italy and made Pope Pius VI a "virtual prisoner of the French."

The defeat of Napoleon in 1814 led to the period of Restoration in the European political order, and rights were restored to the pope, as to other monarchs. However, as one commentator expressed it, "monarchies would never be quite the same or quite so stable."[9] At this time, one recognizes a process of almost reactionary conservativism entering the official teaching of popes. In 1832, Pope Gregory published an encyclical, *Mirari Vos*, where he condemns modern liberal ideas, such as freedom of conscience, as stemming from a "shameful font of indifferentism," and in which he also speaks at length of "obedience owed to princes."[10] This encyclical set the tone for the long pontificate of Pius IX, "Pio Nono" (1846–57). This pope promulgated his *Syllabus of Errors* in 1864, in which he condemned the idea that "the Roman Pontiff can and should reconcile himself and make peace with progress, with Liberalism, and with modern culture."[11]

At a more theological level, Pio Nono supported the emergence of a theological movement called *ultramontanism*. This had emerged during the Napoleonic era among laypeople and the lower ranks of the clergy who were scandalized by the self-interested behavior of nationalistic bishops and higher clergy, whose salaries had been paid by national governments. They turned to the pope as a source of spiritual and moral authority higher than their bishops. This process was assisted by the increasing access to print media, which allowed recent teachings of popes to be widely read. Now, increasingly, to be a faithful Catholic meant obeying what the pope instructed on a variety of day-to-day issues:

> For Catholics the greatest ecclesiastical happening of the long nineteenth century was the almost unmitigated triumph of Ultramontanism, the concentration of authority in the papacy and the unquestioned recognition of other papal prerogatives. This was true not only on a high theological level but also on the level of a corporate consciousness that reached down to ordinary Catholics in the pews and touched them deeply.[12]

The movement of ultramontanism culminated in Pio Nono convoking the First Vatican Council. A central act of this council was to declare a definition of papal infallibility.[13]

In 1907, Pius X had the Holy Office issue a decree, *Lamentabili,* which formulated and condemned sixty-five propositions supposedly held by so-called modernist Catholic theologians. This was followed by an encyclical, *Pascendi Dominici Gregis,* which struck a similar note. Significantly, the pope declared that partisans of the modernist error are to be found not only among the church's enemies but "in her very bosom and heart." For that reason, he added, Catholic modernists were "the most pernicious of all the adversaries of the church." In 1919, Pius required all clerics, and especially teachers of philosophy and theology, to swear a long oath upholding the precepts of the two earlier documents. In 1950, there was a similar publication by Pius XII, *Humani Generis.* This condemned a number of "false opinions" and "novelties" that threatened to undermine Catholic truth. It would result in the censuring of many of the theologians who would subsequently be released from censure and would make key contributions to Vatican II.[14]

Signs of Change

One commentary suggests, "It is all too easy to characterize the response of the Catholic Church to these challenges as ostrich-like, the assertion of fundamental and integralist religious beliefs which championed the traditional and fulminated against the modern." It concedes that this is an accurate description of most papal pronouncements during these years but adds, "other Catholics, scattered throughout all layers of the Church and including members of the laity, ventured an understanding of the new social and economic environment."[15] A key point is that an accumulation of these alternative perspectives had one insight in common: theology needs to adopt a more inductive, historically conscious approach to reasoning, inspired by modern scientific method.

Neo-Scholastic and ultramontanist theology had a geographic center of gravity in Rome. Consequently, it is to different geographical locations that one must turn to notice signs of change. The term *transalpine theology* would later be used to characterize those currents of theology that emerged in France, Belgium, and Germany that would eventually reverse the Roman trend.[16] In the 1940s, these currents of theology would become known as representing *la nouvelle théologie*. The use of this term points to how the question of method was at the heart of the conflict between theologies. One recalls the distinction Lonergan makes between classicism and historical consciousness. For classicism, to speak of novelty in theology is to demonstrate that one is ignorant of what has already been established as eternally true. One recalls that Scholasticism employed an Aristotelian method that seeks to explain things in terms of permanent causes. As a result, "newness," or contingency, is considered a defect. By contrast, a theology that is influenced by more modern methods will adopt a more inductive approach. Above all, a modern study of human institutions, as is included in the remit of theology, will have to study how institutions evolve over time and how progress can occur as institutions develop new and valuable insights about what meanings should constitute community living. In such a situation, a study of change becomes part of the remit of theology, and by no means a defect.

THE "SOCIAL QUESTION"

One of the earliest intellectual currents of Catholic thought that pulled in a different direction than neo-Scholastic ultramontanism was to be found in thinkers who addressed issues of so-called liberal Catholicism and "the social question." Here, a remarkable figure was the Frenchman Félicité Robert de Lamennais (1782–1854). This idealistic diocesan priest, of a nervous disposition, began his career by protesting the worldliness of nationalistic French bishops, especially during the time of Napoleon. He was one of the earliest thinkers to articulate an ultramontanist theology. He proposed that the pope should exercise a spiritual and juridical authority over the bishops of each country and looked to the pope to discipline what he perceived as the worldliness of the French bishops and higher clergy (all of whom received salaries from the French government).

At the same time, Lamennais did not believe that any logical connection existed between an ultramontanist approach to the authority of the pope within the church and a notion that the pope should exercise direct political power. By the 1830s, he observed that political affairs in France had overcome the excesses of the revolutionary era. He now expressed the opinion that "monarchical government had run its course" and, remarkably, that "the Church must now espouse the ideals of freedom and democracy enshrined in the revolution of 1789." He founded a newspaper called *L'Avenir* and began to articulate a philosophy of "Catholic Action" where he proposed that Catholic laypeople should engage actively in the politics of liberal democracies.[17]

Such ideas were never likely to be accepted by the Vatican, and Lamennais was condemned in *Mirari Vos*. However, in certain circles, his ideas had taken root. One such place was Belgium, where the Catholic primate Archbishop Sterckx of Malines had played a role in winning national independence from Spain and in formulating the constitution of a new liberal-democratic state. Movements of liberal Catholicism also began to emerge in Spain, Italy, Germany, and Ireland. In many of these countries, the term *Catholic Action* began to take on a meaning much as Lamennais had hoped it would.[18]

In 1878, the ultramontanist Pope Pius IX was replaced by the more creative thinker Leo XIII. Pope Leo had traveled extensively

41

around Europe and had been affected by the poverty and social unrest he witnessed. He believed that this was related to the oppression of an urban working class that was emerging because of the industrial revolution. He believed that the church needed to speak out in the face of such injustice. He did this in an encyclical "On the Conditions of the Working Classes," called *Rerum Novarum* (1891). Some commentators suggest that this pope, although a philosopher, did not quite recognize the challenge his letter posed for the edifice of neo-Scholastic theology and for current Catholic teaching on church-state relations:

> The unrest of the 1880's…led the pope to react as both a traditionalist and an innovator. He showed himself favourable to organizations of the working classes that strove to ameliorate their situation….This meant that to some extent the social order was to be formed by movements coming from below as well as by authority and power descending from above.[19]

These commentators suggest that the notion of authority coming from below in society comes close to the liberal-democratic idea that moral authority lies with "the people." By contrast, as *Mirari Vos* had emphasized, traditional Catholic teaching held that all legitimate political teaching emanates from a Catholic prince.

LITURGY

Another instance of creative thinking during the nineteenth century occurred in a movement to reform the liturgy. Here again, changes occurred when individuals who considered themselves to be conservative proclaimed ideas that would have unintended consequences. Once again, key developments occur in France.

Dom Prosper Guéranger (1805–75) is described by one commentator as "a Benedictine monk and zealous ultramontanist." However, he held ideas that were in tune with the romantic movement in philosophy, and this led to certain unintended consequences, as his opinions, unwittingly, began to diverge from the version of ultramontanism that was standard in Rome. Together with a group of fellow Benedictines, he was convinced that one of the greatest evils that the French Revolution had perpetrated on society was a corrosive individualism and a loss of a sense of beauty. He founded a monastery in Solesmes that was dedicated to living a liturgical life that would be accessible to modern people "with the idea of providing a model of Christian community united around the liturgy of the church whose beauty would raise to God the souls of all who participated in it or witnessed it."[20] These monks were clear that this return to a past era of celebrating beautiful liturgy involved a prophetic challenge to modern society that could have implications for how that society organized itself.

Commentators note that the opinions of Guéranger exercise an unintended subversion of prevailing Catholic practice. During the ultramontanist era, the notion of liturgy was strictly that which had been articulated in the Council of Trent and interpreted through the lens of neo-Scholastic theology. By contrast, the Benedictines were an ancient religious order, having been founded in the sixth century. However supportive of the pope they wished to be, they could not suppress a memory of how matters had been before the sixteenth century. Consequently, as their liturgical movement spread, first through France and later farther afield, they began to promote practices that had not been encouraged by the official church up to this time: the distribution to laypeople of translations of the Latin Mass into local languages so that the faithful could follow what the priest was saying during the celebration of the sacrament; an encouragement for the congregation to sing during the Mass; and, above all, an encouragement of the frequent reception of holy communion.

The influence of this movement would continue into the twentieth century. Liturgical thinkers of this mode increasingly created links with social Catholicism and other currents of *la nouvelle théologie,* such as the ecumenical movement. Paradoxically, church authorities who were suspicious of these other expressions of creative thinking often remained supportive of these developments in liturgical thinking. In 1947, Pope Pius XII issued an encyclical, *Mediator Dei,* which extended magisterial support to several innovations of Guéranger.

SCRIPTURE

From the 1770s onward, some of the most aggressive onslaughts by Enlightenment thinkers against the truth of Christianity had come from rationalists who turned their attention to the text of the Bible. These authors called into question the extent to which the Bible could be considered to offer a credible account of historical events. Some claimed that Jesus of Nazareth never existed or, at least, that he did not raise from the dead. Similar efforts were made at studying the cultural provenance of the books of the Old Testament and, again, some authors discounted claims that a divine revelation had been at work in the history of the Jews.[21]

Commentators trace how Catholic responses to historical-critical methods in Scripture study came to include efforts to open institutes to study the Bible to refute these attacks on Christian belief. These institutes were expected to make partial use of modern methods of Bible study but never to produce conclusions that would question the neo-Scholastic theological method. Events did not unfold according to this plan. One such institute was the École Biblique founded in 1890 by Dominicans in Jerusalem. The founder of this school was Marie-Joseph Lagrange (1855–1938), who argued that an objective study of the Bible could not be used to "disprove" the Bible. On the contrary, he suggested that, when carefully employed by scholars who were also believers, such a study could help rather than hinder theology. Officials in the Vatican curia had mixed feelings about this Dominican development and tended to prefer sticking with a more neo-Scholastic approach to proving the claims of faith by an appeal to reason and to church doctrines, with only an occasional citation of "proof texts" from the Bible.

The Dominicans were allowed to continue with their institute in Jerusalem, but Pope Pius X then asked the Jesuits to open a Pontifical Biblical Institute (called "the Biblicum") to oppose the methods of the Dominicans with ones more congenial to the practitioners of Roman theology. The Jesuits opened this institution in 1909 but, once again, a series of ironic events followed. Soon, the Jesuits had taken a similar path to the Dominicans in Jerusalem. As O'Malley notes, "When Pius X founded the Biblicum in Rome he had an impact on the future of scholarship that frustrated the ultraconservative goal he had in mind."[22]

ECUMENISM

A formal ecumenical movement began in 1910 but was strictly a movement between Protestant and Anglican churches. The official position of the Catholic Church remained that other ecclesial communities that had separated from Rome should simply "return" to the fold. However, almost accidentally, those involved in some of the areas of renewal of Catholic theology already mentioned became concerned with ecumenism. One example was the area of liturgical renewal. One commentator comments on the apparent contradiction of the otherwise conservative Benedictine liturgist Dom Lambert Beauduin (1873–1960), who became sincerely committed to ecumenism:

> Beauduin saw the liturgy, moreover, as a medium in which Anglicans, Orthodox, and Catholics could meet in friendship....What especially drove Beauduin and other leaders of the movement, however, was the conviction that the liturgy, when properly and fully appropriated by the faithful, was not simply in principle the center of the devotional life of Catholics but the church's most powerful instrument for the spiritual rebirth of society at large.[23]

Implied in this quotation is the fact that Catholics involved in the movement of social Catholicism began to find common cause with Protestants. Another area of convergence, and perhaps the most important one, occurred in the realm of Bible studies. Those involved in the application of modern methods of exegesis to the Scriptures recognized that this represented a moment of a scientific exploration of fact that came prior to reflecting theologically on the doctrinal significance of the texts. In this way, Protestants and Catholics could meet on an equal footing. This, in turn, led to friendships forming and further theological discussions being made possible. One figure who was at the center of many such developments was Augustine Bea, who was rector of the Biblicum, and who Pope John XXIII would eventually appoint as the first president of a newly created Secretariat for Christian Unity that would help to prepare for and to direct the course of events during Vatican II.[24]

RESSOURCEMENT

One of the most important developments that contributed to *la nouvelle théologie* was a process of *ressourcement*, or "resourcing," in theology. In a strict sense, this development involved only the use of modern historical method to study classical authors such as the church fathers and Thomas Aquinas. Broadly, it involved an awareness that is characteristic of modern philosophies of hermeneutics: studying the past can provide new insights for the present. Consequently, it would be from historians and theologians involved in the *ressourcement* movement that the most explicit reflection on theological method would emerge. *Ressourcement* theology unfolded in two steps, one hundred years apart.

The first step occurred in the early 1800s in the Catholic faculty of theology in the University of Tübingen, in southwest Germany. This was the product of a specific history in the German-speaking lands of Europe. Here the teaching of Catholic theology—both for those preparing for priesthood and for laypeople—occurred outside the structure of diocesan seminaries.[25] In these lands, new nation-states were being formed and governments were eager to establish modern educational systems. This included a readiness to support both Protestant and Catholic theology faculties within state universities. At the same time, they required that modern methods be employed within such faculties. In Protestant circles, Friedrich Schleiermacher took a prominent role in the founding of the University of Berlin in 1810 and became a professor in its theology faculty. He took a lead in developing an original approach to a theology curriculum.

In such a national environment, Catholic bishops felt less threatened by modern ideas than was the case elsewhere in Europe. They permitted the forming of government-supported Catholic faculties of theology in state universities. One prestigious example of this emerged in the University of Tübingen. In fact, this university supported both a Catholic and a Protestant faculty of theology. These two faculties shared certain intellectual characteristics. Above all, both were influenced by the thought of German romantic philosophers such as Johann Gottfried Herder, who had opposed the individualistic rationalism of the Enlightenment with an appeal to community, tradition, and the value of popular culture.

As the Catholic faculty of Tübingen took shape during the 1820s and 1830s, a team of theologians began to produce innovative theology that involved both a respectful retrieval of Catholic tradition and new insights into how to apply this to the present. Works produced at this time included work in church history (Möhler's *Die Einheit der Kirche*); New Testament studies (Kuhn's *Das Leben Jesu*); fundamental theology (Drey's *Apologetik*); and moral theology (Hirscher's *Die Christliche Moral*).[26] The most famous theologian in this group was Johann Adam Möhler, a church historian and scholar of the church fathers. In his work, Möhler combined an intimate familiarity with individual church fathers with a study of the development of Christian doctrines over time. The influence of romanticism becomes evident in his book *Unity in the Church*, where he invokes traditional themes such as the church as the people of God and the church as *communio*, themes that would exercise a major influence on Vatican II.[27]

However, impressive as the achievements of Möhler and his colleagues were, their direct influence on Catholic theology elsewhere in Europe was limited. Most faculties of theology and seminaries were funded and directly controlled by bishops. Under the influence of church documents such as *Mirari Vos* and the *Syllabus of Errors*, the approach to theology in most parts of Europe remained one that was found in the theological manuals used in seminaries. These manuals substituted for any direct reading of theological sources and added that "their interpretation can and must lead to nothing less and nothing more than the most recent magisterial statements."[28]

Given this background, one can ask how it was possible that any change would occur. On this question, Pope Leo XIII played a role in encouraging innovation, probably beyond what he intended. Before becoming pope, Leo had been a professor of philosophy. In 1879, he published the encyclical *Aeterni Patris*. More than other popes, Leo recognized that Catholic responses to modern philosophical currents were weakened by not always being well-informed and by not working on a united front. He therefore instructed that less emphasis be placed on diverse approaches within Scholasticism and that Catholic intellectuals unite themselves in promoting the thought of Thomas Aquinas. He also suggested that Catholic scholars should study Thomas directly and not rely solely on the commentaries of seminary manuals. What followed was a renewal of historical studies of Thomas Aquinas, as well as of the church fathers, such as had characterized the faculty of Tübingen.

Early figures in the *ressourcement* process included Étienne Gilson, who published his first work on Aquinas in 1919 and would continue a lengthy career that would include both publishing his own works and opening Catholic centers of medieval studies in more than one country. Austrian Jesuit Josef Andreas Jungmann set about studying how doctrines and practices of the sacraments had developed over the centuries. In a book published in 1932, he pointed out that the form of the sacrament of penance practiced currently had been unknown in the patristic era. He later published a work, *Missarum Solemnia*, that traced how diverse liturgical practice had been before the reforms of the Council of Trent. In the 1940s, Jesuits Henri de Lubac and Jean Daniélou began a multivolume series of Sources Chrétiennes, which provided French translations of the church fathers. The 1950s witnessed an acceleration of publications that studied the historical development of doctrines. This included Yves Congar's book *True and False Reform in the Church*, which pointed out that church reform had been a recurring as well as a necessary and healthy part of church life through the ages.[29]

The Galilean Moment

In the previous section, we observed how modern patterns of thinking—sometimes accidentally—began to encroach on Catholic thought and pastoral practice. From a perspective of Lonergan's analysis of history, it is important to note that in the case of some of the individuals involved in this process of renewal, an awareness grew that theology was facing the need for a shift of methodological paradigm.

In chapter 2, we noted how Lonergan appreciated the account of the genius of Galileo Galilei offered by Herbert Butterfield. This historian of science suggests that Galileo did not make any single scientific discovery comparable to other figures that came before and after him. Rather, Galileo grasped the need to change the "thinking cap" they were using. He grasped that what was needed was a change from a method of searching for permanent causes to one employing empirical method. This is what made Galileo so shocking to theologians.[30]

In the realm of Catholic theology, one can notice something similar occurring. In the years leading up to the Second Vatican Council, steps toward historical consciousness occurred mostly in a piecemeal fashion. However, gradually, some of those engaging in these diverse exercises of applying historical method to theology began to communicate with each other and to recognize that what was afoot in theology was a major shift in the methodological paradigm. Movement in this direction occurred when practitioners of one area of innovation found common cause with one or two others. For example, those involved in renewal of both scriptural and liturgical studies tended to become open to both ecumenism and to social Catholicism. However, Galileo-like figures in Catholic theology also began to emerge. Here we focus on two, Marie-Dominique Chenu and John Courtney Murray.[31]

MARIE-DOMINIQUE CHENU

This gifted Frenchman joined the Dominican Order and was trained in neo-Scholastic theology in the International Pontifical College of the Angelicum, Rome.[32] He was ordained in 1919 and was invited to stay on as a professor in the Angelicum. However, he was an independent thinker and felt that his former professors had not been teaching a version of Aquinas that was as historically accurate as he believed had been called for in *Aeterni Patris*. He asked and was given permission to be transferred to the formation house of the Dominicans in France. There, at a college called Le Saulchoir, he was happy to teach a discipline that was considered of marginal importance: historical theology. In preparing his lectures, he discovered the thought of Johann Adam Möller and the Tübingen school and became enamoured of them. His work in the college was respected by his peers, and in 1932, he was elected regent of studies of the college. In this role, he received his Galilean insight: a historically conscious approach should influence all aspects of theology, much as it did the school of Tübingen one hundred years earlier. In 1937, he published a vision statement to this effect: *Une ècole de théologie: Le Saulchoir*.[33] Here, he outlines how the entire program of theology could be organized along historically conscious lines:

> With the aid of Tübingen…we are able to counter the abstract intellectualism of the Enlightenment and its indifference to history—two related sins—which have not failed to contaminate modern scholasticism, including countless manuals, even the Thomist ones.[34]

As was the case with Galileo, church authorities recognized the significance of the paradigm shift for which this relatively junior churchman was calling. They censured him severely. He was removed from Le Saulchoir, refused permission to teach or to have contact with younger Dominicans, and, of course, refused permission to publish further. In fact, his little book was withdrawn from circulation.

During the years of his official censure, Chenu exhibited a resilient and optimistic personality and began a completely new phase of his life. He deepened an engagement with social Catholicism and, especially, with a movement of "worker priests." These priests took ordinary jobs in factories and farms to work alongside members of the working class who had become alienated from the Catholic Church. These priests began to share a concern about social inequality that was keenly felt by the working class and tended to support socialist political policies in the countries where they worked. For his part, he began to study sociology and, at the same time, to offer a theological reflection to support the direction being taken by the worker priests. While not permitted to publish in academic theological journals, he nevertheless began to deepen his own theological thinking. He became convinced that God's grace was at work in aspects of secular society and culture. He employed a term from the Gospels, "the signs of the times," to capture this phenomenon of God's grace prompting a progress in history that is related to the coming of the kingdom of God. He states,

> Thus all the so-called secular values, built up over the centuries by the consciences of men and women and in their building of the world, are understood anew as various "signs of the times" in the messianic era which has begun. These…already represent the unfolding of the economy of salvation, a process which will culminate eventually in the absolute event of Jesus Christ.[35]

He adds that the church should be clear in its support for these grace-filled developments that have occurred in secular culture. For the church of the 1940s and 1950s, this was radical thinking indeed. However, as will be outlined in the next chapter, with the advent of Pope John XXIII and the Second Vatican Council that he convoked, such ideas would become welcome.

JOHN COURTNEY MURRAY

John Courtney Murray, ten years younger than Chenu, was from the United States and was a Jesuit. However, the trajectory of his life and thought bore similarities to the older Frenchman. Murray was silenced by ecclesial authorities in 1953. Until then, he had focused

on a question of Christian doctrine — religious liberty — convinced that
Catholic teaching on this matter needed to develop. Murray entered
the New York province of the Jesuits and had studied in Rome, where
he was influenced by figures like Jacques Maritain and by the Catholic
Action movement. At first, he had understood himself to be functioning narrowly within the realm of Catholic social ethics and therefore
within what we have broadly described as social Catholicism. However,
the vehemence of the opposition he experienced to his ideas led him
to think more deeply about questions of epistemology and theological
method. From about 1959, he increasingly turned to the thought of
Bernard Lonergan, recognizing that the true drama of the age lay in
"the contemporary clash between classicism and historical consciousness."[36] He explained,

> Classicism designates a view of truth which holds objective
> truth, precisely because it is objective, to exist "already out
> there now" (to use Bernard Lonergan's descriptive phrase).
> Therefore, it also exists apart from its possession by anyone.
> In addition, it exists apart from history.[37]

By contrast, Murray offered a Lonergan-based account of historical consciousness. He explained how intellectual conversion on the
part of the theologian could assist him or her in grasping the aspect of
relativity in Christian doctrines — how they are articulated within a culture, how they are limited by the horizon of meaning of that culture,
and how they can develop over time. At the same time, he recognized
that such an approach could lead to relativism. However, he trusted in
the principle espoused by Lonergan that an authentic exercise of subjectivity (within history, within culture) can lead to objectivity. As one
commentator noted, "Murray thought he had, in Lonergan's notion of
'virtually unconditioned' judgment, a sufficient grounding for the truth
of particular ethical determinations of general value claims."[38]

Murray then began to explore the psychological factors involved
in moving from classicism to historical consciousness. He acknowledged that these are profound. He recognized that a sincere Catholic
who had only known to live within a classicist horizon could be deeply
threatened by an appeal to trust in subjectivity, and to recognize that
understanding truth, even eternal truths revealed by Jesus Christ, is
always historically conditioned and open to further deepening. He

recognized that, to someone of a fearful disposition, shifting beyond classicism could seem like losing one's Christian faith. He suggested that this explained the emotionally charged and not always rational opposition that his ideas could at times provoke. Considering this insight, Murray sometimes spoke of the difficulty of conducting a theological debate on specific issues when what was really at issue was the epistemological horizon out of which the debaters were operating. In one case, he stated, "Our minds are not meeting—in the sense I mean that they are not even clashing (i.e. disagreeing on some technical point of theology)."[39]

Conclusion

Both Chenu and John Courtney Murray would return to public influence in the years when Vatican II was in session. There they would find fellow cause with a remarkable group of capable theological advisors to bishops—*periti*—many of whom had also been silenced by the Holy See during the 1950s. One commentator on the council would assert that a key characteristic all these *periti* had in common was that they were proposing a historical consciousness approach to theology. In an article entitled "Reform, Historical Consciousness, and Vatican II's Aggiornamento," the commentator, John O'Malley, explores how modern philosophies of history influenced the notion of *aggiornamento* that Pope John XXIII introduced to the council. He adds,

> We are not experiencing a "reform" as that term is traditionally understood as a correction, or revival, or development, or even updating. We are experiencing a transformation, even a revolution.[40]

4

Vatican II and the Church in the Modern World

IN JANUARY 1959, the newly elected Pope John XXIII announced that he was convoking an ecumenical council. In September 1962, in his opening address to this council, he called for an updating— *aggiornamento*—in Catholic thinking. According to Lonergan, what unfolded over the course of the next four years represented a breakthrough in the story of Catholic thought toward historical consciousness:

> The massive breakthrough took place at the Second Vatican Council. In general, then, what is going forward in Catholic circles is a disengagement from the forms of classicist culture and a transition into the forms of modern culture.[1]

He added that he hoped that his own thought, as expressed in *Insight: A Study of Human Understanding* and *Method in Theology*, could effectively introduce an explicit concern with theological method into the discussions about the spirit of Vatican II. A reference to the spirit of Vatican II is important here. Lonergan felt that the council represented only the beginning of a process that involved the church passing through an epochal shift in the stage of meaning from which it operated. In the above quotation, note that he shifts to the present tense in suggesting that what is going forward in theology is a disengagement from forms of classicist culture. This article was written in 1969 and implies that Vatican II itself did not complete such a disengagement. Consequently, this chapter proceeds in two parts. First it outlines how the council involved a breakthrough to historical consciousness; second, it identifies ways in which this breakthrough was incomplete.

Breakthrough to Historical Consciousness

A study of the theological breakthrough that is represented by Vatican II needs to attend carefully to the events of the first period and the intersession that followed.[2]

PRELUDE TO THE COUNCIL

On October 11, 1962, some 3,500 council fathers gathered with great pomp and ceremony for the opening Mass. The opening discourse of Pope John XXIII could hardly have been clearer as a call for change in fundamental aspects of the manner of doing theology in the church. Three aspects were especially noted. First, he proposed that the council adopt a new and positive attitude to modern political and economic developments, putting aside a misguided nostalgia. The pope phrased these points, which amounted to a direct criticism of the curial officials sitting by his side, as follows:

> In the daily exercise of our pastoral office, we sometimes have to listen, much to our regret, to voices of persons who, though burning with zeal, are not endowed with much sense of discretion or measure. In these modern times they can see nothing but prevarication and ruin....We feel we must disagree with those prophets of gloom, who are always forecasting disaster, as though the end of the world were at hand. (*Gaudet Mater Ecclesia* 8)[3]

Second, the pope appealed to the council to demonstrate a concern for ecumenism. Finally, he called for the council to support the use of "modern methods of study" of Christian doctrine. On this issue, he remarked,

> The Church...must ever look to the present, to the new conditions and new forms of life introduced into the modern world, which have opened new avenues to the Catholic apostolate....The whole world expects a step forward toward a doctrinal penetration and a formation of consciousness in faithful and perfect conformity to the authentic doctrine, which, however, should be studied and expounded through *the methods of research and through the literary forms of modern thought*. The substance of the ancient doctrine of the deposit of faith is one thing, and the way in which it is presented is another. (*Gaudet Mater Ecclesia* 12, 14 note 4)[4]

THE DOCUMENTS DRAFTED BEFORE THE COUNCIL

It did not take long for the progressive voices among the church fathers to mobilize in response to the speech of the pope. A transformative event occurred when officials of the Vatican curia sought to introduce to the floor of the council a document they had prepared before the council on the theme of revelation.[5] It was formulated in a standard neo-Scholastic set of arguments. Indeed, it adopted a particularly antiecumenical tone.[6]

On November 14, Cardinal Ottaviani, the prefect of the Holy Office, presented the document to the floor. At one stage in the discussion, Bishop De Smedt of Bruges denounced the text for its three "isms": "triumphalism, clericalism, and juridicism." There followed a process of administrative wrangling about whether or not to reject the draft document on revelation. After a complicated series of events, including an inconclusive vote on November 20 by the council fathers, the situation was settled by the extraordinary intervention of Pope John. The pope announced that "yielding to the wishes of many," he was setting up a "mixed commission" made up of members of both the Vatican curia and the newly created Secretariat for Christian Unity. The task of this commission would be to "amend the schema, shorten it, and make it more suitable, with an emphasis especially on general principles."[7] If these terms of reference seemed to indicate little about the theological preferences of the pope, the fact that he appointed Cardinal Bea of the Secretariat for Christian Unity to be cochairman of this commission spoke volumes. Now, a progressive cardinal was taking up a role of equal importance to the prefect of the Holy Office.[8] One journalist wrote,

> The fate of the council was at stake on Tuesday, November 20....With the vote on November 20 we can consider the era of the Counter Reformation ended and a new era for Christendom with unforeseeable consequences, began.[9]

THE INTERVENTION OF CARDINAL SUENENS

With such support from Pope John, a new question now faced the council. If the council fathers were clear what kind of documents they did not want, what then did they want? It was with this question in the air that Cardinal Suenens stood up to speak on December 4. His talk would quickly be another defining moment of the first session of the council.[10]

Cardinal Suenens was the archbishop of Malines, Belgium. As mentioned in chapter 3, this diocese had a long tradition of supporting the social Catholicism and the movement of Catholic Action. Furthermore, earlier in the century, a predecessor of Suenens had encouraged a young priest of the diocese, Joseph Cardijn, to form a movement of "Young Catholic Workers" that had subsequently spread throughout the world.[11] This movement adopted an inductive method of "See-Judge-Act" to help young lay Catholics participate in the mission of the church. In his encyclical *Mater et Magistra*, Pope John had referred explicitly to this method as one of those modern methods that was suitable for helping the church engage with the modern world. Suenens now employed a method that was broadly inductive and historical as he made proposals for the future course of the council.[12]

Suenens began by suggesting that not only the document on revelation but all the documents prepared by the curia be abandoned and a new set be drafted. He suggested that the council should address the theme of the identity of the church ("What do you say about yourself?") and its role in the modern world ("What do you have to say to the world?"). He explained that reflecting on these two questions would involve reflecting about the mission of the church *ad intra* and *ad extra*. He suggested that the council should be organized around three dialogues. The first two of these should address *ad intra* questions: first, the council should dialogue with its own, Catholic, membership; and second, it should be an ecumenical dialogue "with brothers and sisters not now visibly united with it." The third dialogue should address *ad extra* questions of how the church relates to the modern world. He emphasized the importance of the *ad extra* role of the council itself and concluded with an appeal: "that this plan…open a way for a better hearing of the church and understanding of it by the world today and that Christ be for the men and women of our times ever more the way, the truth, and the life."[13]

This intervention was met with immediate and prolonged applause. Evidently, Suenens struck a chord and articulated for most of the bishops a way of proceeding with which they could agree. The first session of the council ended on December 8. Shortly after this date, the ailing Pope John made one final decision that would determine the future course of the council. In place of the mixed commission that had been redrafting only the document on revelation, he appointed a new "coordinating commission" that would take responsibility for redrafting a new set of documents. He appointed Cardinal Suenens as joint chair of this commission, along with Cardinal Ottaviani.[14] The message was clear: the Suenens proposal should be adopted as a plan for the remainder of the council.[15]

During the "intersession," the period between the first and second sittings of the council, the joint coordinating commission created seventeen new committees, each of which would produce a document. One or two members of the coordinating commission were assigned to chair each of the committees, which were then expanded with a variety of bishops and theologians. This committee work proceeded with considerable success, having many documents prepared before the second session of the council in October 1963. One commentator states,

> The Coordinating Commission rode herd on the other commissions. By the time the council resumed on September 29 it had accomplished a wonder. It had reduced the number of schema to a manageable size. It had extracted revised texts from almost every commission.[16]

The next three years would produce many dramatic events, including substantial changes to many of these draft texts. However, the final sixteen documents passed by the council remained substantially those that had been proposed to them at the beginning of the second period. These, in turn, remained largely true to the vision outlined by Suenens in 1962. Before discussing these documents, it is important to note the contribution made by the newly elected Pope Paul VI.

THE CONTRIBUTION OF POPE PAUL VI

During the first period of the council, it was widely understood that Pope John XXIII was a sick man. His death in June 1963 did not come as a surprise. In fact, during the first period of the council, there was much consideration regarding his successor. It had been widely perceived that Giovanni Battista Montini, the archbishop of Milan, was the favorite of Pope John XXIII to succeed him. Montini had said little in the first period, but he had made one brief speech where he lent emphatic support to the ideas of Cardinal Suenens.[17] During the conclave, this speech was regarded as a kind of manifesto for the election of Montini. Those who approved of what Pope John had begun in the council voted for Montini. He was duly elected and adopted the name Paul VI.[18]

As the council proceeded, Pope Paul VI made several gestures that assured its completion. These included his initial permission that the council should be prolonged to take the four years that it did—something that had not been anticipated by Pope John XXIII. In a variety of interventions, he sought to reassure the minority that interpretations of documents would be within the bounds of what they could consider reasonable, without, for the most part, fundamentally alienating the majority. This assured that documents were passed with considerable majorities. He also made visits outside Rome that symbolized the new openness to the world that that council had begun to express. In their turn, these visits reinforced progressive arguments on issues that were still under discussion on the council floor.[19]

THE FOUR CONSTITUTIONS

The sixteen documents of the council comprised four "constitutions," nine "decrees," and three "declarations." The constitutions are intended to be the lens through which the decrees and declarations should be interpreted.[20] They are "On the Church" (*Lumen Gentium*);

"On the Church in the Modern World" (*Gaudium et Spes*); "On the Sacred Liturgy" (*Sacrosanctum Concilium*); and "On Divine Revelation" (*Dei Verbum*).

Lumen Gentium treats the question of the identity of the church *ad intra*. Here, three characteristics exhibit a shift to historical mindedness in the document. First, the preferred image for the church is "people of God." This image is taken from the Book of Exodus and evokes the story of the chosen people traveling for forty years across the desert to take possession of the promised land. This historical image is given priority over the static image of the church as hierarchy, which was the one favored by the draft document on the church prepared before the council. Second, the notion of collegiality is addressed. This explores how the pope shares the responsibility for governing the church with the college of bishops. Third, a renewed emphasis is placed on the role of the laity in helping implement the mission of the church. Here, emphasis is placed on the importance of baptism as involving a "universal call to holiness" for all Christians and prompting all to behave as "priests, prophets, and kings" as they participate in the mission of the church.

Gaudium et Spes, The Church in the Modern World, opens with a statement that reverses the classicist tendency to act as a "prophet of doom" toward the modern world:

> The joys and the hopes, the griefs and the anxieties of the men of this age, especially those who are poor or in any way afflicted, these are the joys and hopes, the griefs and anxieties of the followers of Christ. Indeed, nothing genuinely human fails to raise an echo in their hearts....This community realizes that it is truly linked with mankind and its history by the deepest of bonds. (no. 1)

The document is divided into two parts. Part 1 offers an anthropology that provides a basis for its comments on the role of the church in the modern world. Part 2 proceeds to employ the See-Judge-Act method to discuss "Some Problems of Special Urgency." Section titles include "Fostering the Nobility of Marriage and the Family"; "The Proper Development of Culture"; "Economic and Social Life"; "The Life of the Political Community"; and "The Fostering of Peace and the Promotion of the Community of Nations."

The constitution on the liturgy, *Sacrosanctum Concilium,* began a process of introducing changes that, for many ordinary Catholics, would be the most radical of the council. In its first chapter, it criticized how laypeople had been reduced to playing a passive role in liturgy and called for changes to ensure their active participation. Second, it questioned the "almost absolute value assigned to Latin in the liturgy" in the Roman Rite in recent years and opened the possibility of producing missals in vernacular languages by noting the practice in the Eastern churches of considering "all languages as liturgical." When the constitution was passed by the council, Pope Paul VI moved quickly to form a commission and to produce a series of decrees from 1964 to 1975, including that of translating missals and sacramentaries into vernacular languages and turning around altars so that priests could face the people.[21] This communicated a message that was repeated in other documents: laypeople were now invited to become active participants in the mission of the church.

The document on revelation, *Dei Verbum,* contained several of the deepest shifts in the theology of the council. Instead of exalting the importance of Tradition over that of Scripture, it insisted on a revival of the use of Scripture by lay Catholics. It also shifted the vocabulary by which it spoke of themes such as revelation and faith. Instead of implying, as did neo-Scholasticism, that Jesus Christ communicated a series of supernatural concepts, it spoke of Jesus Christ as the "self-communication of God." Similarly, instead of describing the act of faith as primarily an assent to propositions, it spoke of an act whereby "man commits his whole self freely to God" (*Dei Verbum* 4, 5).[22] Protestant observers at the council noted that the call for such an existential response to the word of God was at the heart of what Martin Luther had been calling for. Some considered this document to be more important for ecumenism than the council document explicitly devoted to the topic.[23]

DECREES AND DECLARATIONS

The remaining decrees and declarations of the council can be understood as expanding on either the *ad intra* or the *ad extra* concerns of the constitutions. The titles of the nine decrees are as follows: on the mass media (*Inter Mirifica*); on Catholic Eastern Churches (*Orientalium Ecclesiarum*); on ecumenism (*Unitatis Redintegratio*); on bishops (*Christus Dominus*); on the renewal of religious life (*Perfectae*

Caritatis); on the training of priests (*Optatum Totius*); on the aposto-
late of the laity (*Apostolicam Actuositatem*); on missionary activity (*Ad
Gentes Divinitus*); and on the ministry and life of priests (*Presbyterorum
Ordinis.*)[24]

The three declarations addressed themes on Christian education (*Gravissimum Educationis*); on non-Christian religions (*Nostra
Aetate*); and on religious liberty (*Dignitatis Humanae*).[25] Technically,
the declarations had the least doctrinal weight of the documents produced by the council. However, as will be discussed later, two of them
included themes that represented the most significant development of
church doctrine to occur in the council: religious freedom, and a positive theological evaluation of non-Christian religions.

Ambiguities about Historical Consciousness

The above account of the first period of the council and the
first intersession explains why Lonergan can describe Vatican II as a
breakthrough to historical consciousness. However, a careful study
of the second, third, and fourth periods illustrates a countervailing
point: the breakthrough was not complete. Ambiguities in the breakthrough manifested themselves in two ways: first, the shift to historical consciousness was vehemently opposed by an influential minority
of council fathers that won several concessions; second, uncertainties
and disagreements emerged among the progressive majority, revealing uncertainty about just what historical consciousness might mean
for Catholic theology.

CONCESSIONS TO THE COUNCIL MINORITY

During the first period of the council, a distinction between two
parties of council fathers emerged—the majority and the minority. The
numbers of these parties could shift according to the issues being debated,
but the majority always comprised at least two-thirds of the council.[26]
Members of the Vatican curia were prominent in the minority, and they
exercised an influence on proceedings that was out of proportion with
their numbers. Much of this influence was exercised by curial officials

having access to private meetings with the pope and being able to persuade him to intervene in council proceedings.

When Pope Paul VI took up his post, he continued and amplified the practice that had already begun with Pope John XXIII of seeking to reassure the council minority. The positive contributions of Pope Paul VI to the successful completion of the council has already been outlined. Several commentators suggest, however, that the support extended by the pope to the council minority went beyond a merely diplomatic concern to avoid schism in the church. One suggests that Pope Paul VI was a man who suffered from a lack of decisiveness, expressed in a "worrisome temperament."[27] Others point out that the indecisiveness of the pope was expressed in a reluctance to clarify what regulations were governing the council and, especially, his relationship to it. They suggest that what resulted was an increasing tendency on the part of the pope to intervene in the deliberations of the council, often favoring the opinions of the council minority.[28]

During the second period, Pope Paul expressed concern about discussions of collegiality—the relation between pope and bishops—in debates over *Lumen Gentium*. When the committee of four moderators of the council decided to hold a straw vote to check what the weight of opinion was among the council fathers on this question, the pope first intervened to forbid the vote, and then allowed it to proceed.[29] Many interpreted this as a desire to protect the influence of conservative members by concealing the fact that they were relatively few. Indeed, some council fathers found it strange that the pope was writing an encyclical on the church, *Ecclesiam Suam*, concurrently with the debates on *Lumen Gentium*. This seemed to imply a sense of competitiveness with the authority of the council.

In the final week of the third period, Pope Paul made his most dramatic intervention of the council. He made a series of requests, including that votes on documents be delayed until the fourth session and that some of these be redrafted. On the important question of how *Lumen Gentium* described collegiality in its second chapter, he requested that an "explanatory note" be added to the text to explain how its comments on collegiality should be interpreted. This note reserved to the pope the right to interpret the meaning of the conciliar statements on this issue. One commentator describes the response of this group as "ecstatic," and adds, "No matter what the pope hoped to accomplish, he in fact gave those who opposed collegiality a tool they could—and would—use to interpret the chapter as a reaffirmation of the status quo."[30] By contrast, the end of the third period was considered by many of the council majority as a low point of the council to date. It became widely known as *la settimana nera* (the black week).[31]

Finally, on the day the fourth period of the council opened, September 14, 1965, Pope Paul issued the document *Apostolica Sollicitudo*. This inaugurated a practice, to begin immediately after the council, of convoking synods of bishops on a regular basis. While this appeared to be a gesture toward collegiality, it was interpreted by some as the very opposite. Commentators note that control of the theme and agenda of such synods remained in the hands of the Vatican curia, as did the power of choosing which bishops should attend, and the writing of the final report on the gathering. One commentator suggests, "With one stroke the text cut collegiality off from grounding in the institutional reality of the church."[32] He suggests that this lessened the overall effectiveness of the council, and concludes,

> On the final outcome of the council the minority left more than a set of fingerprints. On the center-periphery issue the minority never really lost control. It was in this regard so successful that with the aid of Paul VI the center not only held firm and steady but, as the decades subsequent to the council have irrefutably demonstrated, emerged even stronger....Collegiality, the linchpin of the center-periphery relationship promoted by the majority, ended up an abstract teaching without point of entry into the social reality of the church. It ended up an ideal, no match for the deeply entrenched system.[33]

While the above quotation is sharp in its judgment, such criticism should also take note that the council majority was not always clear on just what they were trying to propose.

UNCERTAINTY AND DISAGREEMENT

Concessions to the council minority were not the only factor that introduced ambiguity into Vatican II. Another factor was uncertainty and disagreement within the majority about just what they wanted to say. Such uncertainty became particularly evident when the council reflected on issues of the mission of the church *ad extra* during the third and fourth periods.

Three documents of the council addressed key issues of the *ad extra* mission of the church. As already mentioned, the most important of these was the Pastoral Constitution on the Church, *Gaudium et Spes*. While a declaration was the form of council document deemed to be least important, in fact, two of the three declarations were recognized to touch on issues with major long-term consequences for Catholic theology. In each case, both uncertainty and disagreement were evident amongst progressives on how to proceed.[34]

The Declaration on Religious Liberty, *Dignitatis Humanae*, represented the clearest development of doctrine in the council. For the most part, opposition to the doctrine of religious freedom came from the predictable source, the council minority. Indeed, as already mentioned in chapter 3, the *peritus* who was most involved in producing the various drafts, John Courtney Murray, made explicit use of the thought of Lonergan to explain this opposition. In a lengthy article written to persuade council fathers to accept the declaration, he distinguished between what he called a first view that opposed the declaration and a second view that supported it. Concerning the intense disagreement being demonstrated, he wrote,

> This abortive dialogue seems to indicate where the real issue lies. The First and Second View do not confront each other as affirmation confronts negation. Their differences are at a deeper level indeed, at a level so deep that it would be difficult to go deeper. They represent *the contemporary clash between classicism and historical consciousness.*[35]

At the end of the third period, as noted earlier, Pope Paul VI intervened in the affairs of the council with several requests. One of these was to delay a vote on *Dignitatis Humanae* as well as to reformulate the arguments offered for a change in the doctrine. The pope, in effect, was requesting that the draft of which Murray had been principal author be redrawn. In fact, even among progressive members of the drafting committee there were those who had been uneasy with the degree of historical consciousness being shown by Murray. Even Yves Congar was pleased to have the opportunity to tone down some of the more innovative aspects of Murray's draft. Murray was distressed by this and wrote some articles after the council suggesting that the declaration was weakened by the changes found in its final draft.[36]

In addition to debating the declaration on religious freedom, the third period addressed questions of a theology of non-Christian religions that would culminate in the declaration *Nostra Aetate*. In these debates, considerable disorientation among progressives was also evident. This time, however, the main cause of disagreement was less theological and centered more on questions of a geopolitical nature.

The steps taken in producing *Nostra Aetate* began with the question of how Catholics should relate to Jews. In the light of the horrors of the Shoah during the Second World War, council fathers felt the need to distance the Catholic Church from a long history of Christian antisemitism.[37] However, when governments of Arab states heard that the Vatican Council was considering making a favorable declaration about Judaism, they vehemently objected. These were years of high tension between the Muslim states of the Middle East and the State of Israel. Arab leaders felt that any statement favoring Jews would be interpreted in the current political climate as support for the State of Israel. At this stage, the drafters of the declaration suggested that a way around this problem could be found by adding some positive reference to Islam in the declaration. They suggested that this could be done by stressing those qualities held in common by the three monotheistic religions that claimed roots in Abraham. It seemed unsuitable, however, to make such a point without referring to what is admirable in other world religions such as Hinduism and Buddhism. The final text of *Nostra Aetate* made positive reference to all these religions. Almost by accident, the desire of the council fathers to attend to the signs of the times had shifted the question about just what the signs of the times were.

The process of producing both *Dignitatis Humanae* and *Nostra Aetate* demonstrated that both the bishops and their theological advisors were relatively unprepared to address questions of the mission of the church *ad extra* with any degree of depth. One commentator suggests that "frontiers had been crossed for a voyage into an unknown sea." He adds,

> The problems of religious freedom and of relations with non-Christian religions took the Council to the frontiers of ecclesiastical culture....The vast majority of the Catholic

65

episcopate was caught by surprise and had no sufficient deposit of doctrinal thought to fall back on.[38]

This kind of unclarity was at least as much in evidence when it came to discussing the document that was widely considered to be the most important effort by the council to address questions *ad extra*: The Pastoral Constitution on the Church in the Modern World, *Gaudium et Spes*.

GAUDIUM ET SPES

No such document such as *Gaudium et Spes* had been conceived of in the set of draft documents prepared before the council. Nevertheless, the idea that such a document should be produced was intrinsic to the path-setting speech that Cardinal Suenens had given in December 1962. It made its first appearance as the final of the seventeen drafts that the coordinating commission presented to the council at the beginning of the second period. It was an important document, and for that reason was called a "constitution." However, by the time the council got around to discussing it, time was running out. During the third period, more time than expected had been taken in debating *Dignitatis Humanae* and *Nostra Aetate*. Discussion of the Pastoral Constitution began in the third period and was carried into the fourth period, with much lobbying being conducted in the intersession.[39]

The relatively happy conclusion to the debate on *Gaudium et Spes* stood in contrast to the intense difference of opinions that emerged during the debates that had been devoted to it. As might have been predicted, voices for the conservative minority made their protests. However, what was remarkable about this debate was that most opposition to the draft text came from within the progressive majority. In the end, it became evident to those debating the text that time was running out and that there was a danger of no document of this kind being passed at all. As a result, most council fathers, at the advice of their *periti*, put aside differences about the text and accepted the one that had been presented to them. A reason to explore the details of the debate is that the differences that emerged at this time were significant indicators of how interpretation of the council would unfold in the years after its closure

It was possible to identify at least four currents of progressive thought in the debates over this document. Each represents a different approach to historical consciousness, and it is the fourth of these currents that was the primary influence on the version of the text that was accepted.

The first current of thought concerning *Gaudium et Spes* came from the "Group of the Church of the Poor." This group had formed during the first period of the council. A crucial point of reference for the group was a book written by a worker-priest Paul Gauthier, *Christ, the Church, and the Poor.*[40] This book helped them to formulate three central proposals that they hoped the council would adopt. First, just as there exists an ontological link between Christ and the church, and Christ and the Eucharist, so also there exists "at least a partial ontological identity between the church and the poor." Second, the church should set aside its triumphalist theological attitude, reduce the pomp and ceremony of many of its public and liturgical events, and divest itself of some of its financial wealth. Third, the church should accept modern insights that express a concern for the poor through a concern for social justice: "transform our works of welfare into social works based on charity and justice."[41] The Group of the Church of the Poor exercised some small influence on a variety of documents, and especially on *Gaudium et Spes.* Also, Pope Paul was sympathetic to their arguments and performed a public gesture at the end of the council of selling a papal tiara and dedicating the resulting funds to the poor. The historical significance of this group would become evident in the years after the council, as members of this group would be influential in the way that Vatican II was interpreted in Latin America.[42]

A second current of thought occupied the opposite place on the spectrum of progressive opinion from the Group of the Church of the Poor. It comprised certain *periti* who adopted a neo-Augustinian position. These included Joseph Ratzinger, the future Pope Benedict XVI, and theological experts Henri de Lubac and Hans Urs von Balthasar. Ratzinger began what one commentator describes as "attacking the text radically and violently."[43] The young German *peritus* offered a list of six objections. At the heart of these was an objection to anthropology operative in the first part of the document, an anthropology that offered a fundamentally optimistic account of human nature. Shortly after the council, he would express his objection to part 1 of the document by posing the following sardonic question: "Why exactly the reasonable and perfectly free human being described in the first articles [of

Gaudium et Spes] was suddenly burdened with the story of Christ?"[44] He proposes a major rewrite of the first part of the document, replacing the current anthropological starting point with a "Christological starting point." One of the council fathers, Monsignor Volk, expressed agreement with Ratzinger and added, "The Christian message must not be diluted in order to make it more accessible; there is a darkness in the world that can be dispersed only by Christ."[45]

The third influential group to engage in the debate about *Gaudium et Spes* can be described as German neo-Thomists. These centered around the *peritus* Karl Rahner. Their approach to Thomas bore the signs of their prolonged dialogue with two German thinkers: Martin Luther and Immanuel Kant. Rahner was intensely critical of the draft document, suggesting that it was shallow both philosophically and theologically. He criticized what he suggested was a naïve optimism in the work, saying that it was more a work of sociology than theology. Exhibiting an influence of Luther, he spoke of the need for a theology of the cross to explain the way the church interacts with the world.

The fourth and final current of thought can be described as that of the French Thomists. This group included Jean Daniélou, Yves Congar, Gérard Philips (a French-speaking Belgian), and Marie-Dominique Chenu, a father figure for the others. This group had been responsible for the preliminary drafting of the much-criticized text. During the intersession before the fourth period, Chenu had written an article defending the text, "A Pastoral Constitution of the Church."[46] This then became part of a series of lectures organized by French and Belgian *periti*. One commentator describes the drama of Chenu's intervention in which "the most fully developed part of his lecture had to do with the Christian anthropology contained in the schema"—exactly that which had been criticized by the progressive German *periti* such as Ratzinger and Rahner.[47] In the end, most of the council fathers voted in favor of *Gaudium et Spes*. The following quotation from *Gaudium et Spes* indicates the extent to which Chenu's vision of the signs of the times characterized the document:

> While earthly progress must be carefully distinguished from the growth of Christ's kingdom, to the extent that the former can contribute to the better ordering of human society, it is of vital concern to the Kingdom of God. For after we have obeyed the Lord, and in His Spirit nurtured on earth the

values of human dignity, brotherhood and freedom, and indeed all the good fruits of our nature and enterprise, we will find them again, but freed of stain, burnished and trans-figured, when Christ hands over to the Father: "a kingdom eternal and universal, a kingdom of truth and life, of holi-ness and grace, of justice, love and peace." On this earth that Kingdom is already present in mystery. When the Lord returns it will be brought into full flower. (no. 39)[48]

However, commentators suggest that the vast majority that voted in favor of *Gaudium et Spes* did so in part because they were in a hurry to conclude the affairs of the council. The disagreements that had sur-faced during the debate about the document had not been resolved and would reemerge in the years after the council.[49]

Conclusion: A Positive Evaluation of Ambiguity

The second half of this chapter has been devoted to identifying ambiguities in the documents of the council, not least in those that concerned the *ad extra* mission of the church passed in the third and final periods of the council. Before advancing beyond an account of the final sessions of the council, it is worth noting the reflections of two commentators who evaluate such ambiguity positively. The first, writing in the late 1990s about the debates in the third period of the council, writes,

The comparison and clash between an essentially deductive method and an inductive method, which had already begun during the preparatory work [before the council], manifested itself more obviously during this third period....During the council a transition, imperfect indeed and incomplete, had begun from the former method to the latter. This was a shift of enormous cultural and ecumenical importance, which, over thirty years later, increasingly demonstrates its validity and its fruitfulness.[50]

More recently, another commentator examines the protracted debates that led to the eventual acceptance of *Gaudium et Spes* and states,

> We should never underestimate the importance of the inclusive and intellectually honest synodal processes and their outcomes. The messiness, lengthiness, complexity, and compromises involved can actually be the marks of a virtuous process that goes beyond the easy majoritarianism of what is intellectually fashionable, or the monarchy of an encyclical-based Magisterium, and produces a solid collegial consensus that can withstand the test of time.[51]

Lonergan would agree with both statements. However, he would suggest that employing a theological method based on intellectual conversion could help inductive, synodal processes of reflection arrive at more satisfactory conclusions.

5

The Battle for the Meaning of Vatican II

(1965-2005)

LONERGAN WAS CLEAR that much work needed to be done by Catholic theologians to complete the task begun in Vatican II. He published *Method in Theology* in 1972 and hoped that it would be considered a contribution to this goal. In an article composed while he was writing this book, he explains,

> Classical culture cannot be jettisoned without being replaced; and what replaces it, cannot but run counter to classical expectations. There is bound to be formed a solid right that is determined to live in a world that no longer exists. There is bound to be formed a scattered left, captivated by now this, now that new development, exploring now this, now that new possibility. But what will count is a perhaps not numerous center, big enough to be at home in both the old and the new, painstaking enough to work out one by one the transitions to be made, strong enough to refuse half-measures and insist on complete solutions even though it has to wait.[1]

In this chapter, we begin analyzing the first fifty years of imple-menting the council, drawing both on comments made by Lonergan himself, who lived until 1984, and on my own judgment. Evaluating developments in this way is an exercise in what Lonergan explains as the functional specialty of dialectic. Here one seeks to differentiate ideas that are based on authentic cognitional theory from those that are not. Due to the limits of space, we make some broad judgments, without the nuance that a fuller application of dialectic method would require. The 1970s witnessed ample examples of the emergence of a scattered left. Following this, the next thirty-five-year combined pon-tificates of St. John Paul II and Benedict XVI witnessed an exercise of correcting this imbalance by the magisterium that seemed to favor theologies of the solid right and to employ a theological method that replaced inductive methods with a more deductive approach. In later chapters, we will observe that Pope Francis represents another switch of methodological direction, one closer to the kind of critical realist position outlined by Lonergan.

Tensions between Left and Right (1965–1978)

In the years after Vatican II, there is ample evidence of what Lonergan described as the scattered left and solid right in Catholic theology. Lonergan himself, writing in the 1970s, expressed concern about the emergence of a scattered left. Additionally, the signs of the emergence of a solid right, partly in reaction to excesses on the left, were emerging already during this decade. Consequently, aspects of the subsequent thirty-five years can be understood as a coming to prominence of these tendencies.[2]

A SCATTERED LEFT

Lonergan generally avoided comment on ecclesiastical current affairs. However, it is possible to deduce his views on how theology was developing after the council from a few published comments. Above all, he expressed concern about the emergence of a scattered left in the postconciliar theology.[3] He identifies three tendencies of this kind in Roman Catholic theology.

First, he was alarmed about some theologians who had replaced neo-Scholastic philosophy with approaches that were philosophically superficial and could not support Christian doctrines. In 1979, he speaks of "the debacle that followed the pastoral council," adding, "I would suggest that an outstanding characteristic of the post-Vatican II horizon is a certain disregard of doctrinal issues."[4] He notes that he is not alone in expressing a concern about superficial thinking in postconciliar theology. He comments on how Karl Rahner expressed concern that "a fashionable secularism" was beginning to influence some Catholic theologians, producing "a situation in which genuinely unchristian heresies spring up in the church, whose adherents would not want to leave the church."[5]

A second manifestation of a scattered left during this time, according to Lonergan, concerns certain forms of liberation theology.[6] In his article "Theology and *Praxis*,"[7] Lonergan suggests that certain forms of liberation theology employ philosophical tools that encourage a social activism that is too dependent on the thought of Hegel and Marx. He takes issue with the use of a notion of *praxis* by theologians of liberation and proposes how their concern for issues of social injustice could better be addressed by a theological method based on intellectual conversion. He suggests that theology should engage in a "praxis of meaning" where theologians first seek to influence the meanings and values that constitute a culture, confident that change in this realm will produce change in social structures. On this issue, he adverts to *Method in Theology*, where he had written,

> The family, the state, the law, the economy are not fixed and immutable entities. They adapt to changing circumstances; they can be reconceived in the light of new ideas; they can be subjected to revolutionary change. But all such change involves change of meaning—a change of idea or concept, a change of judgment or evaluation.[8]

Here, there is notable convergence between Lonergan's thought and a letter that would be produced by the Holy See in 1984, the year of his death, "Instruction on Certain Aspects of Liberation Theology."[9]

A third area of concern for Lonergan involved developments in the field of fundamental theology. Here, his criticisms involve more of an invitation to deepening than a major criticism of error. In the late 1970s, he was invited to offer a series of lectures to an Anglican audience in Toronto on the state of postconciliar Roman Catholic theology.[10] One commentator suggests that what Lonergan has to say about Roman Catholic fundamental theology is revealing of his opinions about developments in other theological disciplines. He summarizes Lonergan's view as criticizing "a fundamental theology without philosophical foundations...without paying the price of intellectual conversion."[11]

A SOLID RIGHT

Lonergan had less to say about the persistence of a solid right in postconciliar theology.[12] However, developments that occurred after his death threw light on the significance of developments that were already occurring in the 1970s: the reassertion of a neo-Augustinian position in theology, especially as expressed by contributors to the theology journal *Communio*.

Before we outline the historic details of what unfolded during the pontificates of John Paul II and Benedict XVI, we need to clarify a complex epistemological point: perceptualism is the great enemy of a critical realist approach to theology as proposed by Lonergan and, at least implicitly, by Pope Francis.

In chapter 2, we outlined how Lonergan claims that perceptualism is a biased approach to knowing that has existed from the beginning of philosophy and, as examples, we offered Neoplatonism and medieval nominalism. We then noted that the tendency to perceptualism remained strong in philosophy since Descartes, even though the notion of the "turn to the subject" in the thought of Descartes also made possible an explicit appeal to intellectual conversion by Lonergan. Lonergan believed that the persistence of perceptualism in modern philosophy had much to do with the excesses of the French revolution and with Marxism. A reason for this is that perceptualism can lead to absolutizing certain ideas—such as the priority of the state over the individual—rather than stressing the importance of developing virtuous subjects as the bedrock of authentic decision-making in society.

We also noted how Lonergan believed that the tendency toward perceptualism runs so deep in human nature that it appears also in theology. He identifies this tendency with medieval nominalism, as well as in the neo-Scholasticism of the early modern theology manuals of

Catholic seminaries. While not present in Lonergan's writings, I suggest that a perceptualism with roots in classicism persists in the epistemology underlying the theology of both Pope John Paul II and Pope Benedict XVI, and will examine, how the philosophy of Karol Wojtyla involved an eclectic mix of classicist Thomism, elements of medieval monastic theology, and modern phenomenology. Aspects of this philosophy indicate an openness to critical realism, and more work needs to be done in relating Lonergan's thought to that of Wojtyla, the philosopher. Nevertheless, as pope, Wojtyla relied heavily on the thought of Cardinal Joseph Ratzinger, and consequently, a good deal of neo-Augustinianism entered his teaching magisterium. Neo-Augustinianism has primarily perceptualist presuppositions, similar to those of Neoplatonism described in chapter 2.

It is also important to note that the perceptualism implicit in neo-Augustinianism tends toward a certain deductivist method. In this approach, little attention is paid to the ongoing process of discovery and gradual moral improvement that characterizes human living. Rather, there is a tendency to suggest that the truth is easy to "see" and that the individual Christian must simply decide whether to comply with it or not. Consequently, communicating the contents of the *Catechism of the Catholic Church* as a means of a "New Evangelization" is emphasized. Here, theological method is based on first presenting true ideas—doctrines—and then "deducing" how these can be applied to given situations. From a critical realist point of view, what is missing here is a sense of how human knowing in embedded in historical process. Critical realists value the way liberation theologians employ a method of dialogical interaction with culture, employing terms such as *See, Judge, Act*, and the *hermeneutical circle*.

Of course, Lonergan stresses that much that passes as historically conscious in both philosophy and theology has fallen into another form of perceptualism. Here thinkers fail to distinguish between insight and judgment, and thus become relativist or overinfluenced by rational systems of ideas, such as the thought of Karl Marx. Nevertheless, a study of the pontificates of Popes John Paul II and Benedict XVI must clarify how perceptualism is at work in a solid right in Catholic theology and how this tends to support a deductivist approach to theological method and a centralizing exercise of church authority.

For the remainder of this chapter, we turn to the details of church affairs in the years after Vatican II to illustrate, as Lonergan predicted, the polarization that unfolded between a fragmented left and a solid right.

The Neo-Augustinian Method (1978–2013)

Throughout the 1970s, differences emerged between neo-Augustinian theologians and those who adopted alternative approaches to expressing the progressive vision of the council. Neo-Augustinian theologians had been especially concerned about three developments: the negative reaction of some progressive theologians to *Humanae Vitae*; a book by Hans Küng, *The Church*, which called into question the notion of papal infallibility; and controversies that occurred between the bishops of the Netherlands and the Vatican over a new *Dutch Catechism*.[13] Since 1965, these neo-Augustinian theologians had been board members of the theology journal *Concilium*. The fact that some of the editorial board broke away to form a different journal indicates that differences had begun to run deep. As one commentator subsequently stated, "The theological fault lines between *Concilium* and *Communio* proved to have a long-lasting impact on post-Vatican II Catholic theology."[14]

The opening issue of *Communio* set the tone for much that was to follow. It begins with an article by Hans Urs von Balthasar, "*Communio*—a Program."[15] In this article, he suggests that the process of interpreting the council had been captured by thinkers who employ a philosophy of "evolutionary communism." In consequence, he proposes a neo-Augustinian approach to interpreting the council to counteract this tendency. He concentrates on the ecclesiological dimension of the major texts of the council such as *Lumen Gentium* and *Gaudium et Spes*. He suggests that the theme of the church as people of God was too easily co-opted by thinkers of the evolutionary communist kind and should now be sidelined as a concept. He notes that the title of chapter 2 of *Lumen Gentium* is "On the People of God," but that this chapter also refers to the notion of church as *communio*. He proposes that those seeking to interpret the council should now bring this notion to the center of attention. Such an ecclesiology would have a theological depth that is often lacking in other images of the church. He explains that it has firmer roots in trinitarian theology and in Christology, focusing first on the communion that exists between the church and the Trinity, and only secondly on the communion the church seeks to promote with all peoples. He insists on the christological basis of any notion of communion: "The divine Logos, who as conclusion and culmination of the Old Testament promise has been bestowed on us in Jesus Christ, as grace yet in genuine humanity, making full communion possible."[16]

In the early 1970s, von Balthasar's interpretation of the council was believed by many other theologians to be an inaccurate one, seeking to impose a neo-Augustinian interpretation on an event that had explicitly chosen not to take such a direction. In fact, there is a further irony here. The main references to the church as *communio* in *Lumen Gentium* occur when the document speaks in favor of collegiality between bishops and pope. However, von Balthasar does not explore this point; rather, as subsequent developments would show, he was proposing an understanding of *communio* ecclesiology that placed little emphasis on collegiality. To explain this point, one needs to study the developments during the pontificate of John Paul II.

When the conclave gathered in 1978, many cardinals believed that a pope was needed who would offer a firmer sense of direction to the church than Paul VI seemed to have done in the final years of his pontificate. The decision to opt for a young and strong pope was deepened by the untimely death of the first choice of the conclave, John Paul I, who survived for only one month. As the electors of Karol Wojtyla might have anticipated, being made pope at the age of fifty-eight resulted in his long-lasting pontificate that placed a major stamp on the post–Vatican II era. Furthermore, his pontificate was followed by that of Joseph Ratzinger. Ratzinger had been the prefect of the Congregation for the Doctrine of the Faith under Pope John Paul II and maintained many of his policies. Being elected in 2005 and resigning in 2013 meant that the postconciliar church witnessed a continuity of papal approach for thirty-five years. As noted below, these policies resembled closely those proposed in the theology journal *Communio*.

THE VISION OF POPE ST. JOHN PAUL II

With Pope John Paul II, the world witnessed a man of remarkable energy, ability, and creativity. Being non-Italian was important, as

77

it represented a break with centuries of previous practice. Wojtyla also had a remarkable personal history.[17] With other Poles, he had lived through traumatic experiences under Nazi occupation during the Second World War and Soviet occupation in the years that followed. Unlike many, while undergoing these experiences he believed he heard a call both to become a priest and a philosopher. His attraction to philosophy lay in a conviction that underlying the violently oppressive actions of Nazis and communists lay an intellectual problem. He was convinced that the ideologies behind these political movements resembled each other in opting for false notions of the human person. He believed that there was an immense wisdom in a Christian vision of the human person but acknowledged that this needed to be rearticulated in a modern context. Over time, he developed his own philosophy of the human person that combined aspects of traditional Thomism, the mystical thinking of John of the Cross, and modern phenomenology.[18]

As a philosophy professor, Wojtyla had worked with intellectuals and with youth. However, unlike some more activist priests, he had encouraged an opposition to communism at the level of ideas and he had remained reserved about encouraging direct political confrontation. Government officials (who had placed listening devices in his confessional) misinterpreted him as posing no threat to their interests. Their relationship with church authorities was such that they had the ability to influence the ecclesiastical careers of individual priests. They favored that of Wojtyla, helping him rise to the position of auxiliary bishop and then cardinal archbishop of Kraków. They were destined to be surprised. Soon after Wojtyla was elected pope, the trade union, *Solidarnosc*, began protests about working conditions and, ultimately, against the Polish government. The young pope was swift to recognize in the active nonviolent method of this movement just the kind of activism for which his philosophy called. He lent immediate support to this movement, and, in so doing, it is generally recognized, he contributed to the fall of communism both in Poland and the Soviet Union, an event symbolized by the destruction of the Berlin Wall in 1989.[19]

The pastoral vision of Pope John Paul II was impressive in many respects. However, some commentators found his style of thinking deductivist and, ultimately, not best suited to understanding or implementing Vatican II. One commentator employs Lonergan's dialectic method to study the philosophical thought of Wojtyla. Referring to his use of the phenomenology of Max Scheler, she acknowledges that Wojtyla "adverts to something like self-appropriation in his theory." However, she suggests that he ultimately fails to follow through on this approach and opts instead for a form of neo-Thomistic realism that reveals a perceptualist bias. Parts of Wojtyla's philosophy include what Lonergan explains as a bias of "dogmatic realism":

> This aspect of neo-Thomist cognitional theory "that the real is an aspect of the already out there now to be seen" [in Wojtyla] does manifest itself in a conceptualism that puts a grasp of the real out of our reach as well as contribute to the category error of mistaking doctrine for truth. Not that doctrines are not true, but they are propositions captured in concepts. And the truth cannot be reduced to a concept; it must be kept alive, embodied and incarnate in living, breathing persons intent in achieving their own authenticity.[20]

Another scholar applies this same line of analysis to the encyclicals and exhortations written by Pope John Paul II. Without disputing their authority as magisterial documents, he suggests that the conclusions at which they arrive could be better supported and nuanced by a critical-realist approach. For example, he suggests that CDF declaration published under the authority of the pope, *Dominus Jesus: On the Unicity and Salvific Universality of Jesus Christ and the Church*, represents "an excellent specimen of classicism." In the document, "an overwhelming emphasis is put on truth" without acknowledging that truth comes as a judgment that builds on acts of experience and insight. He recalls that "the conceptualist mind discusses concepts instead of beginning with the data and continuing with questions in order to let insights and judgments emerge."[21]

One can note that there remained some tension in intellectual collaboration between John Paul II and Cardinal Ratzinger. The pope had a more intrinsically optimistic disposition than is normal for a true Augustinian. This tended to make him more progressive than his CDF prefect on issues concerning the relations of the church *ad extra*. However, on issues of church discipline—issues *ad intra*—he found in a neo-Augustinian argument just the intellectual instrument he needed to achieve what he believed was necessary for the church.

AN ALLIANCE WITH JOSEPH RATZINGER

Other commentators on the pontificate of John Paul II suggest that a second explanation of the deductivist tendencies of his teaching and decision-making is related to the choice he made to appoint Cardinal Joseph Ratzinger as prefect of the Congregation for the Doctrine of the Faith. While he was confident in his own abilities as a philosopher, the pope was happy to receive the support of a first-rate theologian such as Ratzinger. Furthermore, he decided that he was in sufficient agreement with the German prefect to form an alliance with him. This implied, in fact, a readiness to implement many of the ideas expressed in the theology journal *Communio*.

One commentator describes Joseph Ratzinger as "having an Augustinian heart, an Augustinian sensibility."[22] Born in 1927, Joseph grew up as a sensitive and artistic boy and part of a loving family with a strong Catholic faith. He was close to his brother and sister. The world he lived in was full of contrasts. His parish enjoyed a rich liturgical tradition, cultivating a sense of the beauty of the sacraments. Otherwise, however, the world seemed to be a dark place. His father, a policeman, refused to collaborate with his Nazi superiors and the family was forced to move regularly during his childhood. His father retired when Joseph was sixteen years old; the family lived quietly as Germany endured the Second World War. Before he ever began the study of theology, his experience of life had encouraged him to think of family and church as places of beauty, truth, and love, and the outside world as a place of ugliness, lies, and violence.[23] When he witnessed the fall of Nazism, he rejoiced. He was proud of how Catholics like his own father had resisted the Nazis. With a phraseology that could have come from Augustine's *City of God*, he stated of the Catholic Church, "It had, with its strength that came from eternity, remained standing in the inferno that had gobbled up the powerful."[24] One commentator comments on the long-term influence the experience of the war would exercise on the thought of Ratzinger:

What the Nazi experience seems to have bred in Joseph Ratzinger, or the preexisting trait it reinforced in him, was a kind of distancing, a pattern of removing himself from unpleasantness, isolating the pure ideal—of the faith, the church, the family, the nation—from the inevitable corruptions of the world.[25]

Joseph joined the seminary shortly after the Second World War. There, like so many intelligent students of his generation, he found the prevailing neo-Scholasticism to be utterly unsupportive of his faith.[26] Commentators suggest that he was not exposed to the phenomenon of a renewal of Thomist studies at this time, but rather accepted at face value the claims of his neo-Scholastic professors to be accurately presenting the thought of this Dominican. By contrast, the academically gifted young Ratzinger was welcomed to study with a Professor Gottlieb Söhngen at Munich University, who guided him to complete a prize-winning doctorate on Augustine. Following German practice, Ratzinger proceeded to study a second doctorate, his *habilitationsschrift*, and this was also directed by Söhngen. This work was on the theology of the history of St. Bonaventure. One commentator identifies characteristics in both doctorates that would characterize Ratzinger's thought in later years. On the one hand, Ratzinger's theology seeks to be affectively and spiritually nourishing, stressing the beauty of the Christian word rather than seeking arid logic system. On the other hand, there is a tendency toward "preferring of the humility of faith over the pride of philosophy; a defense of the 'city of God' against the powers of the 'earthly city'; and a recognition of the duality that lies deep within human beings who, even when desiring the good, cannot embrace it."[27]

As mentioned in the previous chapter, Joseph Ratzinger arrived at Vatican II as a *peritus* and, although still only thirty-five years old, played an active role. He had a major influence on *Dei Verbum*, and on important sections of *Lumen Gentium*.[28] Within the community of progressive *periti* his giftedness was recognized, but not all appreciated his neo-Augustinian approach. As noted in chapter 4, his interventions on *Gaudium et Spes* were not accepted by most council fathers. Some suggested that his tendency to view the church-world relationship in negative terms seemed to resemble the attitude of being "prophets of doom" criticized by Pope John XXIII in his opening address to the council.

A criticism of the Platonism of Ratzinger was made in a public forum by a fellow German priest and academic, Walter Kasper, shortly after the council. In the late 1960s, Ratzinger published a book, *Introduction to Christianity*, and Kasper wrote a robust review of it.[29] This led to Ratzinger publishing a response, and this, in turn, led to two further exchanges of articles. In his comments, Kasper suggests that his own preferred approach to theology is rooted in Aquinas and in Vatican II. He describes his foundational account of the human person as based on "the human being's concrete interwovenness with nature, society, culture, and history."[30] By contrast, he suggests that there is a fundamentally Platonist anthropology underlying Ratzinger's *Introduction to Christianity*. For example, he notes a current of dualism in the following statement:

> Man's center of gravity draws him to the visible, to what he can take in his hand and hold as his own. He has to turn around inwardly in order to see how badly he is neglecting his own interests by letting himself be drawn along in this way by his natural center of gravity....Without this change of direction, without this resistance to the natural center of gravity, there can be no belief.[31]

Kasper recognizes that this kind of dualism has roots in a tradition within Christian theology that passes through Augustine and Bonaventure. However, he suggests that this dualism presents problems for modern theological reflection in that its intrinsic Platonist tendency leads to philosophical idealism that then makes it difficult to establish coherency and objectivity in philosophical statements. He adds that this creates problems for the way theologians who employ this dualistic thinking appeal to the doctrinal authority of the magisterium of the church. Kasper proceeded to outline apsects of Ratzinger's treatment of a variety of doctrinal issues in *Introduction to Christianity* with which he does not agree.[32]

THE CENTRALIZING OF CHURCH GOVERNANCE

As mentioned earlier, Pope John Paul II had an optimistic disposition and a natural gift for leadership. He did not have the same Augustinian "heart" and "sensibility" as did Ratzinger. However, he decided to ally himself with Ratzinger and with the project for church reform outlined by contributors to the theology journal *Communio*. There were two main reasons for this. First the philosophy of John Paul II was eclectic and included Augustinian elements. In fact, in some respects, John Paul II had more reason than Ratzinger to think of the church-world relationship in dualistic terms. During the Second World War, Poland had been on the receiving end of immense violence and ideological control by the Nazis. Then, to add insult to injury, his homeland was "invaded for a second time" after the war, with the Soviet Union imposing another oppressive ideology on the population.[33] More than had ever been the case for Catholics in Germany, the Catholic Church became a place of refuge for much of what the Poles regarded as good and true and beautiful.[34]

A second reason concerned the state of the Catholic Church in the late 1970s when John Paul II was elected. The Polish pope was keenly aware of what has been described in the previous chapter as the presence of a "scattered left" in Catholic theology. With liberal theologians, he was aware that Vatican II had left many unanswered questions and that it needed to be interpreted in a creative way that would generate new insights. However, he also believed that experimentation had gone too far among theologians. Also, he believed that instead of the Holy See correcting these tendencies, a sense of tiredness and drift had characterized the later years of the pontificate of Paul VI. Having reflected much on a philosophy of family life, he disapproved of what he perceived as widespread opposition to *Humanae Vitae*. Above all, he was appalled to witness what he perceived as an encroachment of Marxist thought occurring among liberation theologians in Latin America. For these reasons, he became convinced that a new coherent direction was needed, and that this would require a greater exercise of central authority than had been evident for some time.[35]

On this matter, John Paul found a like mind in Joseph Ratzinger, then the cardinal archbishop of Munich, and according to some commentators, an individual who had persuaded many German bishops in the conclave of 1978 to vote for Wojtyla as pope.[36] One commentator summarizes the opinions of Ratzinger on postconciliar developments:

> In (Ratzinger's) memoirs he speaks of finding on his return
> to Rome in the council's final years a growing impression
> that "everything was open to revision," as well as a grow-
> ing resentment against Rome and the Curia. As theologians
> began seeing themselves rather than the bishops as those
> most expert in the faith, the popular perception grew that

the church and even its creed were subject to change, while
the emphasis on the church as the "people of God" seemed
to suggest a new idea of a "church from below" or a "church
of the people."[37]

On an intellectual level, many of the ideas that would direct the papacy
of John Paul II were announced in his first encyclical, published in 1979,
Redemptor Hominis.[38] However, several commentators point to 1985 as
a defining year for this papacy. By this stage, the pope and his prefect of
the CDF had clarified a strategy for church governance and they looked
to the Extraordinary Synod of Bishops, which was held to commemorate
the twentieth anniversary of Vatican II, to put this in place. One of the
aims of this strategy would be to replace the use of the term *people of
God* to describe the church with a term that had been present but less
prominent in council documents, the church as *communio.*[39]

As the Synod of Bishops began, it was followed with considerable
interest in various quarters. Cardinal Avery Dulles devoted a chapter of a
book to it.[40] This Jesuit theologian from the United States was a staunch
supporter of policies previously undertaken by John Paul II to restore
orthodoxy in Catholic theology. However, he was also in favor of plural-
ism in theological debate. He approved of the way discussion during the
synod (both in documents submitted beforehand and in contributions
on the floor) offered a range of perspectives. Within the debate at the
synod, he recognized "two major schools of thought." He describes the
first as the "Augustinian school" and explains that it "had a markedly
supernaturalistic viewpoint, tending to depict the church as an island
of grace in a world given over to sin." He described the second group as
"communitarian" (unlike other commentators who tend to speak of this
group as broadly Thomist[41]). He explained that this group represented
a "more humanistic and communitarian outlook" and argued in favor
of "further development of collegial and synodal structures so that the
church may become a free and progressive society…in every nation and
every sociological group."[42]

If many commentators were impressed by the proceedings of the
Synod of Bishops of 1985, fewer were impressed by the final report,
or *relatio*, that claimed to summarize the debates. Dulles is cautious
in making a judgment on the *relatio* but asserts, "It is legitimate to ask
whether the Synod documents represent a victory for any particular party
or tendency among the bishops."[43] Other commentators were more

direct in their judgment that the *relatio* privileged a neo-Augustinian perspective.[44] They noted that a notion of the church as *communio* was now proposed as the single best manner of capturing the spirit of the ecclesiology of Vatican II. One states, "The notion of the church as a 'people of God' lost the momentum it had gained twenty years before at the council."[45] Another commentator went so far as to suggest that the synod represented "the beginning of a process of gradual but sure disqualification of some of the interpreters of Vatican II and of a reduction of the possible interpretations of the conciliar documents."[46]

Cardinal Walter Kasper shared the opinion that the final *relatio* of the Extraordinary Synod of Bishops of 1985 represented a watershed in the strategy of governance of the church by Pope John Paul II. In 1999, he published a chapter in a book that identified a process unfolding after this synod, which he considered to be the enforcement of a theology of *communio* on the church. His chapter noted that in 1992, the Congregation for the Doctrine of the Faith issued a letter entitled "Letter to the Bishops of the Catholic Church on Some Aspects of the Church Understood as Communion." He notes how this letter stated that the universal church "is not the result of the communion of the churches, but its essential mystery is a reality ontologically and temporally prior to every individual particular church…and gives birth to particular churches as her daughters."[47] Echoing his comments of the late 1960s about the theology of Joseph Ratzinger, he noted that the letter argues in favor of the priority of the universal church over the local church by invoking a Platonist principle that universals are ontologically prior to particulars. As he had done in the 1960s, he expressed disagreement with such epistemology, proposing instead one that was more rooted in Aristotle and Aquinas. Basing himself on such alternative epistemology, he proposed an "equi-primacy" between the universal church and local churches.[48]

However, Kasper's opinions were not accepted by Pope John Paul II. In 1998, the pope produced a document of higher magisterial authority than the letter of Ratzinger of 1992: a *moto proprio*, or legal instruction, entitled *Apostolos Suos*, "On the Theological and Juridical Nature of Episcopal Conferences."[49] Remarkably, the publication by Kasper in 1999 of a criticism of this document provoked Cardinal Ratzinger to publish a response in a German newspaper. To the fascination of Vatican observers, there followed an exchange of additional articles between the two curial cardinals, much as had occurred thirty years earlier. As had occurred in the earlier exchange, the disputants remained respectful of the argument of the other without arriving at much of a convergence of views.[50]

THE NEW EVANGELIZATION AND THE *CATECHISM OF THE CATHOLIC CHURCH*

Commentators other than Walter Kasper agree that, from 1985 onward, Pope John Paul II, with the close collaboration of Cardinal Ratzinger, implemented with great consistency a strategy of centralized governance and a call on both bishops and theologians to adopt an approach to theology that resembled that found in the theology journal *Communio*. In addition to an appeal to an ecclesiology of *communio*, this strategy included the stressing of certain further themes. Above all, this involved a call for a "New Evangelization." This theme was first introduced in the encyclical that Pope John Paul published in 1990, *Redemptoris Missio*.[51] However, it took on momentum when the bishops of Latin America were requested to adopt it in the final document of their General Assembly held in Santo Domingo in 1992. During the meeting of CELAM, new evangelization was closely associated with preaching the contents of the *Catechism of the Catholic Church*, which was published in that year.

Throughout the 1990s, Pope John Paul focused on the forthcoming celebration of the new millennium. In 1994, he published an apostolic letter, *Tertio Millennio Adveniente* (In Anticipation of the Third Millennium), that announced a program of spiritual and catechetical preparation for the event. In 2001, he completed a series of letters on this theme with *Nuovo Millennio Ineunte* (At the Beginning of the New Millennium). Regional synods of bishops were convoked around the world to anticipate this event. Common to all the final documents was the application of the theme of new evangelization to the mission of the church and an appeal to the *Catechism of the Catholic Church* as a key instrument for implementing this.[52] From a Lonergan viewpoint, both strategies represent a deductivist approach to theology.

POPE BENEDICT XVI

In many respects, the eight-year pontificate of Pope Benedict XVI stood in continuity with that of John Paul II. However, two differences can be noted. First, Pope Benedict was a more coherent and consistent neo-Augustinian than Pope John Paul had ever been. As noted earlier, Pope John Paul II had tended to break ranks with a neo-Augustinian perspective on certain issues, such as interreligious dialogue, that appertained to the *ad extra* mission of the church. A shift of approach to the *ad extra* mission of the church was evident when, in 2012, Pope Benedict published a letter, *Porta Fidei*, which promulgated a "year of faith" to celebrate the fifty-year anniversary of the opening of Vatican II.[53] This letter made the now-standard links between the council, an ecclesiology of *communio*, and an appeal for the use of the *Catechism of the Catholic Church* by those promoting a new evangelization. However, one witnesses also the emergence of a darker view of the church-world relationship. In the opening paragraphs of this letter, Pope Benedict seemed to imply that one of the reasons that the church needed a Year of Faith was to moderate the naïveté of Catholic theologians who adopt a too-optimistic attitude to the *ad extra* mission of the church:

> It often happens that Christians are more concerned for the social, cultural and political consequences of their commitment, continuing to think of the faith as a self-evident presupposition for life in society. In reality, not only can this presupposition no longer be taken for granted, but it is often openly denied....We cannot accept that salt should become tasteless or the light be kept hidden.[54]

A second characteristic that distinguished Pope Benedict from his predecessor can seem, at first glance, to be paradoxical. He insisted less on conformity with his views by theologians and bishops of the world. We will discuss this point further in subsequent chapters because the freer rein given to regional conferences of bishops would be especially significant for the CELAM meeting held in 2007 in Aparecida, in which the future Pope Francis would be active.

Conclusion

At the beginning of this chapter was a quote from Lonergan. Written just after the close of Vatican II, he speculates that unless the church turns to an approach to theological method based on intellectual conversion, Catholic theology is likely to polarize into a scattered left and a solid right, neither of which carry forward the spirit of Vatican II adequately. At the risk of oversimplification, the Catholic Church tended to witness a predominance of the scattered left for the remainder of the pontificate of Pope Paul VI and the magisterial policies of the pontificates of John Paul II and Benedict XVI tended to favor theologies of the solid right.

In this chapter, we have noted that the polarization that Lonergan predicted is as it happened. Diagram 2 summarizes the epistemological issues underlying this theological polarization. Note the connection between the deductivist method of the pontificates of John Paul II and Benedict XVI to epistemological presuppositions (bottom right of the diagram) that are primarily perceptualist (neo-Augustinian, etc.). We recall the comment of Cardinal Walter Kasper in the introduction that to criticize the theological method employed by popes is not the same as failing to respect their doctrinal authority.

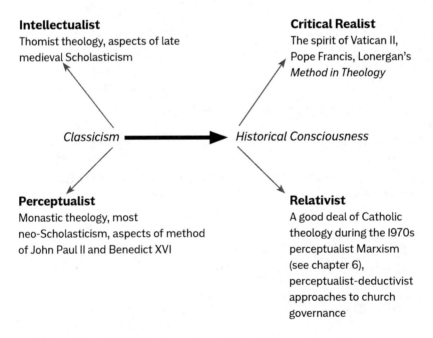

Intellectualist
Thomist theology, aspects of late
medieval Scholasticism

Critical Realist
The spirit of Vatican II,
Pope Francis, Lonergan's
Method in Theology

Classicism ⟶ *Historical Consciousness*

Perceptualist
Monastic theology, most
neo-Scholasticism, aspects of method
of John Paul II and Benedict XVI

Relativist
A good deal of Catholic
theology during the 1970s
perceptualist Marxism
(see chapter 6),
perceptualist-deductivist
approaches to church
governance

Diagram 2: Theological Method through the Ages

The Battle for the Meaning of Vatican II

The combined pontificates of John Paul II and Benedict XVI lasted for thirty-five years. Inevitably, the relatively consistent, neo-Augustinian policies maintained throughout this period exercised a major impact on the way Vatican II came to be interpreted and implemented in most Catholic circles. However, alternative ideas persisted, especially in academic circles. Furthermore, an important locus of alternative ideas was Latin America. Jorge Bergoglio, the future Pope Francis, was an inheritor of such ideas.

6

Vatican II and Latin America

(1965-2007)

IN THE PREVIOUS chapter, we stressed the significance of the Extraordinary Synod of Bishops of 1985 as a moment when Pope John Paul II began to implement his vision for offering firm leadership on the question of how the Catholic Church would interpret and implement Vatican II. We noted that the final documents of the synod presented a primarily neo-Augustinian perspective and that Cardinal Avery Dulles had described two major orientations present at the synod. He described a second orientation as "communitarian" (while most other commentators described this as Thomistic). Dulles added that there was also present a distinctive voice represented by bishops from the so-called Third World countries:

> Not all the bishops and conferences taking part in the Synod could be neatly fitted into one or the other of these two orientations. For example, the leading advocates of liberation theology, coming from Third World countries, shared neither the sacralism of the Augustinians nor the secular

optimism of the communitarians. They wanted a politically involved church that was confrontational and militant.[1]

In the years following the synod of 1985, liberation theology was not given much opportunity to thrive. However, twenty-eight years later, it would show its resilience when Pope Francis was elected and began to express views that demonstrated its influence on him. In this chapter, we examine the history of liberation theology in the fifty years after the council, and in the following chapters, we discuss the thought of Jorge Bergoglio, the future Pope Francis.

The Roots of Liberation Theology

Liberation theology represents a distinctively Latin American application of Vatican II. At the same time, one can notice significant differences between different currents of liberation theology.

Walter Kasper suggests that two distinct forms of liberation theology emerged in Latin America that have roots in the two European philosophical traditions of rationalism and romanticism. In chapter 2, we outlined some aspects of these currents of thought: how rationalism based itself on the use of reason evident in the first wave of the Scientific Revolution, and how it developed expressions in the realm of political philosophy. In fact, two diverse expressions of such political philosophy emerged. The first was a liberal-democratic one represented by figures such as John Locke, David Hume, and Thomas Jefferson. The second was a more radical one that was identified with the French *philosophes* and with Jean-Jacques Rousseau. This latter line of thinking has been called the "Radical Enlightenment" and exercised an influence on both the leaders of the French Revolution and on Karl Marx. Kasper suggests that it is this form of rationalism that has influenced the forms of liberation theology that "are generally better known to us." He explains that they proceed "from an analysis of sociopolitical and economic relations or from antagonisms in society in order then to interpret them with Marxist categories."[2]

However, Kasper also suggests that a distinct philosophical tradition from Europe, romanticism, also exercised an influence on liberation theology. While this influence is less well known, it is essential to understanding the thought of Pope Francis.[3]

ROMANTIC PHILOSOPHY AND LIBERATION THEOLOGY

In chapter 2, we commented briefly on how romanticism was a cultural movement that was an early contributor to the second wave of the Enlightenment, which was characterized by historical consciousness. In chapter 3, we noted how romanticism influenced Catholic theologians in the School of Tübingen in the nineteenth century. Kasper notes that, for several reasons, Argentine culture was particularly influenced by romantic philosophy. Argentine theologians developed a distinctive form of liberation theologian known as *la teología del pueblo*, or "the theology of the people." He suggests,

> The parallel between this Romantic teaching of the early Tübingen theologians about the national spirit, which goes back to Johann Gottfried Herder (1744–1803), and the Argentine theology of the people are striking and clearly not accidental.[4]

Johann Gottfried Herder (1744–1803) was one of the first thinkers to encourage Germans to be proud of their language and culture. Like all romantics, he explained his thinking by contrasting it with liberal rationalism. He reacted against the capitalist economic policies of the reigning Bourbon princes, and recognized that these policies were defended as having a basis in rationality, but he believed that they were, in fact, serving the interests of a rich elite. He especially disliked the way this elite sought to mimic the cultural mores of France and England and to look down on the popular culture of the German peoples. In reaction, he stressed the concepts of community, solidarity, nationality, and patriotism. Above all, Herder introduced a notion of the *Volk*, the people, that became an idealized notion of a community that enjoys a unity of culture. He stated, "There is only one class in the state, the *Volk* (not the rabble), and the king belongs to this class as well as the peasant." He suggested that to impose rationalistic ideas on the local German people would be to alienate them:

The happiness of one single people [*Volk*] cannot be imposed onto, talked onto, loaded onto the other and every other. The roses that for the wreath of freedom must be picked by a people's own hands and grow up happily out of its own needs, out of its own desire and love.[5]

The thought of Herder and other German romantics was communicated to the Spanish-speaking world largely through the thought of Karl Christian Friedrich Krause (1781–1832). The works of this German romantic philosopher had been translated into Spanish and had inspired a movement of "Krausismo" in Spain and Latin America, just as countries on the different continents were looking for philosophies for nation-building.[6] Currents of romantic nationalism became evident across Latin America, but especially in Argentina. One reason for this was the publication in 1879 of a book, *El Gaucho, Martín Fierro*, which quickly became a national epic. This book, written by an author deeply affected by Krausismo, describes the adventures of a wandering gaucho who represents a way of life that was passing. In fact, *El Gaucho, Martín Fierro* resembles the literature about cowboys of the "Wild West" that was emerging in the United States at the same time. However, it retains characteristics specific to Iberian culture and is explicitly Catholic in several of its themes. At the end of World War II, a political movement of Peronism emerged in Argentina that had roots in the gaucho political culture of the country. In addition to, and at times apart from, being identified with the political career of President Juan Domingo Perón, Peronism developed as a political philosophy. This, in turn, had a direct influence on the Argentine response to Vatican II.[7]

THE GROUP OF THE CHURCH OF THE POOR

Having outlined the currents of thought that influenced the less well-known theology of the people of Argentina, it is now important to study the form of liberation theology that is considered the mainstream expression of the movement in the 1960s and 1970s. This had roots in more socialist, or Marxist, thought and was associated with a lobby group in Vatican II known as "the Group of the Church of the Poor."

One commentator, Gerd-Reiner Horn, explains how the first wave of liberation theologians tended to be more influenced by Marxist and socialist currents of thought than romantic ones. He describes how the 1950s witnessed the emergence of a movement of "Left Catholicism."[8] After the war, reflecting tendencies in general voting populations in Europe, social Catholicism tended to adopt socialist thinking. Horn notes that the movement of worker priests in France and elsewhere seemed to present an impressive application of the ideas being expressed by Left Catholicism, and recounts how this movement did not maintain an important influence for many years in Europe, as factors such as the Cold War and a postwar economic boom soon reduced interest in socialism. However, he also notes that, by coincidence, when Left Catholicism was at its height, many young priests from Latin America arrived to pursue doctoral studies in Europe. An explanation of the reason for this is simply that travel to Europe had been impossible during the war years and Latin American seminaries needed professors who held reputable doctorates.

Left Catholicism held a special appeal for students from Latin America. These regarded Marx-influenced approaches to social analysis as particularly relevant to Latin America, which was characterized by poverty, inequality, and oppression. Horn describes how Gustavo Gutiérrez was representative of this generation:

> In the dark decade of the 1950s, many extra-European Catholics had come to study at world-renowned European centers of Catholic learning such as Leuven or Lyon. One should note for instance the personal and theological itinerary of perhaps the most well-known figure in Latin American liberation theology, the Peruvian Gustavo Gutiérrez, who studied in Lima, Rome, Leuven and Lyon. He later repeatedly expressed his admiration for the worker priest experience, which had profoundly shaped his own theological education.[9]

In chapter 4, we mentioned briefly how the Group of the Church of the Poor was a group of bishops and theologians that met regularly throughout Vatican II and tried to influence its various documents.[10] This employed, as a point of departure for their worldview, a book written by a worker-priest, Paul Gauthier: *Christ, the Church, and the Poor*. Consequently, the Group can be understood as carrying forward to the debates of the council the perspective of postwar, European, Left Catholicism. At the end of the council, Group members produced a thirteen-point declaration that would influence the way *Gaudium et Spes* was interpreted across Latin America. It stated,

> We will do everything possible so that those responsible for our governments and our public services establish and enforce the laws, social structures, and institutions that are necessary for justice, equality, and the integral, harmonious development of the whole person and of all persons, and thus for the advent of a new social order, worthy of the children of God.[11]

Liberation Theology Established: Medellín (1968)

While intellectual roots of liberation theology can be traced to Europe, there should be no doubt that, soon after Vatican II, theologians in Latin America produced something distinctive. Furthermore, liberation theology went through a complex development in the decades following Vatican II, with three phases of development being notable: early development, including diverse tendencies (1965–79); near suppression by the Holy See (1979–2003); and a recovery of energy in a more mature form (2007–13). As previously noted, Kasper points to two main currents in liberation theology: that version "generally better known to us," and a less well-known version that emerged in Argentina.[12] The General Assembly of CELAM held in Medellín, Columbia, in 1968 would express the former current; that held in Puebla, Mexico, in 1979 would witness to the emerging influence of the latter current. The Argentine influence would become predominant in the assembly held in Aparecida in 2007.

MEDELLÍN

The generally better-known liberation theology had begun to emerge before Vatican II in countries such as Brazil. There, figures such as Hélder Câmara had returned from studies in Europe eager to apply principles of See-Judge-Act to their home contexts.[13] This decade also witnessed the forming of a group of Catholic and Protestant theologians in several Latin American countries called "Church and Society." They included thinkers such as Gustavo Gutiérrez (Peru), Segundo Galilea (Chile), Juan Luis Segundo (Uruguay), and Lucio Gera (Argentina). The developments in the first session of Vatican II gave a new impetus to such thinkers and in March 1964, a meeting was held in Petrópolis, Rio de Janeiro, that some consider a founding event of liberation theology. Significantly, it was at this meeting that Gutiérrez described theology as "a critical reflection on praxis."[14] In 1967, liberation theologians felt encouraged by the publication by Pope Paul VI of the social encyclical *Populorum Progressio*. This letter echoed the tone of the Group of the Church of the Poor rather more than *Gaudium et Spes* did.

A seminal moment in the history of liberation theology occurred in 1968 with the holding of the Second General Assembly of the Latin American Episcopal Council, CELAM (*Consejo Episcopal Latinoamericano*), in Medellín, Columbia. This assembly was supposed to occur every ten years and to coordinate national processes of pastoral planning at national levels.

The final document of Medellín was entitled "The Church in the Present-Day Transformation of Latin America in the Light of the Council" and demonstrated that both the method and content of liberation theology had found approval by CELAM. The document identified *Gaudium et Spes* as its guide and suggested that a key characteristic of the signs of the times in Latin America was the "cry of the poor":

> The bishops of Latin America cannot remain indifferent in the face of the tremendous social injustices existent in Latin America, which keep the majority of our peoples in dismal poverty, which in many cases becomes inhuman wretchedness. A deafening cry pours from the throats of millions of men, asking their pastors for a liberation that reaches them from nowhere else.[15]

The structure of the document strictly followed the See-Judge-Act format. Part 1 was entitled "Pertinent Facts" and was based primarily on a lengthy sociological analysis of the reality of Latin America that had been presented to the bishops during the assembly. Part 2, "Doctrinal Basis," asserts that "the Latin American Church has a message for all people on this continent who 'hunger and thirst for justice,'" adding that God the Father sent God the Son "so that he might come to liberate everyone from the slavery to which sin has subjected them: hunger, misery, all oppression and ignorance." Part 3, "Projections for Social and Pastoral Planning," presents an extensive list of pastoral actions, including the formation of basic Christian communities, and a form of education favored by liberation theologians known as "conscientization."

GUSTAVO GUTIÉRREZ

Another important moment in the history of liberation theology was the publishing of the book by Gustavo Gutiérrez a year after the event of Medellín: *Teología de la liberación*.[16] Three main characteristics can be recognized in this book: the promoting of a notion of preferential option for the poor; the use of dependency theory in social analysis; and the adopting of theological method based on the See-Judge-Act method. Regarding the first of these, his work is a deepening of the insight of Paul Gauthier, who inspired the Group of the Church of the Poor at Vatican II and who suggested that there exists "at least a partial ontological identity between the church and the poor."[17] The second characteristic of the theology of Gutiérrez is an employment of a Marxist-inspired "dependency theory" as a means of studying the situation of the poor. This sociological theory was inspired by a book that had been published in 1916 by Vladimir Lenin, *Imperialism the Highest Stage of Capitalism*.[18] This extended a Marxist analysis of class oppression within societies of Europe to a geographical analysis of the relations between developed economies and the colonies within their empires. Lenin spoke of how, in capitalist systems, a central "core" exploits a "periphery" of colonized countries.[19]

The third dimension of the theology of Gutiérrez involved the application of a sophisticated notion of the method of See-Judge-Act to all theology. He referred to this as a "hermeneutical circle." Here, he expands upon what the method Judge involves. He stresses that it should include a dimension of what Marx called "ideological suspicion." This involves being aware of the implications for social and political practice of certain theological ideas. He adds that certain approaches should be "unmasked" as implicitly supporting an unjust status quo. By contrast, he suggested that themes and emphases should be drawn from Scripture and Tradition that serve the purpose of transformative social action. In fact, the term *liberation theology* originates from this insight. Gutiérrez suggests that the theme of Moses leading the chosen people out of Egypt and into the promised land offers a sufficient notion of liberation to motivate transformative political praxis in Latin America. He touches more briefly on a theme that would soon be developed by other liberation theologians such as Leonardo Boff and Jon Sobrino: the historical Jesus can be understood as a subversive figure for the political and economic status quo of his time.[20]

Liberation Theology Consolidated: Puebla (1978)

If Gutiérrez is considered the father figure of the more well-known branch of liberation theology, Argentine theology had its own father figure: Lucio Gera (1924–2012).[21] Gera had similar credentials to Gutiérrez. Like his Peruvian colleague, he had been sent to Europe for studies in the 1950s. He had also become enamored of the Young Christian Workers movement and had recognized how their pastoral method of See-Judge-Act could be applied to the way theology was conducted. In March 1964, he was present at the meeting of theologians—already mentioned—that was held in Petrópolis, Brazil, where he presented a paper entitled "The Meaning of the Christian Message in the Context of Poverty and Oppression."[22]

However, if Gera seemed to hold similar opinions to others at the meeting of 1964, significant differences were already present in his thought. As Kasper points out, during his studies in Europe, Gera had been drawn to explore the relevance of the philosophical tradition of European romanticism more than traditions of rationalism and Marxism. Before long, the differences between Gera and his fellow Latin American theologians began to emerge. In 1967, he was invited to attend a meeting of Third World Priests (MSTM), which was an organization that coordinated the development of liberation theology and would play a key role at Medellín. During the meeting, he objected to aspects of the consensus agreement that was being prepared. He then left before the end of the meeting and asked that his name not be added to the list of signatories of the final document. He stated that he did this in protest over "an unacceptable embrace of Marxism" in the final document.[23]

While Gera was widely considered to be a father figure for an Argentine postconciliar theology, what emerged is more correctly explained as a product of a cooperative effort by several Argentine thinkers. In 1966, the Episcopal Conference of Argentina established a commission to produce a pastoral plan for the country. This commission, the *Commissione episcopale di pastorale*, or COEPAL, presented its findings to the bishops in 1972, who accepted them and began to implement its proposals. The members of the commission continued afterward as an informal group promoting publications and continuing to act in a consultative role to the bishops. In effect, they became the nucleus of a distinctive school of Argentine liberation theology. In addition to Gera, two other thinkers also emerged as leading voices: the Jesuit philosopher Juan Carlos Scannone and another diocesan priest and theologian, Rafael Tello.[24]

COEPAL had a richly interdisciplinary makeup and was closely connected with the faculty of social science of the Catholic University of Buenos Aires. Scannone points out that at this time Argentina had a more developed education system than many other countries in Latin America. He suggests that this resulted in COEPAL theologians interacting with philosophers and social scientists in a way that was not always possible elsewhere in the subcontinent. One immediate consequence of this was that they avoided using the simplistic theory of dependence as an instrument of social analysis. Other commentators suggest that this complemented the fact that Argentine culture was already influenced by romantic nationalism and so Argentine theologians were already disposed to be suspicious of Marxism.[25]

Before long, other Latin American theologians began to recognize the distinct direction being taken by their Argentine colleagues. Among the most critical of responses was offered by Juan Louis Segundo, a Jesuit from Uruguay. It was he who first coined the term *theology of the people* to describe the new Argentine theology. He recognized that Argentines were speaking with respect of the popular culture of the Argentine poor, especially the popular religiosity of these masses. He recognized an influence of romanticism here and stated that the over-idealized notion of "the people" employed by them was "verbal terrorism." In contrast, he suggested the poor masses of Latin America should be understood in terms of a Marxist notion of a proletariat, and pointed out that within such an analysis, the culture of the poor is best understood in terms of the "false consciousness" created by an ideology of the ruling class. He considered a good deal of popular religion to represent a kind of privatizing and depoliticizing of religious sentiment, and thus in need of correcting. He invoked a Leninist notion of revolutionary elite to describe the role that theologians should play in helping the poor recognize their need for liberation.[26]

Segundo's comments clarify the key difference between Argentine and other currents of liberation theology. It appertained not just to the use of dependency theory in social analysis but to the very understanding of what solidarity with the poor might mean. One commentator explains the contrast between the branches of liberation theology as follows:

> Who is *el pueblo*?...Gera defined it in terms of the despised and marginalized majority, from whom comes the desire for justice and peace. For Gera, *el pueblo* is an active agent of history, not, as liberals and Marxists view it, a passive mass needing to be made aware. "The people have a rationality," wrote Gera, "they have their project; we don't give it to them." The role of theologians was not to impose categories, be argued, but to interpret the people's project in the light of its salvation history. Gera put it starkly, "Either theology is the expression of the People of God or it is nothing."[27]

In this matter of distinguishing a theology of the people from Marxism, it is important to recognize the contribution made to the theology of the people by Rafael Tello.[28] Tello's distinctive contribution had two characteristics. First, he had a vigorous training in Thomism and was alert to the epistemological issues that underlie the difference between Marxism and a theology of the people. He recognized how Aquinas relies on the cognitional theory of Aristotle and how this differs in important ways from that of Plato. Aristotle explains that the thinking mind creates a phantasm in the imagination based on what is received by the five senses. He then describes an act of insight that occurs into the phantasm.[29] Tello explains that this gives a concrete quality to the epistemology of Aristotle. By contrast, Plato had employed a cognitional theory of applying universal ideas to specific situations. Drawing on Aquinas, Tello recognized that currents of nominalism, rationalism, and Marxism in modern philosophy tend to employ this Platonic approach of applying universal systems of concepts to specific situations. Adopting a Thomist position, he insisted that the object of Christian care is "not an abstract person, considered as some idea or conception," but rather, "the entire human person, in all his or her dimensions—eternal, temporal, spiritual and corporal, individual and communitarian." He further suggested that even the uneducated poor have a practical wisdom that deserves respect.[30]

A second characteristic of the theology of Tello was that he devoted attention to the popular religiosity of indigenous peoples. He explained how this religiosity is rooted in the experience of the Jesuit "Reductions" of the seventeenth century and how, for all its devotional and sometimes superstitious characteristics, it is not without a political sensibility. One commentator outlines the aspect of Tello's thought that identifies how popular religion is concerned with questions of social justice:

> A simple visit to the web sites of San Cayetano and of Our Lady of Luján today reveals the distinctive character of these places of devotion and pilgrimage decades later. They are at once expressions of a community's deep piety and faith, especially of the most needy, but also impressive instruments of social service where food, clothing, housing, and medical needs are readily available. Nor are they merely concerned with charity but also with advocacy and even empowerment of the community. They serve as centers of political (but not partisan) mobilization. Accordingly, the way to go about abetting social awareness and action is suggested by the popular solidarity expressed in customs, rituals, art, and music of the community itself rather than by the cold, rationalist pragmatism and vanguardism of modern political and intellectual elites.[31]

THE PUEBLA DOCUMENT

Argentine theology exercised little influence on the CELAM assembly held at Medellín. However, by the Third General Assembly of CELAM in Puebla, Mexico, in 1978, the Argentine perspective had become more influential. One reason for this is that other forms of liberation theology were witnessing increasing opposition from the official church. Another was that the Argentine approach to liberation theology had begun to win the approval of Pope Paul VI.

Soon after Medellín, bishops in several countries of Latin America began to feel uneasy about the direction that liberation theology was taking. They noted that some authors were employing a notion of class conflict to describe bishops as an oppressive class that suppressed a "true Church of the poor."[32] By contrast with such developments, the bishops in Argentina were supportive of the locally developed theology of the people. They communicated this enthusiasm during synods of bishops in Rome in 1971 and 1974. Pope Paul VI became aware of this difference within Latin American theologies and began to express support for the Argentine approach.[33] In his apostolic exhortation of 1975, *Evangelii Nuntiandi*, he first offered broad insight for insights held by all liberation theologians: "Between evangelization and human advancement—development and liberation—there are in fact profound links." However, echoing Argentine theologians, he adds, "What matters is to evangelize man's culture and cultures" (nos. 31 and 20). As the date for the General Assembly at Puebla approached, the bishops of CELAM read this apostolic exhortation with interest and followed its lead. They decided against adopting the policies being proposed by the more aggressive opponents of liberation theology.

The final document of Puebla devoted a full chapter to "A Preferential Option for the Poor" and stated,

> With renewed hope in the vivifying power of the Spirit, we are going to take up once again the position of the Second General Conference of the Latin American episcopate in Medellín, which adopted a clear and prophetic option expressing preference for, and solidarity with the poor.... We affirm the need for conversion on the part of the whole Church to a Preferential Option for the Poor, an option aimed at their integral liberation.[34]

In this quotation, reference to "integral liberation" exhibits the influence of Gera and *Evangelii Nuntianti*. Other terms used in the document indicate a similar broadening of the perspective of Medellín: the "evangelization of culture" and "the commitment of solidarity."

As one commentator put it, "The *Puebla Final Document* echoes the thought of Gera."[35]

Liberation Theology Reversed: Santo Domingo (1992)

By 1978, John Paul II had been elected pope. While the CELAM assembly at Puebla in 1979 was held during his pontificate, he had not yet begun to exercise an effective influence on the affairs of CELAM. It would be 1985 before he and Cardinal Ratzinger began to fully establish the approach they expected to guide the church in its interpretation and implementation of Vatican II. Inevitably, this Polish pope and philosopher was going to take notice of the Marxist tendencies in Latin American liberation theology and seek to correct them. Unlike Pope Paul VI, he did not concern himself with differences that might exist within the liberation theology movement, or whether a self-correcting process might already be underway where theologians and bishops were finding ways to free liberation theology of Marxist presuppositions.

TENSION WITH ROME

Pope John Paul decided that one of the priorities of his pontificate would be to correct the Marxist tendencies of theology in the Latin American church. He visited Central America in 1983, where the press was fascinated to see him publicly rebuke Ernesto Cardenal, a priest who had become a minister in the left-wing Sandinista government of Nicaragua. In 1984, he approved a letter produced by Cardinal Ratzinger and the CDF, "Instruction on Certain Aspects of the 'Theology of Liberation.'" This document warned against "the temptation to reduce the Gospel to an earthly Gospel" and any tendency to imply that "the class struggle is the driving force of history."[36]

Argentine proponents of a theology of the people were pleased with this letter. Indeed, some suggested that it expressed just what theologians such as Gera and Tello had been saying for years. Elsewhere in Latin America, responses varied. Gustavo Gutiérrez proved to be humble in responding to such critique. Already in the 1970s, he had been more tolerant of Argentine theology than some.[37] After 1984, he underwent a remarkable change of opinion. He accepted that he had been mistaken in his use of dependency theory. In an introduction to a revised edition of *Theology of Liberation* published in 1988, he acknowledged the "simplistic position we were perhaps in danger of initially adopting in analysing situations of poverty," and adds, "it is clear that the theory of dependence, which was so extensively used in the early years of our encounter with the Latin American world, is now an inadequate tool."[38]

However, concessions such as these were not about to change the policies of the Vatican. As noted in chapter 5, a new centralization was emerging in church governance, and episcopal conferences would be expected to employ a deductive approach to theology and pastoral planning, similar to that of Pope John Paul II.

PAPAL POWER ASSERTED

From the late 1980s onward, Pope John Paul relied on figures such as Archbishop López Trujillo as trusted agents of his plans for the Latin American church.[39] Alfonso López Trujillo had taken an aggressive stance against liberation theology, but his ideas had not prevailed at Puebla.

As the 1980s unfolded, officials within the secretariat of CELAM noticed an increasingly directive approach from Rome, communicated to them by officials of the Pontifical Commission for Latin America. They were instructed to postpone the next General Assembly by four years, from 1988 to 1992. It was explained that this would make it possible for the CELAM assembly to coincide with the five-hundred-year anniversary of the discovery of the Americas by Christopher Columbus. In this way, they were told, CELAM could focus on the theme of "New Evangelization," implying a project for the next five hundred years of evangelization of the subcontinent. Next, as usual, the officials of CELAM began to consult the national episcopal conferences regarding their national processes of pastoral planning to compile a working document as a basis for discussion during the assembly.

When CELAM officials presented their draft of a working document to Rome, it was rejected. The Pontifical Commission for Latin America presented the officials with an alternative document that they themselves had composed. It removed reference to a method of See-

Judge-Act and provided a document that, instead, was "rich in quotes from John Paul II."[40] Next, when CELAM appointed twenty theologians as *periti* for the assembly, the Commission rejected eighteen of them and replaced these with Vatican appointees.[41] When the General Assembly at Santo Domingo opened in 1992, John Paul II arrived to open it and stayed for three days. Remarkably, on the first day of the conference, the working document that had been provided by Rome was itself withdrawn. Delegates to the assembly were left to read the opening address of the pope until a new working document was provided. When the pope did leave for Rome, he left Cardinal Sodano, his secretary of state, to control proceedings, along with Cardinal Trujillo. At this stage, the bishops present began to show signs of restiveness. What followed were a remarkable series of events. One commentator describes them as follows:

> Toward the end of the gathering, CELAM rebelled. When the Vatican appointed five members to redact the final declaration, CELAM, bishops voted on a sixth member, the president of the Brazilian bishop's conference, Luciano Mendes de Almeida. As the conference drew to a close, the CELAM bishops through Archbishop Mendes tried to counter the Rome version but were continually blocked by Sodano. Eventually Mendes, with the CELAM bishops stayed up all night to redact their alternative version, which was a defense of the approach the Latin-American bishops had taken at Puebla and Medellín. The next day he went straight to the microphone and read it. "Sodano could do nothing," recalls a bishop prominent in CELAM at the time, who is now a key cardinal in the Francis papacy. "He just sat there, powerless, while the whole auditorium broke into applause.[42]

Nevertheless, signs of rebellion such as this did not have much effect in the short and medium term. The document the bishops approved at Santo Domingo remained largely similar to the working document that had been provided by the Pontifical Commission for Latin America. It avoided reference to a See-Judge-Act method; it stressed the theme of a New Evangelization; and it replaced most references to the church as people of God with references to the church as *communio*.[43]

SIGNS OF OPENNESS

Commentators are clear that Santo Domingo represented a reversal of many aspects of the trajectory of the development of liberation theology that had been evident in Medellín and Puebla. However, in both the pontificates of John Paul II and Benedict XVI there also occurred signs of a readiness to dialogue with aspects of liberation theology. These signs are significant because they would be developed further by Pope Francis.

Already in 1984, the CDF document "Instruction on Certain Aspects of the 'Theology of Liberation'" stated that the warnings it offers about tendencies toward imbalance in liberation theology "should in no way be interpreted as a disavowal of all those who want to respond generously and with an authentic evangelical spirit to the signs of the time on the sub-continent." It stated, "More than ever before," the church intends "to struggle, by her own means, for the defense and advancement of the rights of mankind, especially of the poor."[44] Next, in 1986, Pope John Paul asked the CDF to produce a second letter on liberation theology, "Christian Freedom and Liberation," which would take a more positive stance toward liberation theology.[45]

One commentator, Rohan Curnow, suggests that on one issue, Pope John Paul II allowed his thinking to be enriched by liberation theology. He traces how the pope wrote two social encyclicals, *Solicitudo Rei Socialis* (1987) and *Centesimus Annus* (1991), each of which employed the terms "preferential option for the poor" and "a love of preference for the poor," which the pope had borrowed from liberation theology. He notes that reference to this option was reproduced in the *Compendium of Social Doctrine of the Church* (2004). Here it was defined as "an option, or a special form of primacy in the exercise of Christian charity, to which the whole tradition of the Church bears witness."[46] He concludes that these references mark the "definitive appropriation of the Preferential option for the Poor" in the ordinary magisterium of the church.[47]

However, Curnow adds a qualification to this assertion. He suggests that the way that John Paul II employed the term *preferential option for the poor* represented only a limited concession to liberation theology. The understanding of the term by the pope remains within the context of deductive reasoning. He states, "For John Paul II, the Option remains understood as a particular emphasis in the exercise of charity in the context of Christian social ethics." He adds, "At Santo Domingo, the tight control the Vatican exercised over CELAM's meeting resulted in the preferential option for the poor being expressed dominantly in terms of Christian Social Ethics to the exclusion of any explicit link to the fullness of Christian conversion and the hermeneutics of history."[48] Studying reference to an option for the poor during the subsequent pontificate, he states, "Benedict continues in the tradition of John Paul II, without representing either a development or repudiation of that tradition."[49]

If Pope Benedict XVI was lukewarm on the notion of an option for the poor as a principle in theology, in other respects, he exhibited an openness to and a kindness toward liberation theology. Scannone reported how, during the 1990s, as prefect of the CDF, Ratzinger established a practice of holding informal meetings with liberation theologians. A private conference organized by the prefect, held in Schönstatt, Germany, in 1996, included theologians such as Gustavo Gutiérrez, Carlos Galli (a successor to Lucio Gera), and himself. Cardinal Ratzinger acknowledged that liberation theology would be a central influence on Latin America in the new millennium, and stated that the purpose of such conferences was to explore ideas together, so as to avoid future misunderstandings between liberation theologians and the CDF.[50]

Conclusion

The story of the general assemblies of CELAM takes a further dramatic step at Aparecida, Brazil, in 2007. To some extent, this is a development of the signs of positive regard toward aspects of liberation theology in the previous two pontificates. However, one cannot ignore the fact that it also involved a quiet rebellion against the conclusions of Santo Domingo and a return to a trajectory of development that passes through Medellín and Puebla. To explain the significance of Aparecida, it is necessary also to recount biographical details of the person who played a key role in it: Cardinal Jorge Bergoglio of Buenos Aires, the future Pope Francis.

7

Bergoglio's Theological Vision

UNDERSTANDING THE THEOLOGY of the people of Argentina and the significance of the Aparecida general assembly of CELAM brings one a long way to understanding the theology of Pope Francis.[1] From his time as a theology student near Buenos Aires, Jorge Bergoglio had been deeply influenced by the theology of the people. He would go on to become a prime mover at the CELAM conference at Aparecida.

Establishing a Theological Identity (1936–1973)

Jorge Bergoglio was born in 1936 in Buenos Aires. He joined the Jesuits when he was twenty-one and was ordained at the age of thirty-three. As is the way with Jesuits, who devote more years to training, or "formation," than most other priests or religious, these years are considered a valuable time for establishing a pastoral identity that would direct one during subsequent years of active work.

CHILDHOOD AND ADOLESCENCE

Jorge's parents were the descendants of immigrants who had traveled from northern Italy in the 1800s.[2] His mother worked outside the home for the first five years of his life. During these years, she would drop Jorge off with his paternal grandparents on her way to work and collect him upon her return. In their house, his grandparents, Rosa and Giovanni Bergoglio, spoke Piedmontese, a dialect from northern Italy, and the young Jorge learned this from them. Rosa influenced him. Before leaving Italy, she had been an active member of the Catholic Action movement, taking on national responsibilities as a public speaker. She had experienced firsthand the violent disruption of Catholic Action meetings by Mussolini's fascists. One reason she and her husband chose to immigrate to Buenos Aires was to get away from such political repression. Jorge would speak often of the influence of Rosa on his life—broadening his horizons, giving him an appreciation for social Catholicism, and, above all, developing in him a sense of God as merciful.[3]

As a teenager, Jorge attended a school run by the Salesian fathers. This school offered technical training as well as general education to its students. He studied to be a laboratory technician and, upon leaving this school, worked in the research section of a food company. After a few years, at the age of twenty, he joined a seminary to train as a diocesan priest and, after a year, transferred to a Jesuit novitiate. At the level of national politics, these were turbulent times in Argentina. The dominant political figure was Colonel Juan Domingo Perón, who represented a form of romantic Catholic nationalism that was attractive to Argentines, especially of the lower middle class. Jorge formed political opinions and attitudes that can broadly be described as Peronist.[4] However, Peronism was a complex phenomenon and needs careful explaining.

Colonel Perón rose to power after the Second World War, first by a military coup and then by democratic election. He drew on the currents of romantic nationalism already present in Argentine political culture.[5] He formed alliances with Trade Unions and small-business people and employed economic policies that made explicit reference to Catholic social teaching. His economic policies involved encouraging import substitution in Argentina and considerable government intervention in the economy. He spoke of "humanizing capital" and "dignifying labor" and recruited young leaders of the Catholic Action movement to propose specific economic policies. He began to nationalize industries, raised the minimum wage, and developed a social welfare system. For a period of about five years, these policies met with singular success. One commentator identifies 1950 as a "high noon" for Peronism. It is the memory of these years that helped form a political philosophy of Peronism, a philosophy that sometimes detached itself from supporting the actual behavior of Juan Diego Perón. Perón's initial economic successes began to reverse themselves and he became increasingly despotic. In 1955, he was overthrown in a military coup. One commentator explains that, by the 1950s, there existed in Argentina a "paralyzing political paradox" that is difficult for foreigners to grasp: "the antiliberals (the nationalists, the Peronists) were popular and came to power by winning elections, while the liberals—the democrats, the pluralists—used dictatorship to keep the Peronists out of power."[6]

The family of Jorge Bergoglio, like most of his class, were solidly Peronist in political loyalty.[7] Throughout his school years, he remained an active member of a Catholic Action study group in his parish. There he imbibed principles of Catholic social teaching and a general orientation toward Peronist political philosophy.[8] However, he was not overtly political and, unlike some of his friends, chose not to become a member of the Peronist youth movement that emerged during these years, which sought to aid the return of Perón from exile so as to engage again in Argentine politics.

In other respects, Bergoglio grew up as a normal teenager, liked by his friends, who recognized in him gifts of intelligence and leadership. Biographers describe him as enjoying music, dancing, and soccer, although he was not especially athletically gifted. Being twenty years old when he joined the seminary, he had time to experience the world of work as a laboratory technician and to have some serious relationships with women. A woman biographer states, "Jorge Bergoglio—who, like John Paul II, became a seminarian when he was an adult—had normal relations with his women friends, to the extent that one of them made him doubt his vocation."[9]

TRAINING FOR THE JESUIT PRIESTHOOD (1958–1968)

At first, Bergoglio did not choose to become a Jesuit, but rather a diocesan priest. Indeed, at this stage, he did not have a deep familiarity with Jesuits. In 1957, he entered a seminary of the Archdiocese of Buenos Aires, which was, however, run by Jesuits. After a brief time there, he fell sick with a serious case of pneumonia. He experienced much pain, was at risk of dying, and eventually had an operation that removed a part of one lung. He prayed through this experience and found that his faith life deepened considerably. His spiritual director at this time was a Jesuit, and he was grateful for the guidance he received from this man. In addition, during this year, he learned of the missionary charism of the Jesuits and was attracted to it. As he began to recover, he decided to leave the seminary and to apply to enter the Jesuits (ironically, his weak lungs would later cause his Jesuit superiors to refuse to send him on the missions).[10]

In 1958, Bergoglio entered the Jesuit novitiate. The formation regime of the 1950s for young Jesuits was strict, and most of the young men had a feeling that "all this could be done another way." At the same time, as noted in chapter 1, Bergoglio had a positive experience of following the *Spiritual Exercises of St. Ignatius*, with a director who had benefitted from the renewal of understanding that was ongoing in the Jesuits regarding how to direct this experience. After novitiate, he traveled with his fellow scholastics to study humanities for a year in the Jesuit college of philosophy and theology in Chile, near the capital city, Santiago. In the community where he lived, he was required to combine studies with a considerable degree of work with the poor. In fact, he witnessed among the Jesuits of Chile a particularly strong commitment to working with the poor, something Bergoglio enjoyed and admired. The combination of pastoral and academic work that was required of him at this time would later bring such practices to formation structures in Argentina.[11]

In 1960, when Bergoglio returned to Argentina, he began formal studies in philosophy in the Jesuit Colegio Máximo de San Miguel, near Buenos Aires. In 1964, he spent two years in direct pastoral work—teaching in a Jesuit high school—before returning to the Colegio

Máximo for theology studies and being ordained in 1969. While a good deal of the philosophy and theology was neo-Scholastic, these were also times of change. Vatican II began while he was in philosophy studies, and he became aware of currents of *ressourcement* in Catholic theology. As noted in chapter 1, Bergoglio felt especially attracted to studying how new approaches to theology had an impact on the understanding of the *Spiritual Exercises*.[12] He began to imagine what Jesuit formation might be like if it were more comprehensively based on such innovative approaches.

In addition to reflecting on Ignatian spirituality, during Bergoglio's theological studies, he undertook another lifelong commitment. At this time, a small number of his professors at the Colegio Máximo were directly involved in the bishops' commission, COEPAL, described in chapter 6 as a founding place of a theology of the people. This was especially the case with one full-time member of staff, the young Jesuit philosopher Juan Carlos Scannone. In addition, however, figures such as Lucio Gera came as visiting professors from nearby seminaries to lecture there. Bergoglio became deeply persuaded by the value of the new theology of the people that these academics were beginning to formulate.[13]

Bergoglio was recognized by his superiors as being gifted. A year after being ordained a priest in 1969, he was appointed as novice master. By this time, he had begun to establish his own theological vision. His use of themes from a theology of the people is evident in this description of his thought at this time:

> There was a lot of talk at that time about *el pueblo*...the politicians talked about *el pueblo*, the intellectuals talked about *el pueblo*, what *el pueblo* was calling for...but what did they mean? We priests must talk to a "people" but a very special people. In the Bible we appear as a "holy people"....
> I started to talk about...God's holy faithful people.[14]

In addition to these basic concepts, he employed an Ignatian notion of discernment of spirits to specify just how such an option of solidarity with God's holy people should be exercised.

Opposing Marxist Method (1973–1986)

After ordination, Bergoglio was quickly assigned to positions of responsibility, first as novice master and then as provincial superior. In these roles, he would be obliged to articulate his theological vision in opposition to a major tendency in the Society of Jesus at this time: a more Marxist-influenced liberation theology.[15]

ARGENTINE JESUITS AND MARXISM

Commentators describe a complex situation in the Jesuit province of Argentina as Bergoglio was appointed provincial superior. First, they note that the upper middle and upper classes in Argentina tended not to be Peronist. Many of these adopted right-wing opinions and were supportive of military dictatorships and neoliberal economic policies. Some members of these classes were offended by the degree of inequality of wealth in the country and tended to adopt Marxist views. By contrast with both these positions, the lower middle and lower classes tended to be Peronist. As noted earlier, the views of romantic nationalists like these were opposed both to neoliberalism and Marxism, both of which were considered as ideological systems not appropriate for local conditions.

In a country so divided by issues of class and political ideology, it was inevitable that the Jesuits would reflect these tensions. A Jesuit from Chile who knew the Argentine province during those years describes "a lack of togetherness" among young Jesuits, adding, "Those who came from the popular classes were staunch Peronists, while those from the upper class who had come through the [Jesuit] Colegio del Salvador were strongly anti-Peronist."[16] Some of these Jesuits from the upper classes would remain highly conservative, at times serving as chaplains to the army. However, others would opt for socialist or Marxist positions. Such Jesuits were aware that their opinions were close to those of liberation theologians outside of Argentina. In addition, they were aware that, at an international level, the Jesuits had officially adopted an understanding of their mission within the church that resembled such a position.

In the late 1960s, a center for social research known as El Centro de Investigación y Acción Social (CIAS) had been established in Buenos Aires by the Jesuits.[17] This was part of a network of similar centers that had been established by Jesuits in different countries of the world in an effort to promote the mission they would soon articulate for themselves as "the service of faith and the promotion of justice that this entails."[18] Within the Argentine context, the work of CIAS formed an alternative school of thought to the members of COEPAL.[19] Unlike the theology of the people that was emerging in that group, the members of CIAS began to articulate theological ideas of a kind more familiar in Latin America beyond Argentina. All this occurred as a civil war broke out in Argentina. This conflict, known as the "Dirty War," lasted from 1974 to 1983. In such a context, Marxist-leaning expressions of liberation theology were easily perceived as expressions of support for the Marxist guerrillas, known as *montoneros*.[20]

In the late 1960s, a provincial superior was appointed to the Argentine province, Ricardo O'Farrell, who had close associations with CIAS. This appointment provoked sharp reactions and the Argentine province of the Society of Jesus became intensely divided. This was associated with a departure of priests and a decrease in vocations. By 1973, the province numbered only 243 members, with nine in formation. To a certain degree, these statistics reflected trends elsewhere in the world in the wake of Vatican II. However, they were more extreme. By the early 1970s, Argentina had perhaps the most divided Jesuit province in the world. In 1973, the superior general, Pedro Arrupe, asked O'Farrell to submit his resignation.[21]

JESUIT LEADERSHIP (1973–1982)

When Bergoglio became provincial in 1973, divisions in the province lay primarily between conservatives, who supported the military dictatorship, and progressives, who held views with Marxist tendencies. He believed that he could introduce a "third way" of proceeding by proposing a vision of Jesuit mission based both on the *Spiritual Exercises* and on the theology of the people.[22] In 1974, Bergoglio gave his first address to the province in which both these dimensions of his thinking were evident.

At the beginning of this address, he invited his fellow Jesuits to overcome their "sterile intra-ecclesiastical contradictions" in order to embark on a "true apostolic strategy."[23] Before elaborating on what such a strategy might be, he reflected on a dimension of the *Spiritual Exercises* that speaks about the subtle temptations of the "Enemy of Human Nature." He reminds his listeners that at times the enemy can manifest himself in the form of what Ignatius describes as an "angel of light." Here, the individual is tempted to confuse the apparently good with the truly good—one's own plan with God's plan. Bergoglio stated, "The only real enemy is the enemy of God's plan. The real problem is the problem raised by the Enemy in order to impede God's plan." He then named temptations into which the enemy tends to lead Jesuits: "a certain 'avant-gardism' and 'elitism' as well as a fascination for abstract ideologies that do not match our reality." Coming close to quoting Gera and Scannone, he proposed that Argentine Jesuits should exhibit "a healthy allergy to theories that have not emerged from our national reality."[24]

In this talk, Bergoglio remained at a general level of description of the strategy he was proposing for the province. However, it did not take long for him to make decisions that rendered this general vision concrete. His strategic reform had three dimensions. The first area of reform involved administrative issues. It included confronting a looming fiscal crisis in the province by selling property. It also involved handing over the management of the university, USAL, to members of the moderate Peronist movement Guardia de Hierro, a step that was widely regarded as "depoliticizing" the university and altering the left-wing direction it had been taking. A second reform regarded redeploying Jesuits to work in poverty-stricken areas. This included expanding and opening new missions in remote rural areas, as well as founding a series of new pastoral activities in the barrios of Buenos Aires. In these commitments, he insisted that Jesuits focus on sacramental work and a direct care of the poor. He did not welcome Jesuits making political statements, as he believed that this was likely to provoke a violent government response.[25] A third area of reform was one that was close to Bergoglio's heart: the recruiting and formation of young Jesuits. Here, he pursued policies that met with considerable success. The Colegio Máximo, which had housed nine scholastics in 1972, would be home to two hundred a decade later.[26]

The influence of Bergoglio on the Argentine province of the Jesuits continued for six years after his period as provincial. This was because his friend and supporter, Novice-Master Andrés Swinnen, was appointed provincial. Bergoglio was then appointed rector of the Colegio Máximo, where he concentrated on completing a reform of the curriculum that had begun during his time as provincial.[27] Commentators note that it was at this time that Bergoglio began to repeatedly summarize his vision in a set of four aphorisms, which he would continue to enunciate as pope. As outlined in chapter 1, these state, "Time is more important than space"; "unity prevails over conflict"; "realities are more important than ideas"; and "the whole is greater than the part."[28] Bergoglio remained popular at this time among most Argentine Jesuits, who were primarily young. However, trouble was brewing for him.

THE REJECTION OF BERGOGLIO (1986–1992)

Members of CIAS, along with a small number of other members of the province, had maintained a constant criticism of Bergoglio's policies during his period as provincial and as rector of the Colegio Máximo. They suggested that the direction in which he had been leading the Argentine province for twelve years was inappropriate to the needs of the country and out of step with the practice of the Society of Jesus elsewhere. Members of this group had long criticized the policies of Bergoglio as "sacramentalist, a-critical, and assistentialist."[29] In 1986, the general superior of the Jesuits, Fr. Peter Hans Kolvenbach, decided to act on these complaints. He appointed a provincial who had worked in CIAS, who, in turn, set about reversing the policies of Bergoglio. Bergoglio, himself, was invited to leave Argentina and to pursue doctoral studies elsewhere.[30] The next six years (1986–92) were ones of great suffering for Bergoglio. After a period in Germany, where he began his doctoral studies in theology, he decided to abandon this project and to return to Argentina. There he lived in the Jesuit community at Cordoba, without a clear ministerial appointment. His isolation continued for five more years until he was appointed auxiliary bishop of Buenos Aires.[31]

Even if Bergoglio experienced much suffering during his "Cordoba years," this was also a time of human and spiritual deepening for him. At a psychological level, he grew in humility. He reflected on his years in power and noted that he had exhibited authoritarian characteristics. He found the freedom to acknowledge that he bore a share of guilt in provoking such a negative response to himself at this time. Later, he would reflect,

> My authoritarian and quick manner of making decisions led me to have problems and to be accused of being ultra-conservative. I lived a time of great interior crisis while I was in Cordoba. To be sure, I have never been a Blessed Imelda (a goody-goody), but I have never been a right-winger. It was my authoritarian way of making decisions that created problems.[32]

Of note, here, is the statement by Pope Francis, "I have never been a right-winger." This indicates that he is aware that he was accused of this by those who did not understand the nature of the Argentine theology of the people. While he acknowledges personal failings during his time in Jesuit leadership, he does not express regret for his commitment to a theology of the people.

At a spiritual level, Bergoglio describes how he went through some experiences of deep consolation amid his suffering during his Cordoba years. At an intellectual level, one commentator has stressed that during this time, Bergoglio developed his theological thinking in a way that echoed his devotion to Our Lady Untier of Knots, passing through a "dialectical and mystical deepening."[33] He traces how Bergoglio read extensively the twentieth-century theologians Romano Guardini and Henri de Lubac. Both these were influenced by romantic philosophy, and also appeal to a mysterious reality whereby a respectful holding of opposites in tension can eventually produce solutions to problems. He concludes by suggesting that it is by developing such ideas as these that Bergoglio would increasingly speak about the importance of dialogue as a remedy for situations of conflict. He adds that, as bishop, Bergoglio would speak increasingly of "a culture of encounter."[34]

Opposing Neoliberalism (1992–2013)

In 1992, Bergoglio was appointed auxiliary bishop of Buenos Aires. This occurred largely because the current archbishop of Buenos Aires, Cardinal Antonio Quarracino, "move[d] heaven and earth" to make this happen.[35] This churchman pressed Pope John Paul II to make this appointment. John Paul, who had been seeking to correct what he perceived as Marxist leanings at the highest levels of the Jesuits, was sympathetic to the fact that Bergoglio had suffered the disapproval of Jesuit superiors and was open to the argument in Bergoglio's favor made by Quarracino.[36]

Bergoglio would remain in the role of auxiliary bishop until 1997, at which point he succeeded Quarracino.[37] Throughout these years, his pastoral decision-making exhibited continuity with his approach when he had been in Jesuit leadership. He was given special pastoral responsibility for the quarter of Buenos Aires called Flores. One commentator notes, "What he was doing in Flores was almost exactly what he had done at the Maximo—an intense pastoral focus on the poor by mobilizing the young."[38] However, he was also appointed vicar general of the archdiocese, where he was required to administer its finances. This would introduce him to a new set of challenges, contributing to development in his pastoral vision. He came to recognize that the neoliberal government of the time had been systematically setting out to corrupt higher churchmen with financial inducements. He believed that this, in turn, was related to an inherent encouragement to selfishness involved in the prevailing political philosophy of neoliberalism.

BERGOGLIO AND PRESIDENT MENEM (1992–1999)

For the first seven years of Bergoglio's ministry as bishop, the president of Argentina was Carlos Menem. As Bergoglio began to shift his horizon from being concerned with Marxism to being concerned with neoliberalism, it was often with respect to relations with the Menem government that he worked out his stance.

In his role as vicar general, Bergoglio became convinced that the Archdiocese of Buenos Aires had become involved in irregular financial dealings, both in the private sector and with the government, in a way that compromised its ability to speak out prophetically against corruption. He learned that President Menem had employed a close aide, Esteban Juan Caselli, to oversee relations with the church. In government circles, Caselli was nicknamed "el Obispo" (the bishop) because he was so successful in establishing close relations with high churchmen. Bergoglio became convinced that the methods of Caselli were unethical and, at times, illegal. He began to extricate the archdiocese from several financial entanglements, some of which would become public scandals shortly after the death of Archbishop Quarracino.[39] Such was Bergoglio's success in instigating financial reform as soon as he was appointed archbishop that one commentator states that his elevation to that role was "a major setback for the Menem/Caselli strategy of co-opting the church."[40]

Soon after this elevation to archbishop, Bergoglio had an experience of an international nature that clarified for him that his disagreement with the Menem government lay not only over issues of corruption but also over issues of economic philosophy. This experience encouraged him to focus on the problem of a reigning neoliberal orthodoxy in international economic institutions, which exercised an influence on Argentina. In 1998, he was invited to accompany Pope John Paul II on a historic visit to Cuba. The visit included a series of philosophical discussions between the pope and Castro, as well as between officials of the Vatican curia and the Cuban government. These discussions had a serious intellectual quality and moved beyond simplistic condemnations of one another's positions. After the event, Bergoglio was requested to write a reflection on these dialogues. He published a book entitled *Diálogos entre Juan Pablo II y Fidel Castro*.[41] Commentators suggest that while the book primarily quotes the thought of John Paul, it also expresses the maturing thought of Bergoglio. One commentator notes how the book follows a critique of Marxism with an equivalent critique of neoliberalism:

> The book also strongly objects to neoliberalism. The Church, Bergoglio pointed out, had no difficulty with capital accumulation that increases productivity—what he calls "capitalism as a pure economic system"—but rather "the spirit that has driven capitalism, utilizing capital to oppress and subject people, ignoring the human dignity of workers and the social purpose of the economy, distorting the values of social justice and the common good." Although neoliberalism respected religious values, it did so by relegating them to the private sphere, he went on, adding that "no one can accept the precepts of neoliberalism and consider themselves Christian." The opposite [to Christianity]

was neoliberalism, which "brings about unemployment, coldly marginalizing those who are superfluous," empties economic growth of human content, is "concerned only for numbers that add up," and "corrupts democratic values, by alienating from these the values of equality and social justice."[42]

From an early stage as archbishop, Bergoglio included such criticisms of neoliberalism in public criticisms of the Menem government. In a homily given in 1999 on the national feast day of Argentina, Bergoglio declared that "the system has fallen into a period of dark shadow," and added, "only a few benefitted" from current economic development and "the social fabric was being destroyed." Echoing the theology of Lucio Gera, he insisted, "Our people has soul," and suggested that the "true revolution" in politics will be based on listening to the deeper desires and values of this people.[43]

ECONOMIC RECESSION AND THE KIRCHNER GOVERNMENTS (1999–2013)

The sustained criticism Bergoglio had been leveling at the Menem government seemed justified when the Argentine economy collapsed in 2001. The causes of this collapse are complex. In part, it was the result of misjudged and heavy borrowing by the Menem government. However, Bergoglio was persuaded that part of the problem was the neoliberal economic policy of international bodies such as the IMF, which allowed such borrowing to occur and was then quick to punish a lack of repayment. He recognized that part of the inability of the Argentine government to repay loans was a downward shift in the prices it was receiving for export goods, something over which Argentina had no control. Consequently, he believed that economic policies that had encouraged export-led and highly indebted growth had contributed to Argentina's problems.[44]

From 2001 to 2003, the Argentine economy shrank rapidly. Now it was not only the poor who suffered but also large sections of the lower middle classes, which descended into a state of unemployment. Also, a wide range of government services were cut. The Episcopal Conference of Argentina was quick to respond. It coordinated food kitchens and centers of material assistance in parishes across the country. Commentators noted that while "the state shrank," the church "hugely expanded its activity." Direct engagement by church groups in the economy extended from "building schools, clinics, and drug rehab centers," to assisting vulnerable groups such as "garbage collectors, prostitutes, trafficked workers, undocumented migrants" to organize themselves in self-help cooperatives, as well as to campaign for their rights before the government. One commentator concluded, "The Church became, in effect, the host space for the national recovery."[45]

President Menem had already stood down from power before the economic crisis of 2001. However, his policies were blamed for it. A new era began when President Nestor Kirchner came to power in 2003. He would remain in power until 2007, followed by his wife, who continued in power until 2015. These leaders adopted a more left-wing set of policies, offering intense criticism of the Menem era. While Bergoglio agreed with some of these criticisms, he distanced himself from the Kirchner governments, much as he had done with that of Menem. He disliked the rhetoric of the new government, criticizing their tendency to employ a "friend-enemy logic," "pitting 'people' against a series of foes: the 'corporations,' the armed forces, the agro-export sector, the big industries," and, not least, the church.[46]

As the first decade of the new millennium advanced, Bergoglio remained a respected figure in Argentine politics. In 2010, Argentina began a multiyear process of celebrating its independence from Spain. Bergoglio took this as an opportunity to support the writing of a detailed document that would describe a new *Proyecto de país* (country project) that would add some concrete proposals to a more general call for dialogue for the common good. One commentator describes it:

> The document identified core Argentine structural failings: stubbornly high unemployment despite economic growth, deep-seated public corruption, political clientelism, an explosion of drugs and gambling, a lack of respect for life and family, and, of course, a growing population of *los descartables*, "throwaway people." The new country project was an invitation to learn from the dialogue and solidarity that emerged in the crisis of 2002, and to tackle together Argentina's

121

failures, mobilizing the energies of civil society and renewing public life.[47]

Officially, the Kirchner government maintained a distance from these proposals. However, in private, many politicians took them seriously and consulted Bergoglio about them. One such politician stated, "He understands politics. He understands the logic of power. You can really talk to him." One commentator suggested that what resulted was "a very Bergoglio paradox" where "the austere, incorruptible mystic at war with spiritual worldliness" was nevertheless "the most astutely political Argentine since Perón."[48]

Opposition from within the Official Church

As a proponent of a theology of the people, it was natural for Bergoglio to find himself in opposition to both Marxism and extreme neoliberalism. It came as more of a surprise for him that a third source of opposition to him would emerge from the Vatican.

THE VATICAN, POLITICS, AND ARGENTINA

A chapter of the biography of Pope Francis by an Argentine journalist, Elisabetta Piqué, is entitled "Clerical and Political Adversaries." Here the author outlines how, from the beginning of his time as an auxiliary bishop, Bergoglio was regarded as not only making enemies in the Menem government but also among officials of the Vatican curia and among Argentine bishops closely associated with this curial group. Piqué describes how certain bishops were allied to a "Caselli-Sodano alliance," referring to the Argentine government minister and the current Secretary of State of the Holy See.[49]

Bergoglio opposed the efforts of Menem's aide, Caselli, to use government money to build a friendship with him. Having witnessed the financial entanglements of his predecessor, Archbishop Quarracino, he was determined to avoid accepting such gestures. Equally, he could not but become aware that Caselli continued to enjoy a close relationship with other Argentine bishops.[50] He was made aware that his appointment as auxiliary bishop of Buenos Aires came through the campaigning of Archbishop Quarracino directly with Pope John Paul II, and over against the preference of a "powerful nexus" that included Cardinal Sodano and his assistant Archbishop Sandri and certain Argentine bishops. Bergoglio, no stranger to intraecclesial conflicts as a Jesuit, now found himself embroiled in new ones.

Commentators explain that by the late 1990s, a complex situation had emerged in the Vatican. In addition to clear policy lines being offered by Pope John Paul II, relying often on the theological support of Cardinal Ratzinger, more institutional dynamics were also at play.[51] Here members of the Vatican curia began exercising a certain autonomy in their actions and to exercise a degree of interference in the affairs of local churches beyond what the pope intended. Cardinal Sodano played a key role in this dynamic. He coordinated a network of papal nuncios around the world, and this gave him a strong influence in the nomination of bishops. Such a situation explains how Bergoglio, who enjoyed the support of Pope John Paul II, could also find himself treated in an unfriendly manner by elements of the Vatican curia, and by some Argentine bishops who were close to them.[52] This opposition increased as Pope John Paul successively nominated him as coadjutor with right of succession to Archbishop Quarracino, archbishop, and then cardinal.

While Vatican officials operated with a certain autonomy from the pope, it must also be acknowledged that the explanations they offered for their interventions in the affairs of local churches referred to the deductivist and neo-Augustinian teachings of the two popes who were in office during the time that Bergoglio was a bishop. What had emerged in the church was a narrow set of criteria for what was considered the appropriate behavior of a bishop. Piqué recounts,

> Bergoglio is accused of not defending doctrine, of making pastoral gestures that are too daring, and of not arguing publicly and with greater determination with the Argentine government of the time [on issues of sexual morality]. In other words, they criticize his ways of being a pastor and of understanding the church.[53]

On a variety of issues, the Vatican curia began to interfere in what Bergoglio considered his prerogatives of governing his own archdiocese. A particularly obvious one occurred late in his tenure as archbishop when he appointed Father Victor Manuel Fernández to be rector of the Catholic University of Argentina. For two years, the Vatican delayed any confirmation of the nomination. Bergoglio left Fernández in place for all this time and repeatedly protested to Rome, without winning a hearing. Bergoglio was angry about this and confided with Fernández that he believed that such behavior by the Vatican was a classic example of "seeking space" in the church, and a refusal to respect local processes of people-building (i.e., appreciating that "time is more important than space"). When he was elected pope, one of the first actions that Pope Francis undertook was to confirm Fernández in his post. Piqué notes that, in addition, he ordained Fernández a bishop "in a direct message to those who waged war against Bergoglio about that nomination."[54]

After his nomination as bishop, Fernández published an article. He suggests that ever since the conclave of 2005, officials of the Vatican curia had been stepping up their opposition to Cardinal Bergoglio, perceiving him as promoting a significantly different vision of the church from what they wished to maintain. He describes their efforts at "concentration of power" in their own hands and how, at a local level, this had created an "impossibility of solving all problems with such a Roman centralization." He adds that several Argentine bishops agreed with this authoritarian approach of the Holy See, holding an ecclesiology where they understood themselves as "implacable judges" of the people. After 2012, when Bergoglio turned seventy-five years old, a number of these bishops had felt confident that he would soon retire and withdraw from public life. Together with officials of the Holy See, these began to criticize Bergoglio more openly than before. Fernández recounts,

> I personally took part in a meeting where a number of the Argentine bishops and some important representatives of the Holy See...enjoyed themselves by criticizing him shamelessly. They reproached him for not being demanding enough with the faithful, for not showing clearly his identity as a priest, for not preaching enough on questions of sexual morality.[55]

In the context of such tension, the story of how Bergoglio came to be elected pope is even more remarkable.

Conclusion

By the time Bergoglio was appointed cardinal, in 2001, his theological vision was well established. As outlined in chapter 1, its main characteristic was that it employed a method with three dimensions: discernment of spirits, an inductive approach, and a preferential option for the poor. In this chapter, we have traced how it was forged in a crucible of conflict with three approaches to thinking: Marxism, unrestricted neoliberalism, and a deductivism and centralization that emanated from the Vatican. Bergoglio believed that there was a strange similarity in all these opponents. All tended to adopt an ideological system and to impose it, inappropriately, on the situations they faced. In terms of the four dicta he held dear, his opponents preferred space to time, considered conflict preferable to unity, preferred ideas to reality, and found the parts more important than the whole.

8

Pope Francis and Theological Method

HAVING LIVED FOR so much of his life in Buenos Aires, Jorge Bergoglio considered himself a man of deeply local concerns. However, he was an intelligent man and recognized that even his concern to govern his archdiocese well made it inevitable that he should broaden his focus to include wider affairs of the church in Argentina, Latin America, and even the world. As noted in the previous chapter, Vatican politics had begun to impinge on him from the time of his first ordination as auxiliary bishop of Buenos Aires. However, when he was elected cardinal in 2001, he appreciated that it was part of his responsibility to be concerned for the well-being of the universal church.

Broadening Horizons

To understand the development of the international ecclesial vision of Bergoglio, it is necessary to understand the influence on him of his mentor, Alberto Methol Ferré.[1]

ALBERTO METHOL FERRÉ

Methol Ferré was a layman from Uruguay who lived from 1929 to 2009. One commentator describes him:

> Methol Ferré was arguably the most significant and origi-
> nal Latin-American Catholic intellectual of the late twen-
> tieth century. A writer, historian, journalist, theologian and
> autodidact—he described himself as a "wild Thomist with-
> out either seminary or academy"—converted to Catholicism
> by the writings of G. K. Chesterton while working in the
> port authority of Montevideo. A follower of Étienne Gilson
> and Perón, his two passions were the Church and Latin
> American integration, which came together in his work for
> CELAM over twenty years, between 1972 and 1992.[2]

Uruguay is close both geographically and culturally to Argentina, and Methol Ferré had been a supporter of the theology of the
people from its origins. In 1972, he found employment in the offices
of CELAM. Here, he promoted the idea that the Argentine theology
of the people had a relevance for the whole of Latin America. He was
a critic of Marxist tendencies in liberation theology, which he believed
had been uncritically accepted in the final document of Medellín.
He was committed to a notion of a united Latin America—*la patria
grande*, which had been promoted by romantic nationalist philosophers in the subcontinent since the nineteenth century—and believed
that such political unity could be supported by a church that adopted
an Argentine-initiated theology of the people. In fact, the vision of
Methol Ferré also extended to the universal church.

Methol Ferré studied the way new ideas (which he described as
"fire and energy") had renewed the universal church over the course of
history. Following studies by Yves Congar in *True and False Reform in
the Church*, he reflected on how ideas always emerged in some periph-
eral region of the church, only subsequently moving to the center. In
this respect, Methol Ferré noted how Congar describes the influence
of Alexandria and Antioch in the early church, of Spain and Italy on
the Council of Trent, and of the *nouvelle théologie* of northern Europe

on Vatican II. Methol Ferré's own contribution to this analysis was in one sense simple: he asserted that it was the turn of the church in Latin American to become the next "source church" for renewal in the universal church.[3]

Methol Ferré had exercised a considerable influence in drafting the final document of the general assembly of CELAM at Puebla in 1979. During the 1980s, he founded an academic journal, *Nexo*. During this time, he was distressed to witness how Pope John Paul II exercised an increasingly centralized governance over the church, marginalizing institutions such as CELAM. He was present at the General Assembly of CELAM held at Santo Domingo in 1992 as one of its organizing officials. He resigned from CELAM immediately afterward. This was the year when Bergoglio was ordained auxiliary bishop of Buenos Aires. Methol Ferré was quick to recognize the abilities of this young Argentine and cultivated a friendship with him.

Methol Ferré's writings of the 1990s were more somber than those of previous decades. Like other observers on international affairs, he had beheld with fascination the collapse of communism. However, he became convinced that the danger of Marxist influence in Latin America was being replaced by the danger of an all-pervasive culture of neoliberalism.[4] He considered this to produce materialistic and divided societies, and increasingly came to propose his notion of *la patria grande* in contrast to "the failures of both the North Atlantic model of economic growth and the Cuban-style socialism."[5] A second theme that he regularly treated was ecclesiology. One of his criticisms of the meeting in Santo Domingo was that it abandoned the inductive method that had characterized CELAM up to that point. He added that the lack of attention to the signs of the times, of which the church was now guilty, was leading to certain unintended consequences. The Vatican was beginning to encourage episcopal conferences to soften their criticism of unjust economic policies when governments who were implementing them were adopting policies on sexual ethics that were relatively close to a Catholic position.[6]

However, Methol Ferré remained an essentially optimistic thinker. He suggested that the pontificate of John Paul II was merely causing a delay in the process by which Latin America would convey its gifts to the wider church. As the health of John Paul II began to decline, he suggested that there would be a need for a transitional papacy, with another European pope, to follow John Paul II. He suggested that during such a papacy, CELAM should hold a new General Assembly that would reverse the trend of Santo Domingo and help the bishops of Latin America coordinate among themselves a return to the tradition of Puebla. After such an assembly, Latin America would be ready to provide a pope to the church. Remarkably, Methol Ferré had been proposing such ideas since the early 1990s. For reasons of health, he was not able to attend the CELAM assembly held in Aparecida in 2007. However, one commentator on that assembly describes it as, in fact, the expression of what Methol Ferré had been hoping for since the early 1990s:

> Like Moses on Mount Nebo glimpsing the Promise Land at the end of his life, the Uruguayan prophet lived to see it happen. In his intellectual testament, *Latin America in the Twenty-First Century*, which Bergoglio would distribute to many friends when it came out, Methol Ferré had predicted that Benedict XVI's engagement with the Latin-American church in the 1980s would bring about a new spring of Latin American Catholic thinking loyal to the Magisterium. That, essentially, is the story of Aparecida.[7]

Methol Ferré did not live to see the election of Jorge Bergoglio as pope, as he died in 2009. However, there is no question about the influence he bore on the Argentine. Bergoglio had been aware of the writings of Methol Ferré from the time of his theology studies before ordination. He first met the Uruguayan in the late 1970s, when he was Jesuit provincial. Subsequently, he referred to articles from *Nexo* when he was rector of the Colegio Máximo. However, it was above all when he was archbishop of Buenos Aires that he and Methol Ferré began to meet regularly and to form a fast friendship. Methol Ferré cultivated this friendship assiduously, traveling often from nearby Uruguay to visit Buenos Aires.

BERGOGLIO'S RISING INTERNATIONAL PROFILE

Assisted by the vision of Methol Ferré, Bergoglio began to accept a growing role in the church beyond the boundaries of his archdiocese. In 2001, he was made a cardinal. In the same year, he found himself appointed as a member of a synod of bishops in Rome. The theme of the synod was on the role of bishops. This was a neuralgic topic with some members of the synod, who believed that the centralized policies of John Paul II were not consistent with the notion of collegiality that had been approved of in *Lumen Gentium*. In chapter 6, we outlined how Cardinal Walter Kasper had protested publicly in 1998 about a *moto proprio* that had been produced by the pope on this topic. By the time of the synod of 2001, it was clear that Kasper and others had developed an additional strategy to registering their disagreement: they began to look for a possible successor to Pope John Paul II who would adopt different policies. Kasper became part of a group of senior churchmen who began meeting informally in St. Gallen, Switzerland. Their aim was to coordinate themselves in advance of a future papal conclave. The figurehead of this group was Cardinal Carlo Maria Martini, the Jesuit archbishop of Milan, and other figures, including Cardinal Godfried Danneels of Brussels, and Cardinal Lehmann of Mainz, Germany.[8]

At the beginning of the synod of 2001, Bergoglio was appointed rapporteur of the document the synod would forward to the pope for his reflection.[9] During the course of the synod, he communicated an opinion to a member of the St. Gallen group that he did not think that the issue of collegiality could be treated with adequate depth in a synod whose results would be controlled by the current Vatican curia. He added that, in his opinion, only a radical reform of the curia would permit the question of collegiality to be treated in a way that was genuinely open to the spirit of *Lumen Gentium*.[10] This response came as a surprise to members of the St. Gallen group, as the new cardinal had a reputation of being a conservative. They began to consider promoting his name as a potential future pope.

In 2005, Pope John Paul II died. During the conclave that followed, members of the St. Gallen group, without consulting Bergoglio, began to propose that cardinals vote for him. In the early ballots, an increasing number of votes were cast for the Argentine cardinal. At this stage, a remarkable event occurred. Bergoglio "begged the other cardinals 'almost in tears' to vote for Ratzinger." Cardinal Ratzinger was duly elected pope.[11] Members of the St. Gallen group were disappointed and would remember in the future not to act without first informing Bergoglio. Various explanations have been offered for the reluctance of Bergoglio in the conclave of 2005. The most convincing is the following:

> [Bergoglio] believed he was not ready: more important, Latin America wasn't. His Uruguayan philosopher friend, Alberto Methol Ferré, explained as much in an interview just days after John Paul II's death. Latin America, as the oldest of the non-European Churches, had been moving from a "reflection Church" to a "source Church" that would in time invigorate the universal church; but that process had been halted, even reversed, in the 1980s and 1990s. Until the continent's bishops came together through the next CELAM General Conference—it had been thirteen years since the disaster of Santo Domingo—any pope elected from Latin America would represent only his nation's reflection of the European Church.[12]

This explanation of Bergoglio's apparent timidity at the conclave of 2005 explains why it was followed by a remarkable apostolic boldness on his part immediately afterward.

APARECIDA

In 2005, Bergoglio was appointed president of the Episcopal Conference of Argentina. The fact that he had received votes at the conclave of that year had increased his profile among Latin American bishops. He used this position to campaign actively for the holding of a general assembly of CELAM.[13] It was partly because of his efforts that the Fifth General Assembly of CELAM was convoked in 2007 in Aparecida, Brazil.

Because Bergoglio had been an active promoter of Aparecida, it was not a surprise that he was also elected to be the chairman of the drafting committee of the final document.[14] Two Argentine priests were key collaborators in the drafting process. As already mentioned, one of these was Victor Manuel Fernández, then the vice rector of the Catholic University of Argentina. The other was Carlos Galli, considered to be the premier interpreter of the theology of Lucio Gera. Describing Bergoglio's performance at Aparecida, Fernández stated, "It was amazing to watch him move in Aparecida, to see his ability to knit together a consensus, to create the right atmosphere, to instill trust."[15]

Commentators agree that the final document of the assembly represented a polite rebellion against Santo Domingo.[16] Also, as anticipated by the conferences held between Cardinal Ratzinger and liberation theologians in the late 1990s, it represented an arrival to prominence in CELAM of the Argentine perspective on liberation theology. Differences between the documents of Santo Domingo and Aparecida are immediately evident. The latter document opens with an emphatic restatement of the value of inductive method:

> In continuity with the previous general conferences of Latin American Bishops, this document utilizes the see-judge-act method....This method has been helpful for living our calling and mission in the church with more dedication and intensity. It has enriched theological and pastoral work.[17]

The final document of Aparecida was itself organized according to the See-Judge-Act method. Aparecida treats many of the issues already familiar from Medellín and Puebla, including poverty, injustice, and the need to respond pastorally to youth. However, one issue received a new prominence: a concern for the environment. This concern was driven by an awareness of the damage being done to the ecosystem of the Amazon region, as well as the Antarctic. Consequently, this issue, which (like the notion of the option for the poor) appertains to the first step, See, also informs the later steps of Judge and Act in the document.[18]

The Argentine character of the inductive method employed in the Aparecida document was evident in two ways. The first was its approach to a preferential option for the poor. Echoing Lucio Gera, it states,

> Only the closeness that makes us friends enables us to appreciate deeply the values of the poor today, their legitimate desires, and their own manner of living the faith. The option for the poor should lead us to friendship with the poor. Day by day the poor become agents of evangelization and of comprehensive human promotion: they educate their children in the faith, they engage in ongoing solidarity among relatives and neighbors, they constantly seek God,

and give life to the Church's pilgrimage. In the light of the gospel, we recognize their immense dignity and their sacred worth in the eyes of Christ, who was poor like them and excluded among them. Out of this believing experience, we will share with them the defense of their rights.[19]

In its treatment of a preferential option for the poor, the document also echoes the analysis of culture of Rafael Tello. It states, "We must consider that culture with empathy in order to understand it, but also with a critical stance to discover whatever within it is the product of human limitation and sin."[20] Furthermore, it devotes a section to the complex question of ministering to culture in urban slums: "The city has become the proper site of the new cultures which are coming into being and imposing a new language and new sets of symbols. This urban mindset is also spreading even in the countryside."[21]

Entering deeply into the complexity of the first step, See, the document struggles with a further question: how to combine a use of social science with a theological perspective that is convinced that God's grace is already at work in all situations. After some rather intense debate, it was agreed to insert a section, "The Reality that Confronts Us as Disciples and Missionaries," before an in-depth analysis of the situation. This section asserts that, as Christians, our ability to study a situation is illuminated by "the love received from the Father through Jesus Christ, by the anointing of the Holy Spirit."[22] Those who at first objected to this approach had suggested that such statements might represent a return of deductivist thinking, where theological concepts are imposed in an abstract way on empirical reality. However, they were persuaded that it need not be deductivist to speak of studying a situation "with the eyes of discipleship," and that, conversely, there were limitations to the value-free methods of the social sciences, which could only offer an "antiseptic, detached, and disengaged" method of studying social reality.[23]

Chapters 4 and 5 of the document are devoted to the step Judge. Here biblical references are employed to study the practice of Jesus and a notion of church is invoked that describes it as a "communion of missionary disciples." Also included is a section with the heading "Popular Piety as Space of Encounter with Jesus Christ."[24] Chapters 6 and 7, devoted to the step Act, stress the importance of formation of laity as well as clergy in a spirituality of missionary discipleship.

The participants at Aparecida were aware that they had produced something new. They were discreet in their criticism of Santo Domingo, but the way they ignored its statements spoke volumes. At the same time, they sought to strike a reconciliatory tone with those who have been offended by the Marxist tendencies of liberation theology in the past. Rather than blame specific theologians for such excesses, the bishops of CELAM confessed that they themselves had previously made exaggerated statements. They stated that experience "has taught us to look at reality more humbly, knowing that it is greater and more complex than the simplistic ways in which we used to look at it in the not very distant past."[25] One commentator concludes his account of Aparecida:

> The Aparecida document was the fruit of the Argentine Church carrying the flame of Latin-American theology over twenty years, safeguarding the insights of liberation theology from the pitfalls of liberal and Marxist thinking. It had done so by sticking close to the poor and their culture—the *pueblo fiel* hermeneutic—which [the]...Argentine team ensured took pride of place in the document.[26]

A New Papacy; A New Methodological Paradigm

When Pope Benedict XVI resigned in February 2013, he surprised just about everybody. This followed on a series of scandals that involved the Vatican curia. The worst of these was the case known as "Vatileaks," which involved the leaking of confidential papal documents to the press by a papal butler. However, this scandal was just the culmination of what diplomats seconded to the Vatican had been describing for some time as an air of "implosion" and an "end of regime" in the Vatican curia. It had become clear to many that the policy of centralization of power in the Vatican had culminated in a curia that was out of touch with the signs of the times and embroiled in a series of scandals.[27]

For his part, Bergoglio, like everyone else, was surprised with the rapid turn of events. Just before Aparecida, he had turned seventy-five years old. As is the norm in the church, he had written a letter of resignation to Pope Benedict. Given his lack of popularity among Vatican officials, he had expected a rapid acceptance of this resignation. He had already identified a simple apartment where he expected to spend his retirement. In fact, no response came to his letter of resignation and he found himself still as archbishop when the conclave of 2013 gathered. During the conclave, he came to accept that, in spite of his earlier thoughts about being too old, he being the next pope was God's choice.[28] He would later describe how he first experienced anxiety after being elected, how he went to pray in the nearby chapel, and how "a great sense of inner peace and freedom came over me, which has never left me."[29] This joy, as well as a novel informality of style, communicated itself immediately to the world as television cameras portrayed him standing on the papal balcony and greeting the crowds in St. Peter's Square.

While Bergoglio had not expected to become pope, he did in fact arrive in the post well prepared. One commentator states, "Unwittingly, Bergoglio had for some time been preparing to lead the Catholic Church. Like a shepherd who takes care of his sheep, but also reading, studying, and gathering information."[30] Another suggests that Bergoglio believed that he had received "two mandates." The first of these was "the mandate of the conclave," which appertained to a reform of the Vatican curia and the decentralization of governance in the universal church. The second mandate "could appropriately be called popular." This involved a call to employ an inductive approach to pastoral reflection and so to engage with the signs of the times as he continued to perceive them and as they pertained to the universal ministry that he now held.[31]

Once elected, Pope Francis moved quickly to implement his two mandates. Commentators note the novelty of his immediately appointing a group of eight cardinals to consult with him on issues of strategy, thus building a process of dialogue into the highest level of his decision-making.[32] Journalists have followed how he moved quickly to address issues in the Roman curia that had been causing scandal: financial transparency, and questions of the protection of children. I suggest that one can offer an analysis of these fundamental characteristics of the papacy of Francis by studying the three main teaching documents he has produced: *Evangelii Gaudium* (2013), *Laudato Si'* (2015), and *Amoris Laetitia* (2016).[33]

Evangelii Gaudium

Evangelii Gaudium was published in the same year that Pope Francis was elected. It bears a remarkable resemblance to the Aparecida document and can be regarded as a manifesto for the Francis papacy.[34] In fact, already before publishing this first apostolic exhortation, Pope Francis had stated to a meeting of the bishops of Brazil, "Aparecida offers us a perennial teaching about God and about the Church."[35]

As with the Aparecida document, interpreting *Evangelii Gaudium* is assisted by tracing how it contrasts with previous documents. Whereas the final document of Aparecida contrasts with that of Santo Domingo, *Evangelii Gaudium* contrasts with writings of Pope John Paul II and Pope Benedict XVI. As is customary in magisterial documents, a pope takes care not to explicitly criticize his successor. However, the writings of Pope Francis exhibit a shift of method that is impossible to miss. As Kasper points out, this shift includes that of replacing a deductive approach with an inductive one, and the replacement of a neo-Augustinian perspective with a Latin American one more rooted in Aquinas. Similarly, Carlos Galli, the coauthor with Bergoglio of the Aparecida document, points out that Pope Francis avoids the use of the vocabulary of New Evangelization, so favored by his two predecessors. He adds, "With Francis there reappears the theology of the People of God thus recapturing the centrality conferred on this notion by Vatican II, a centrality which, since 1985, had been obscured in the documents of the Pontifical Magisterium."[36]

THE DOCUMENT

Despite its similarities with Aparecida, *Evangelii Gaudium* differs in one striking respect: it offers swinging criticism of clericalism and the centralization of church governance. This development is easy to understand in the light of developments already described in the previous chapter. Clearly, Bergoglio felt a freedom to comment on these matters as pope that he did not feel as a representative of CELAM.

Chapters 1 and 2 of the apostolic exhortation constitute the step See in inductive method. Chapter 1 echoes the Aparecida document in the way it initiates this step with a theological consideration. Here, as I have already pointed out with respect to Aparecida, an implicit point made is that the eyes of faith—and not only social sciences—influence how we attend to a situation. Such a position tries to find a via media between imposing abstract and universal theological ideas on situations and adopting a reductionistic approach to social analysis—as do Marxists. In the Aparecida document, this point was made by introducing the notion of "missionary discipleship" to the perspective involved in how we study the situation. In the apostolic exhortation *Evangelii Gaudium*, Francis refers to the title of the document itself, "The Joy of Evangelization," to make a similar point. Furthermore, such is his eagerness to arrive at one of the main points of the document that, already in this first chapter, Francis moves straight to commenting on how certain structures and attitudes within the church "can hamper efforts at evangelization" (no. 19).

At the beginning of the encyclical, Pope Francis lists how church governance is too centralized to attend appropriately to pastoral situations. He begins with a comment on how clericalism can affect both parish and diocesan life. Moving to higher structures, he suggests that increasing authority should be delegated to national conferences of bishops by the Vatican. In striking contrast to the *moto proprio* on episcopal conferences issues by Pope John Paul II in 1998, he states, "A juridical status of episcopal conferences which would see them as subjects of specific attributions, including genuine doctrinal authority, has not yet been sufficiently elaborated." Next, he suggests that making changes such as this will involve nothing less than a conversion of self-understanding by the papacy: "The papacy and the central structures of the universal Church also need to hear the call to pastoral conversion" (nos. 24, 30, 32).

In addition to such statements about the organizational structure of the church, Pope Francis also asserts that pastoral conversion at all levels of the church should be motivated by a preferential option for the poor:

> But to whom should she go first?…Today and always, "the poor are the privileged recipients of the Gospel."…We have to state, without mincing words, that there is an inseparable bond between our faith and the poor. May we never abandon them. (no. 47)

In a narrow, logical sense, it might have seemed better for Francis to have delayed these comments about church structure and guiding theological perspective until after a more neutral study of the signs of the times, an analysis that would employ social science. However, as evidenced in the Aparecida document, this is not his style. He believes in including a degree of theological reflection even in the first step of inductive method, See. However, a more classic expression of this first step does arrive in chapter 2. The first part of this chapter is entitled "Some Challenges of Today's World." Here Francis offers an analysis of the social and cultural context in which the church finds itself, while continuing to express himself in an exhortative mode—keeping an eye to the kind of pastoral proposals he will be offering in step 3, Act. He speaks of the need to offer a prophetic denunciation of economic inequality in sections entitled "No to an Economy of Exclusion," "No to the New Idolatry of Money," "No to a Financial System which Rules Rather Than Serves," and "No to the Inequality which Spawns Violence" (nos. 53–60). All these positions stand in continuity with his statements on economic and political issues as archbishop of Buenos Aires. The rest of part 1 explores questions of culture. "Some Cultural Challenges" identifies cultural problems that make evangelization difficult, including secularism, individualism, and family breakdown. The next two sections, "Challenges to Inculturating the Faith" and "The Challenge of Urban Cultures," take up themes that were explored in the Aparecida document and state, "A uniform and rigid program of evangelization is not suited to this complex reality" (nos. 53–60, 75). Such analysis is a classic expression of a theology of the people.

Remarkably, the second part of chapter 2 returns to the issue of those characteristics of the church that can hamper efforts at evangelization. Here, Pope Francis borrows the notion of "spiritual worldliness" from Henri de Lubac, a term he had been using since his speeches as Jesuit provincial. Now, however, expressed within a papal document, his words have an extraordinary directness:

> This insidious worldliness is evident in a number of attitudes which appear opposed, yet all have the same pretense of "taking over the space of the Church." In some people we see an ostentatious preoccupation for the liturgy, for doctrine and for the Church's prestige, but without any concern that the Gospel have a real impact on God's faithful people and the concrete needs of the present time. In this way, the life of the Church turns into a museum piece

or something which is the property of a select few. In others, this spiritual worldliness lurks behind a fascination with social and political gain, or pride in their ability to manage practical affairs, or an obsession with programs of self-help and self-realization. It can also translate into a concern to be seen, into a social life full of appearances, meetings, dinners and receptions. It can also lead to a business mentality, caught up with management, statistics, plans and evaluations whose principal beneficiary is not God's people but the Church as an institution. The mark of Christ, incarnate, crucified and risen, is not present; closed and elite groups are formed, and no effort is made to go forth and seek out those who are distant or the immense multitudes who thirst for Christ. Evangelical fervor is replaced by the empty pleasure of complacency and self-indulgence. (no. 95)

The third chapter of *Evangelii Gaudium* constitutes the more formally theological moment of Judge. It can be understood as a classic presentation of a Latin American theology of the people. In many respects, it takes up the ecclesiological reflection that was begun in chapter 1. The first part of chapter 3 echoes the theology of Lucio Gera and is entitled "The Entire People of God Proclaims the Gospel." Here, Pope Francis stresses that all the baptized are the agents of evangelization. He suggests that notions of infallibility in matters of faith in Catholic theology should first and foremost be attributed to the whole people of God. Speaking of this infallibility, he describes it as related to the "instinct of faith *sensus fidei*—which helps them to discern what is truly of God...even when they lack the wherewithal to give them precise expression" (no. 119). He states that "expressions of popular piety have much to teach us; for those who are capable of reading them, they are a *locus theologicus*" (no. 126). As stated earlier, one commentator suggests that this return to an ecclesiology of people of God is a particularly distinctive characteristic of the theology of Pope Francis, one that stands in contrast with the preferred approach of his two predecessors.[37]

Continuing his exploration of questions of culture, Pope Francis echoes the theology of Raphael Tello. He asserts, "The People of God is incarnate in the peoples of the earth, each of which has its own culture," and adds, "no single culture can exhaust the mystery of our redemption in Christ." He also acknowledges that evangelizing practices in the past have at times represented "a needless hallowing of our own culture," which, in fact, demonstrated "more fanaticism than true evangelizing zeal." In a section important for academic theologians, he addresses the role of "professional, scientific, and academic circles" in the process of evangelization. He criticizes a merely "desk-bound theology," but acknowledges that academic theology has a key role to play in dialogue with culture and science. He acknowledges that "the other sciences and human experiences [are] most important for our discernment on how best to bring the gospel message to diverse cultural contexts and groups." Finally, having made it abundantly clear that the priest is not the only agent of evangelization, he devotes a lengthy reflection to the importance of the homily and to the role of the priest in adult catechesis (*Evangelii Gaudium* 115–18, 132–34, 133, 143, 160–75).

Chapter 4 has four main parts, all of which constitute the moment of Act in inductive method. They each stress distinct aspects of Catholic social teaching and return to the importance of pastoral action that helps the poor: "this is why I want a Church which is poor and for the poor." It is in this chapter that he outlines the four main pastoral principles that should characterize pastoral action that we have discussed already in previous chapters. Commentators suggest that these principles have long acted as a shorthand summary of Bergoglio's mode of theological reflection and pastoral decision-making: "time is greater than space"; "unity prevails over conflict"; "realities are more important than ideas"; and "the whole is greater than the parts" (nos. 198, 224–34, 238, 239). In concluding the chapter, the pope treats the question of dialogue. He identifies three areas of dialogue that are of importance: "dialogue with states, dialogue with society—including dialogue with cultures and the sciences—and dialogue with other believers who are not part of the Catholic Church." He implies that a key outcome of the pastoral action of the church is to initiate processes of dialogue in society, and admonishes church leaders to remember that "we do not speak for everyone." Rather, he calls for dialogue that exhibits a "profound social humility" and that hopes to find agreement with non-Catholics around broad principles such as "subsidiarity and solidarity" (nos. 240–41).

Laudato Si'

If *Evangelii Gaudium* represents a general manifesto for the Francis papacy, *Laudato Si'* represents something more specific: a discussion of the mission *ad extra* of the church. Here Francis demonstrates how he is responding to the second, "popular," mandate of his papacy, that of responding to the signs of the times as he continues to become aware of them. Questions of ecological concern had been present in his earlier thought, but never so central. Raphael Tello had included a concern for the destruction of the environment as he reflected on factors that were forcing indigenous peoples of Argentina to migrate to cities. Also, Cardinal Bergoglio's involvement with CELAM had increased his awareness of threats to the survival of ecosystems in the Amazon basin and Antarctica. However, it is only as pope that Bergoglio places ecology as a central concern of his preaching.[38]

From the time of his election, Pope Francis had been aware that two years later—in November 2015—there would occur a major conference on climate change in Paris, COP 21, where political leaders from around the world would decide whether or not to sign an agreement on limiting carbon emissions. He recognized that such a gathering was an impressive example of the kind of social dialogue that he wished to encourage. The publication of *Laudato Si'* was timed to occur a few weeks before the Paris conference and is judged to have exercised a certain influence on the positive outcome of that event.[39] However, within the church, the encyclical is also regarded as one of the major social encyclicals, introducing a significant development of doctrine in the realm of Catholic social thinking.

THE DOCUMENT

Predictably, *Laudato Si'* is organized according to a structure of See-Judge-Act, with chapters 1 and 2 constituting the first step, See.[40] As usual, Pope Francis does not limit himself to a narrow use of the social sciences in his conducting of this first step. He begins with an appeal to affectivity and values in outlining how the signs of the times should be studied. In his explicitly theological works such as the Aparecida document and *Evangelii Gaudium*, he had spoken of "missionary discipleship" and "the joy of the Gospel" as influencing this step. In *Laudato Si'*,

141

he recognizes that he is speaking as much to a non-Christian audience as to a Christian one and that it is appropriate to adopt the language of philosophy. However, he notes that St. Francis of Assisi is a figure who is universally appreciated and invokes the memory of this saint to make some preliminary comments. He points out that the title of the encyclical is taken from a hymn written by the medieval saint that declares, "Praise be to you, my Lord, through our Sister, Mother Earth, who sustains and governs us." He then suggests that St. Francis "shows us just how inseparable the bond is between concern for nature, justice for the poor, commitment to society, and interior peace" (nos. 1, 11). Next, he explains the actual threat humans pose to the natural environment. In preparing these reflections, Pope Francis had conducted an extensive, if confidential, dialogue with a wide range of experts. Problems identified include climate change, issues of water, a reduction of biodiversity, and factors affecting human society including inequality and war. Qualified commentators are agreed that the description of the ecological crisis facing the world offered in the first two chapters of the encyclical is both comprehensive and scientifically accurate.[41]

Chapters 3 and 4 represent the second step, Judge. Here, Francis continues a reflection that is primarily philosophical but is not shy about acknowledging that his philosophy is influenced by theology. Some recognize that the pope employs a terminology that is common in current debates in secular academic circles, but also recognize that the pope has something original to say. To those familiar with the theological background of Francis, the influence of a theology of the people here is evident. In chapters 3 and 4, the pope stresses that humans have a unique role to play in the history of the universe. Commentators recognize that his argument can be located within a group of opinions described as "moderately anthropocentric." They contrast such views, first, with an extreme anthropocentrism that is responsible for the ecological crisis, and second, with "biocentric" arguments.[42] Biocentric arguments hold that there is little that is normatively superior about the human species, that all species should be treated with equal respect, and that humans should extend their notion of human rights to include the rights of the environment. Some biocentric arguments seek to incorporate a notion of the rights of "Mother Earth" into national constitutions. Commentators recognize that Pope Francis offers an eloquent criticism of such arguments:

This situation has led to a constant schizophrenia, wherein a technocracy which sees no intrinsic value in lesser beings coexists with the other extreme, which sees no special value in human beings. But one cannot prescind from humanity. There can be no renewal of our relationship with nature without a renewal of humanity itself. There can be no ecology without an adequate anthropology. When the human person is considered as simply one being among others, the product of chance or physical determinism, then "our overall sense of responsibility wanes." A *misguided anthropocentrism need not necessarily yield to "biocentrism," for that would entail adding yet another imbalance,* failing to solve present problems and adding new ones. Human beings cannot be expected to feel responsibility for the world unless, at the same time, their unique capacities of knowledge, will, freedom and responsibility are recognized and valued. (*Laudato Si'* 118 [Italics added])

When Pope Francis outlines what he claims to be an "adequate anthropology," he calls for an "integral ecology." Two characteristics of his argument are evident: first, his anthropology has a "sacramental" dimension; and second, it includes an account of the importance of a preferential option for the poor. Concerning the first point, he draws on the teaching of St. Francis of Assisi to suggest that we can praise God by means of our attitude to the natural environment. He explains, "Developing the created world in a prudent way is the best way of caring for it, as this means that we ourselves become the instrument used by God to bring out the potential which he inscribed in things" (nos. 1, 124).[43] Concerning the second point, he speaks of the importance of culture in any consideration of changing social structures such as economic systems to protect the environment. He adds that a measure of the health of any culture is the respect it shows for the poor. He again echoes St. Francis when he stresses that a tension exists in human living between a sinful self-centeredness and a liberating other-centeredness. He notes that cultures can encourage one or other of these dispositions and suggests that the former attitude is fundamentally violent both to one's neighbor and to the natural environment. Conversely, he explains that the latter attitude is fundamentally peaceful: seeking to include marginalized groups in the material well-being of the community and respecting the natural environment. He adds that today, an extreme anthropocentrism is producing a "throwaway culture" eschewing wisdom traditions in many cultures that proposed different values. He suggests that "together with the patrimony of nature, there is also an historic, artistic and cultural patrimony which is likewise under threat" (nos. 11, 22, 143).[44]

Chapters 5 and 6 represent the third step, Act, and are entitled "Lines of Approach and Action" and "Ecological Spirituality and Education." Several commentators have noted that these chapters do not offer detail about solutions to the ecological crisis. Rather, they recognize that the chapters represent primarily a call for dialogue. A few criticize the pope for not being more specific. Most recognize that the encyclical lies more at the level of moral exhortation to the international community and to various other communities. Many accept the value of the five areas of dialogue that the pope distinguishes: within the international community (as in the Conference in Paris, 2015); at the level of national and local politics; for "transparency in decision-making"; between economics and politics; and between religions and science. Some recognize how the pope's proposals in the realm of "Ecological Education and Spirituality" draw on a philosophical tradition with roots in Aristotle when it suggests that, to be capable of authentic dialogue, citizens need to be virtuous. Consequently, many appreciate a concluding statement of the encyclical: "Many things have to change course, but it is we human beings above all who need to change"; and also, "A great cultural, spiritual and educational challenge stands before us, and it will demand that we set out on the long path of renewal" (no. 202).

Conclusion

Studying the writings of Pope Francis with an awareness of his intellectual biography before being pope is revealing. Certainly, the closeness of *Evangelii Gaudium* to the final document of Aparecida is striking. By contrast, in some respects, *Laudato Si'* comes as a surprise. Archbishop Bergoglio had not produced reflections quite like this. However, at second glance, one recognizes that this important encyclical is the fruit, simply, of Pope Francis continuing to employ the inductive method that had guided him for his whole priestly life. With the issue of the environment, he recognized a sign of the times that, especially with his new universal responsibilities, was necessary to address.[45]

Concerning both these documents, note that, ever since his work on the final document of Aparecida, Pope Francis had insisted upon adding a theological dimension to the first step of inductive method, See. This becomes apparent in the early chapters of both *Evangelii Gaudium* and *Laudato Si'*. This instinct is supported by Lonergan. Implicitly, Pope Francis is seeking to recognize that each situation is constituted not only by dimensions of progress and decline, but also by redemption. It is important to recognize how each of these dimensions is already present in any situation before one reflects on how the church can be a catalyst of further redemption, reversing decline, and promoting progress. As one Lonergan scholar states,

> The structure of history cannot be understood correctly if one prescinds from the realities affirmed in the Christian doctrines of grace and sin, in the theological doctrines of the natural and the supernatural, and in the religious doctrines of radical evil and gratuitous redemption.[46]

Pope Francis employs his characteristically inductive method in the third document, *Amoris Laetitia*, which treats the pastoral care of families. This document has provoked a remarkable degree of opposition within the Catholic Church. Discussing this topic in the concluding chapter of this book is appropriate because these controversies bring into focus issues we have been discussing throughout this book: that Pope Francis is the most historically conscious pope yet seen by the Catholic Church, and that this is provoking resistance by the forces of perceptualist classicism that remain in the church.

9

The Test of a Papacy

IN THIS CHAPTER, we examine the apostolic exhortation *Amoris Laetitia* and the controversies that have emerged over it. These controversies bring to a climax tensions between classicism and historical consciousness in the Catholic Church that have been evident since Vatican II. They now present an opportunity for the Catholic Church. Hopefully, both conservatives and progressives in current debates might find agreement based on an interiorly differentiated consciousness.

Amoris Laetitia

In the previous chapter, we described *Evangelii Gaudium* as a manifesto for the Francis papacy and *Laudato Si'* as the document that treats one dimension of the broad proposal of *Evangelii Gaudium*: the mission of the church *ad extra*. By contrast, the apostolic exhortation *Amoris Laetitia* turns attention to issues that are proposed primarily *ad intra* to the church. As with Vatican II, it was the changes proposed *ad intra* to the church that were destined to cause the most controversy. *Amoris Laetitia* can be understood as representing a direct application of principles outlined in *Evangelii Gaudium* to the question of the pastoral care of families.

THE SYNODS

While composing *Evangelii Gaudium*, Pope Francis began planning the next series of synods of bishops. This apostolic exhortation had stressed the importance of "collegiality and synodality," and synods of bishops were an obvious structure to begin acting on this vision. Pope Francis approached Archbishop Lorenzo Baldisseri to invite him to be general secretary of the Synod of Bishops. Baldisseri, an Italian, had spent many years as papal nuncio in Latin America and, in his capacity as nuncio to Brazil, had attended the CELAM conference in Aparecida in 2007. Together, they planned new developments. They would hold two synods on the question of the pastoral care of families, and before each synod, they would conduct an elaborate process of consulting the opinions of people in all the dioceses of the world.

In February 2014, in advance of the first of these synods, Pope Francis convoked a consistory of cardinals where he explained his plans for the synods. Significantly, he invited Cardinal Walter Kasper to offer a long theological reflection to launch the discussions of the cardinals. Kasper's talk to the cardinals included two key elements. First, he spoke of the need for a paradigm shift toward a more pastorally minded theological method that spent more time listening to the reality of family life today and the difficulties couples had in living up to the fullness of Catholic teaching. Essentially, this was a call for a shift from a deductive to an inductive approach to theology. He then explored the possibility of accepting divorced and remarried couples to receiving communion—a topic considered highly controversial, at least before the pontificate of Francis.[1]

In October 2014, an Extraordinary Synod of Bishops opened with the theme "The Pastoral Challenges of the Family in the Context of Evangelization." Pope Francis offered an opening address. He stressed the importance of conducting a frank exploration of the reality of family life today to arrive eventually at insights into what pastoral policies should be adopted for the better pastoral care of families. He spoke of the importance of the questionnaire process that had preceded this event and of the importance of a "dynamic" of "collegiality and synodality" in the church. He invoked a term from Greek philosophy, *parrhesia*, which means "direct speaking" or "apostolic boldness," and invited the synod members to employ this, along with "listening with humility," as their guiding attitudes. He acknowledged that he was introducing a new approach to synodal debates and noted that when he had introduced this to the consistory of cardinals the year before, some had found this difficult. One cardinal had written to him saying that some cardinals found it difficult to express their own opinions for fear that they might differ from what the pope wanted them to say. Pope Francis declared that "this is not good, this is not synodality!"[2]

As the synod proceeded, it became evident that a novelty in its rules of proceeding was proving significant: much of the synod was conducted in the form of small discussion groups, with plenary sessions devoted to synthesizing the results of these discussions. This altered the dynamic of the synod. In previous synods, most sessions had been plenary sessions and relatively few individuals got to speak.[3] By the time the Ordinary Synod of 2015 was to begin, certain conservative bishops had begun to feel deeply unhappy about the method being promoted by Pope Francis. A group of thirteen cardinals expressed their discontent in a private letter to the pope, which was then released to the press. Pope Francis was quick to insist that it was his prerogative to organize synods along these lines and that he intended to continue as he had begun.[4] As the synod unfolded, those who opposed the method of the pope became increasingly identifiable as a distinct group, especially by means of consistent leaks to newspapers. Apart from having problems with the discursive nature of the synod, the group expressed displeasure with the proposal that German bishops had already been presenting for years: that under certain circumstances couples that included individuals who had been divorced and remarried could be admitted to the Eucharist.

When it came time to summarize the results of group discussions in a final document, it was difficult for the synod secretaries to find formulas of words upon which many of the synod fathers could agree. Consequently, the final document avoided making clear proposals on controversial topics. Attention now turned to Pope Francis and the positions he would take in the apostolic exhortation that would follow the two synods.

THE DOCUMENT

Amoris Letitia was published in March 2016. It has similarities and differences from the previous two magisterial letters of Pope Francis.

Like the others, it follows an inductive method, employing the steps of See, Judge, and Act. However, unlike the others, it is a long—over 250 pages—and not tightly argued document. In some respects, it reflects the ambiguity of the final documents of the synods by not adopting clear dogmatic proposals. At the same time, for all its ambiguities, the exhortation was immediately considered to be a highly significant moment in magisterial teaching in pastoral and moral theology—both by its supporters and by its critics. Many recognized that applying an inductive approach to questions of pastoral and moral theology represented a shift from the practice of the previous two pontificates.[5]

Pope Francis makes no apologies for not writing a document that gives definitive answers to diverse questions. In introducing the document, he praises the kind of exploration of issues that occurred during the synod and notes that "the complexity of the issues that arose revealed the need for continued open discussion of a number of doctrinal, moral, spiritual, and pastoral questions." In a classic statement of an inductive approach to theology, he adds that not all moral and pastoral issues need to be treated by the papal magisterium:

> Since "time is greater than space," I would make it clear that not all discussions of doctrinal, moral or pastoral issues need to be settled by interventions of the magisterium. Unity of teaching and practice is certainly necessary in the Church, but this does not preclude various ways of interpreting some aspects of that teaching or drawing certain consequences.... Each country or region, moreover, can seek solutions better suited to its culture and sensitive to its traditions and local needs. For "cultures are in fact quite diverse and every general principle...needs to be inculturated, if it is to be respected and applied." (*Amoris Laetitia* 3)

Chapters 1 and 2 represent the first step, See, of inductive method. As customary with the writings of Bergoglio, he delays a sociological analysis of the current situation with reflections so that we approach such empirical data "through the eyes of faith." The first chapter is entitled "In the Light of the Word" and elaborates on how "the Bible is full of families, births, love stories and family crises." The second chapter, "The Experience and Challenges of the Family," advances to a more sociological commentary and takes care to do justice to the vast variety of family life situations that were described during the synods. Here, Francis notes a paradox: the culture in rich countries often presents young people "with so many options that they too are dissuaded from starting a family," while in poor countries—as well as often among the poor in rich countries—society "pressures young people not to start a family, because they lack possibilities for the future" (no. 13). Similarly, he takes note of a variety of difficult situations in which families find themselves, including families torn apart by migration and those living in "a blended or reconstituted family" (nos. 45–46).

Pope Francis makes it clear that his inductive pastoral approach does not imply a compromise of doctrinal clarity. He demonstrates what some would call a doctrinal conservativism and a continuity with the teaching of Pope John Paul II when he addresses the question of "gender ideology" in current culture. He criticizes a line of thinking that "denies the difference and reciprocity in the nature of a man and a woman and envisages a society without sexual differences, thereby eliminating the anthropological basis of the family." He adds,

> It is one thing to be understanding of human weakness and the complexities of life, and another to accept ideologies that attempt to sunder what are inseparable aspects of reality. Let us not fall into the sin of trying to replace the Creator. We are creatures, and not omnipotent. Creation is prior to us and must be received as a gift. (no. 56)[6]

Chapters 3, 4, and 5, representing the second step, Judge, of inductive method, offer a theological reflection on marriage and the family. Here again, Pope Francis demonstrates a clarity about the obligation to accept church doctrine. He acknowledges that the Catholic Church has been failing in its efforts to persuade both Catholics and non-Catholics that its teaching on sexuality and marriage is reasonable, attractive, and true; as a result, the church has tended to retreat to authoritarian declarations and an appeal to obedience. However, he also insists, "We have been called to form consciences not to replace them" (no. 37). Consequently, when he discusses what Christian teaching on marriage and family is, one cannot help but notice the change in tone in his explanation of Christian doctrine.

The third chapter, "Looking to Jesus, the Vocation of the Family," begins with a biblical treatment of its theme and proceeds to a survey of recent church teaching. Recalling his belief on the importance of trying to persuade rather than to impose, he states that "the Gospel of the family also nourishes seeds that are still waiting to grow, and serves as the basis for caring for those plants that are wilting and must not be neglected." The fourth chapter, "Love in Marriage," offers a lyrical reflection on what is called the "Gift of Love," which states, "Love is patient, love is kind…" (1 Cor 13:4–7). Commentators have noted how this chapter draws on personalist philosophy and diverges from recent papal documents in making little reference to natural law. The fifth chapter, "Love Made Fruitful," is devoted to the theme of the role of children in the family.

The next three chapters represent the third step, Act, of inductive method. Here, Pope Francis offers proposals for the pastoral care of families. The sixth chapter, "Some Pastoral Perspectives," takes care to quote the proposals of the two synods at length. It stresses the importance of accompaniment of families and expresses hesitation in making any universal proposals about how the local parish and diocese should care for individual families. Rather, the pope encourages local decision-making in finding the best way to accompany families (no. 199). The seventh chapter, "Towards a Better Education of Children," takes up themes introduced in chapter 5 and reflects on questions of the education of the young.

The eighth chapter, "Accompanying, Discerning, and Integrating Weakness," was always destined to become the most controversial of the document. It includes sections with titles such as "Gradualness in Pastoral Care" and "Discernment of 'Irregular' Situations." In the latter of these sections, the pope makes a distinction that will be grasped only by those who recognize the inductive character of moral reasoning. He states that, at times, individuals who have good intentions will simply not be able to appreciate the truth of Catholic moral teaching in such a way as to incorporate it into their process of decision-making:

> What is possible is simply a renewed encouragement to undertake a responsible personal and pastoral discernment of particular cases, one which would recognize that, since "the degree of responsibility is not equal in all cases," the consequences or effects of a rule need not necessarily always be the same. Priests have the duty to "accompany [the divorced and remarried] in helping them to understand

151

their situation according to the teaching of the Church and the guidelines of the bishop. (no. 300)

He expands on the idea that "the degree of responsibility is not equal in all cases" in subsequent sections entitled "Mitigating Factors in Pastoral Discernment" and "The Logic of Pastoral Mercy." In fact, while exploring this point, he makes statements that seem to indicate that he is in agreement with the proposal of the German bishops that, under certain circumstances, divorced and remarried couples could be admitted to the sacrament of the Eucharist: "I am in agreement with the many Synod Fathers who observed that 'the baptized who are divorced and civilly remarried need to be more fully integrated into Christian communities in the variety of ways possible, while avoiding any occasion of scandal.'" He then adds, "Their participation can be expressed in different ecclesial services, which necessarily requires *discerning which of the various forms of exclusion currently practiced in the liturgical, pastoral, educational and institutional framework, can be surmounted*" (no. 299 [author's emphasis]). Furthermore, when he makes the comment already noted earlier that "the degree of responsibility is not equal in all cases," he adds a footnote: "This is also the case with regard to sacramental discipline, since discernment can recognize that in a particular situation no grave fault exists" (no. 300; note 336).

RECEPTION

It was inevitable that *Amoris Laetitia* would provoke controversy. Pope Francis invited Cardinal Christoph Schönborn of Vienna to make the official presentation of the text to journalists, in March 2016.[7] In presenting the exhortation, the cardinal praised its spirit of merciful accompaniment of couples in imperfect situations and expressed relief at its personalist and nonjudgmental tone. He also acknowledged that there were "hot potatoes" in the last chapter that would inevitably provoke debate. In this and subsequent comments, Schönborn suggested that, more than for some other papal documents, the effectiveness of *Amoris Laetitia* would depend on how it was received by episcopal conferences around the world. The reason for this was that the text itself insisted on introducing a principle of synodality and collegiality into the heart of the pastoral care of families. He added that Pope

Francis had thus handed responsibility over to local churches to appropriate what the exhortation had only stated in general terms. Some journalists interpreted the cardinal as implying that Pope Francis was asking episcopal conferences, at least in certain countries, to take the lead in making concrete decisions on receiving certain "irregular couples" into receiving the Eucharist.[8]

How, then, did episcopal conferences respond to *Amoris Laetitia*? Most conferences issued loyal statements of acceptance and approval of the exhortation. However, a closer analysis of statements and policy decisions indicates that some conferences embrace its novelty more than others. In some cases, conferences have explicitly spoken of a readiness to address the question of admitting divorced and remarried couples to the Eucharist. Among these are those of Argentina, Brazil, and Chile and, significantly, these have received warm replies from the pope.[9] In September 2016, Pope Francis instructed that his response to the Episcopal Conference of Argentina should be included in the *Acta Apostolica Sedis*, the official record of Vatican documents and acts. This implies that he considers both the guidelines for implementing the exhortation, and his response approving these guidelines, should now be considered part of the "authentic magisterium" of the church.[10]

Apart from the question of responses to *Amoris Laetitia* from episcopal conferences, much has also happened at other levels. This has included a litany of protests in social media and in blogs of traditionalist Catholics. Negative opinions have also been expressed by a small number of bishops and cardinals, as well as by some Catholic academics.[11] On the other side of this debate, supporters of the apostolic exhortation have also been publishing their thoughts. Emanating from the German-speaking world, a book was published whose title translates as *Amoris Laetitia: A Leap forward for Moral Theology?* Here a group of prominent moral theologians suggest that, despite a studied ambiguity of the apostolic exhortation, it represents a significant shift of paradigm from the approach to moral theology exhibited by previous popes.[12] Two years after the publication of *Amoris Laetitia*, the question remains somewhat open regarding just what will be the long-term impact of this apostolic exhortation. In the opinion of some, this will be the touchstone of the success of the Francis papacy.

A Lonergan-Based Analysis of Current Controversies

Of importance for an academic study of the significance of Pope Francis is the fact that some respected Catholic intellectuals have also voiced opposition. I discuss one such contribution at relative length, and then compare it with a letter supporting the exhortation written by Walter Kasper.

FINNIS AND GRISEZ

In December 2016, John Finnis and Germain Grisez published an article on the internet entitled "The Misuse of *Amoris Laetitia* to Support Errors against the Catholic Faith: A Letter to the Supreme Pontiff Francis, to All Bishops in Communion with Him, and to the Rest of the Christian Faithful."[13] The authors purport not to criticize Pope Francis directly, but rather to criticize those who misinterpret him. Their argument identifies eight "erroneous positions" they suggest are current in the church; points out how each can claim justification in one or other "unclear" statement in *Amoris Laetitia*; and explains how such positions are not in keeping with "the New Testament and Tradition." They then request that Pope Francis make a public statement refuting the eight possible misreadings of *Amoris Laetitia*.[14]

According to Finnis and Grisez, the first error into which readers of *Amoris Laetitia* might fall is to believe that the exhortation supports the following proposition: "A priest administering the Sacrament of Reconciliation may sometimes absolve a penitent who lacks a purpose of amendment with respect to a sin in grave matter that either pertains to his or her ongoing form of life or is habitually repetitive."[15] The second error is close to the first: "Some of the faithful are too weak to keep God's commandments; though resigned to committing ongoing and habitual sins in grave matter, they can live in grace." The third error holds, "No general moral rule is exceptionless. Even divine commandments forbidding specific kinds of actions are subject to exceptions in some situations." The fourth error is, in effect, a restatement of the third one: "While some of God's commandments or precepts seem to require that one never choose an act of one of the kinds to which they refer, those commandments and precepts actually are rules that

154

express ideals and identify goods that one should always serve and strive after as best one can, given one's weaknesses and one's complex, concrete situation, which may require one to choose an act at odds with the letter of the rule."

According to Finnis and Grisez, the fifth error into which readers of *Amoris Laetitia* might fall touches on how to understand the Christian notion of conscience: "If one bears in mind one's concrete situation and personal limitations, one's conscience may at times discern that doing an act of a kind contrary even to a divine commandment will be doing one's best to respond to God, which is all that he asks, and then one ought to choose to do that act but also be ready to conform fully to the divine commandment if and when one can do so." The remaining three errors identified by Finnis and Grisez express opinions that are so extreme that one can legitimately question how such errors could even appear to be supported by *Amoris Laetitia*. Such errors include the following: an extreme view on sexual license (the sixth error); a lack of belief that the indissolubility of marriage is a doctrine (the seventh error); and a lack of belief in the existence of hell (the eighth error).

RESPONDING TO FINNIS AND GRISEZ

The first five possible errors in reading *Amoris Laetitia* outlined by Finnis and Grisez are worthy of consideration. At first reading, the authors may seem to make a convincing argument. One can perhaps agree that certain readers might fall into the kind of interpretation of the exhortation that Finnis and Grisez criticize. Certainly, one can agree that the positions outlined as errors are indeed so, However, when one reads the texts from *Amoris Laetitia* that the two authors cite as being ambiguous and open to such misinterpretation, an alternative insight emerges. Finnis and Grisez are conducting a consistent misinterpretation of Pope Francis. On no occasion do they grasp the significance of the comment the pope makes in chapter 8 that "the degree of responsibility is not equal in all cases" (*Amoris Laetitia* 300). Here the pope does not dispute the objective truth of church teaching on issues such as the indissolubility of marriage. Rather, he suggests that, subjectively, there are many forces in culture and personal psychology mitigating against couples having a fully informed conscience when they make decisions. It becomes evident that in each of the first five erroneous readings of *Amoris Laetitia* listed by Finnis and Grisez, the authors are not considering such situations of poorly formed conscience. Rather, they are assuming that individuals have full and clear understanding of Catholic moral teaching and wilfully choose to ignore it.

Such misinterpretation of Pope Francis is primarily unwitting. Finnis and Grisez operate from a perceptualist and classicist presupposition about moral reasoning. Their understanding of how we make moral judgments considers the act of knowing a moral truth to be analogous to "seeing" an object. They look to an encyclical of Pope John Paul II such as *Veritatis Splendor* as offering a clear statement of Catholic moral teaching. They then believe that with such clear propositions on offer by the magisterium, it can only be by culpable ignorance that couples are not able to "see" the truth.[16] Their notion of moral reasoning is based on assent to or rejection of propositions. Using Lonergan's terminology, they are adopting the "counterposition" of an inaccurate cognitional theory.

By contrast with this analysis of moral reasoning offered by Finnis and Grisez, it is worth recalling the approach to moral reasoning offered by Lonergan, who explains how moral reasoning involves a process of moving through four levels of consciousness and following the transcendental precepts: be attentive, be intelligent, be reasonable, be responsible. Within such a cognitional theory, one can recognize how easy it is for individuals to fail to observe one or other of the transcendental precepts—and to make poor decisions. As a result, the sins of such individuals have often not been those of a person making a clearheaded decision to commit mortal sin. Therefore, to suggest that *Amoris Laetitia* promotes the forgiving of an unrepentant person in a state of mortal sin is unfair.

WALTER KASPER: DEFENDING *AMORIS LAETITIA*

Another example of how a Lonergan-based approach can illuminate debates over *Amoris Laetitia* comes from an article that supports the exhortation. Close to the time that Finnis and Grisez published their thoughts, Cardinal Walter Kasper published an article in German, the English translation of which is, "*Amoris Laetitia*: Rupture or New Beginning?"[17]

When one reads Kasper's article, one is immediately struck by its tone. In contrast to that of Finnis and Grisez, Kasper adopts an inductive approach to his argument. The starting point of Kasper is the degree of resistance that had emerged against *Amoris Laetitia*. This lends a controversial and rhetorical tone to his article. He begins by suggesting that those who are critical of the exhortation represent a "party" within the church that "has alienated itself from the faith and the life of the People of God."[18] Echoing a theme already noted in chapter 1, Kasper suggests that the major novelty of Pope Francis lies at the level of theological method and not of doctrine:

> One will understand *Amoris Laetitia* only if one follows the paradigm change that this writing undertakes. A change of paradigm does not change the previous doctrine; but it brings them into a larger context. So *Amoris Laetitia* does not alter an iota of the doctrine of the Church, but it changes everything.[19]

Kasper then argues that what is new about the exhortation of Pope Francis is that "*Amoris Laetitia* takes a distance from the primarily negative, Augustinian view of sexuality and turns to the creative affirmation of the Thomistic view."[20] For much of the rest of his article, he explains how *Amoris Laetitia* is rooted in a perspective close to that of Aquinas. He recalls that the medieval doctor holds a fundamentally positive view of nature, while acknowledging that nature is marred by sin. He suggests that reference to the thought of Aquinas can support statements made in *Amoris Laetitia* on questions of conscience, discernment, and gradualism. He explains that the medieval saint employs the philosophy of Aristotle to speak of how a "'final cause' is a 'causative cause,' which sets all other causes to work." These other causes are what Aquinas calls efficient causes. He suggests that in *Amoris Laetitia*, Pope Francis considers the fullness of Catholic doctrine to function as a final cause on the moral conscience of Catholics.[21] He suggests that such a final cause can often fail to exercise its causative influence successfully over efficient causes. He explains that it is this breakdown that prompts Pope Francis to claim that in moral decision-making, "the degree of responsibility is not equal in all cases" and to call for empathy and flexibility in the pastoral care of such cases. He stresses that decisions such as to admit divorced and remarried couples to receive the sacraments should only be made on a carefully discerned, case-by-case basis. He adds that this process should never be understood as rejecting the basic Catholic doctrine of the indissolubility of marriage.

RESPONDING TO KASPER

Kasper offers an impressive guide to the thought of Pope Francis, offering helpful insights into links between *Amoris Laetitia* and an authentic Thomism. Above all, his explanation of final cause as causative cause is illuminating. It reveals that already in the thought of Aquinas there was an inductive dimension to his cognitional theory. He identifies how, for Aquinas, the way that final cause interacts with the other causes of moral reasoning is time bound. Consequently, moral reasoning involves more than a simple intellectual assent or rejection of propositions. The way that Kasper applies such an understanding of Aquinas to *Amoris Laetitia* is persuasive.

However, I suggest there are also limits to the value of the strategy adopted by Kasper in this article. Essentially, he opposes perceptualist classicist arguments with intellectualist classicist arguments (see the diagram in chapter 2). To begin with, as noted earlier, he opposes an authentic Thomism to a "primarily negative, Augustinian view of sexuality." On this issue his argument states that it is not valid for opponents of *Amoris Laetitia* to invoke orthodox Catholic tradition when, in fact, they are only invoking those aspects of tradition that follow the tradition of neo-Augustinianism that emerged in the thirteenth century. He explains that, if anything, Thomist philosophy has a stronger claim to represent traditional Catholic philosophy than does neo-Augustinianism. However, our study of Finnis and Grisez raises a complication for this aspect of Kasper's argument. These authors claim to be experts on Aquinas and employ their own interpretation of the medieval doctor to support their criticisms of *Amoris Laetitia*. It becomes evident that in the case of Finnis and Grisez, the problem is with their perceptualist reading of Aquinas.[22]

One can extend Kasper's argument to suggest that Kasper is proposing an intellectualist interpretation of Aquinas to counteract all perceptualist interpretations of Christian tradition, whether they claim origin in Aquinas or Augustine. This raises the question, "Is it likely that a perceptualist—of either an Augustinian or Thomist stripe—will be persuaded to change their position by offering an intellectualist reading of Aquinas?" I am not convinced that it is.[23] I suggest that, in the end, the best way to defend *Amoris Laetitia* is to do so in a way that employs an argument based explicitly on interiorly differentiated consciousness. Kasper is not incorrect to relate a notion of gradualism in *Amoris Laetitia* to a correct understanding of what Aquinas has to say about final cause as the causative cause. However, such metaphysical terminology is a poor substitute for modern insights, informed by psychology and cultural analysis, about how our freedom can be limited when we make moral decisions and how most of our lives involve a struggle between an ideal and our achieved performance.

Conclusion

How important is it for theology today to be conducted based on interiorly differentiated consciousness? We have perhaps already explained sufficiently how important it is for theologians of conservative tendency to shift from classicism to a historical consciousness grounded in intellectual conversion. Let us now complete a point begun in the previous section: it may be equally important for progressive supporters of Pope Francis to take a similar, explicit step toward intellectual conversion.

There are two reasons for this. First, adopting this stance can be the most effective way of addressing some of the key concerns of conservatives. Note that Lonergan agrees with conservatives who suggest that most of those who appeal to historical consciousness are relativist. Only an appeal to intellectual conversion can clarify the distinction between insight and judgment and explain how it is possible to employ both in a historically conscious manner. Second, an appeal to intellectual conversion may help overcome some superficialities in the arguments of those who adopt a progressive stance toward theology today.

On this issue, we note that while Lonergan admired the effort to be historically consciousness on the part of Marie-Dominique Chenu, he nevertheless found Chenu's analysis of history excessively optimistic. He suggested that Chenu failed to grasp "the many ways in which progress is corrupted by bias and turned into decline." He implied that Chenu needed to undergo an intellectual conversion to accurately understand "the redemptive role of religion in overcoming bias and restoring progress."[24] Turning to debates about *Gaudium et Spes*, by implication, Lonergan's argument applies also to the inadequate treatment of the reality of decline in this document. Note that many *periti* at the time were quick to spot the excessive optimism of the document. However, many of these used such a criticism to justify a refusal to move from one or other form of classicism to a historically conscious horizon. Without wishing to make anachronistic suggestions about what should have been said fifty years ago, the critics of *Gaudium et Spes* might have found arguments grounded in Lonergan's heuristic theory of history more convincing than the ones they were offered.

Conclusion

Beyond the Pontificate of Francis

THIS BOOK IS not intended primarily as a book about Pope Francis. Nor does it seek simply to suggest that classicist approaches to theology must give way to a version of historical consciousness understood in a generic way. Rather, it proposes that historical consciousness, as Lonergan understands it, can make a key contribution to Christian theology. This includes recognizing the importance of intellectual conversion for creating a world culture based on interiorly differentiated consciousness and the way that a theology based on functional specialization can help to serve as a catalyst for this. Proceeding in such a way would be with the deepest spirit of Vatican II. At the same time, this book does suggest that the pontificate of Francis represents an especially opportune time—a *kairos*—for a wider acceptance of a Lonergan-based approach. By identifying this *kairos* for what it is, my hope in writing this book is to contribute to the way Christian theology is conducted long after the pontificate of Francis. Looking to the future, I sketch some broad lines of how theology might unfold.

The Abiding Significance of Liberation Theology

I would like to think that the vision of Alberto Methol Ferré, out-lined in chapter 7, will prove to have been prophetic. From the late 1960s onward, Methol Ferré believed that the interpretation of Vatican II being developed in Latin America could serve as a source of renewal for the universal church. He qualified this insight by affirming that lib-eration theology needed first to mature—above all to be freed from an overreliance on Marxism—before it would be ready to render this ser-vice. Already in the 1970s, he recognized that such a maturing process was occurring in Argentina. He died in 2009, but he looked forward to the election of a Latin American pope who could be the agent of this renewal in the universal church for which he hoped.

In this book, we have maintained that a Lonergan-based approach to theological method can help to bring yet further explanatory depth to "a new phase in the reception of Vatican II"[1] that has been initiated by Pope Francis and follows the vision of Methol Ferré. At this point, we need to clarify a technical point: developments in liberation theol-ogy also serve as a challenge to Lonergan studies. Recent developments of Lonergan's thought by some of his students have accepted this chal-lenge. Robert Doran is one such student of Lonergan. He speaks of the need for a "psychic conversion" as well as intellectual conversion and explains how both these taken together can ground a notion of a pref-erential option for the poor in transcendental method. Similarly, he stresses a theme that remained underdeveloped in Lonergan: "that the situation which a theology addresses is as much a source of theology as are the data provided by the Christian tradition."[2] Doran concludes by claiming that his own work helps to affirm "the permanent validity of two emphases of the theology of liberation—the preferential option for the poor and their privileged position in the interpretation of contem-porary situations, and ultimately of the tradition itself."[3]

The contribution of Doran achieves more than simply helping Lonergan studies catch up with insights that have long since been commonplace in liberation theology. Rather, by anchoring key notions of liberation theology in acts of psychic and intellectual conversion,

Doran's thoughts can consolidate the long-term influence of the liberation theology of Latin America on all continents.

Decision-Making *Ad Intra* to the Church

Let us briefly indicate how a theological method grounded in functional specialization can provide a base for theology in the future. Regarding the role of theology helping the *ad intra* mission of the church, we have already noted how an interiorly differentiated horizon can help the church reflect on the pastoral care of families, in the spirit of *Amoris Laetitia*. We now address one further issue. After decades of centralized governance, the Catholic Church seems to be headed into a period of decentralization. Hopefully, the call that Pope Francis makes in *Evangelii Gaudium* for improved collegiality and synodality will continue to influence future popes. In such a context, the church will have to address questions of the relative roles of laypeople and the magisterium. On this issue, we recall a contribution John Courtney Murray had already begun to address before his sudden death in 1967.

Murray's explanation of the appropriate relationship between laypeople and the magisterium begins with the blunt statement: "There exists among the people no *right* to judge, correct and direct the actions of the teaching of authority."[4] This statement is more carefully explained in an article entitled "Freedom, Authority, Community."[5] Referring to developments in Vatican II, Murray explains that he is in favor of a major expansion of the role of laypeople in the church and believes that bishops have an obligation to consult the faithful before making most important decisions. However, he employs the epistemology of Lonergan to suggest that the involvement of laypeople in decision-making within the church appertains primarily to helping the emergence of insight within the church about appropriate ways of responding to the signs of the times. He suggests that it remains the prerogative of the magisterium to judge what insights are valid and to decide on actions to be undertaken by the church. On this matter, Murray invoked the encyclical of Pope Paul VI, *Ecclesiam Suam*

(1964). Pope Paul VI indicates that bishops who do not comprehensively and sincerely consult the faithful will be guilty of provoking a *"crisis of community"* that will inevitably result.[6]

Finally, the notion of dialogue understood in these terms will be able to assist in the realm of ecumenism. Here, the churches will benefit from basing discussions on an interiorly differentiated consciousness—and on theology grounded in functional specialization—as they explore how to reach a unity based on "reconciled diversity."[7]

Interdisciplinary Collaboration and the *Ad Extra* Mission of the Church

Turning to questions of the *ad extra* mission of the church, we note, first, the importance that Pope Francis places on this issue and, second, the potential of Lonergan's thought to support such a vision.

A constant refrain of the teaching of Pope Francis is the need for dialogue at many levels as the church engages with society at large. He devotes chapter 6 of *Laudato Si'* to discussing five areas in which the church hopes to dialogue with secular society: within the international community; at the level of national and local politics; for "transparency in decision-making" (which relates also to the dialogue of the church with politicians); between economics and politics; and between religions and science."[8] However, the comments of the pope on such matters remain at a general level. In *Evangelii Gaudium*, he acknowledges that it is not the responsibility of the papal magisterium to prescribe the content of such dialogues. Rather, he notes that this is where Christian academics must assume a key role:

> When certain categories of reason and the sciences are taken up into the proclamation of the message, these categories then become tools of evangelization; water is changed into wine....The Church, in her commitment to evangelization, appreciates and encourages the charism of theologians and their scholarly efforts to advance dialogue with the world of cultures and sciences. (*Evangelii Gaudium* 132–33)

Conclusion: Beyond the Pontificate of Francis

In this statement, the pope recognizes that a key function of academic theology is to negotiate the challenges of interdisciplinary collaboration. He confirms this insight and adds to it in a document published in December 2017, *Veritatis Gaudium*. This is an apostolic constitution on the governance of ecclesiastical universities and faculties. Here the pope speaks of four criteria of the theology he hopes to witness being conducted in ecclesiastical universities: first, that it begin with a contemplation and presentation of Jesus Christ, informed by an intrinsic option for the poor; second, that it be characterized by "wide-ranging dialogue"; third, that it include "interdisciplinary and cross-disciplinary approaches"; and, fourth, that ecclesiastical universities collaborate with each other (*Veritatis Gaudium* 4). In response to this appeal, a Lonergan-based method can help implement the criteria for theology for which the pope calls. In fact, what Lonergan has to say on interdisciplinary collaboration will be seen in the future as particularly innovative and helpful.

Chapter 1 presented only a brief account of Lonergan's thought. As one can imagine, Lonergan explains matters in greater depth in works such as the 800-page work *Insight: A Study of Human Understanding*. There, after inviting readers to an act of intellectual conversion, he proceeds from this epistemological step to develop a metaphysics. He understands metaphysics as developing a set of heuristic categories by which we can anticipate the broad lines of all future acts of insight and judgment into the universe of "proportionate"[9] being:

> Thoroughly understand what it is to understand and not only will you understand the broad lines of all there is to be understood but also you will possess a fixed base, an invariant pattern, opening upon all further developments of understanding.[10]

Lonergan's approach to metaphysics leads him to explain the actual order of the universe in terms of a notion of "emergent probability" that has immense explanatory power. It is because of such a metaphysics that Lonergan offers an account of how different academic disciplines should relate to each other. He first speaks of a "general empirical method" that underpins all academic disciplines and then explains how the more specific, particular method of different disciplines is anchored in this general empirical method. He states that becoming aware of the deeper methodological and metaphysical questions underlying their disciplines can help academics to "curb one-sided totalitarian ambitions" where they tend to exaggerate the competence of their discipline. By contrast, Lonergan suggests that intellectual conversion and the use of a notion of general empirical method can help academics to recognize the boundaries of their disciplines and how a comprehensive study of proportionate being must be conducted in an interdisciplinary manner.[11]

Within his account of different academic disciplines that study different "levels of being," Lonergan locates the human and social sciences, as well as theology. This, in turn, allows him to speak of three heuristic categories of progress, decline, and redemption, as the basis for analyzing any historical situation. He explains that these three heuristic categories can provide a foundation for interdisciplinary dialogue between religion and other social actors. In an article written toward the end of his life, entitled "Healing and Creating in History," he stressed that it is not enough for theologians to communicate a message of healing that identifies sinfulness and decline, with a promise of restoration of right order in a distant, eschatological future. Rather, theologians are obliged to engage also in the "creative" task of cooperating with experts in other disciplines to find solutions to current problems and to promote progress. He adds, "For just as the creative process, when unaccompanied by healing, is distorted and corrupted by bias, so too the healing process, when unaccompanied by creating, is a soul without a body."[12]

It was with the view of engaging in the practical task of finding solutions to current problems besetting the poor that Lonergan devoted years of his life to studying the academic discipline of economics. In fact, the notions of progress and decline in history that he explains at a philosophical level in *Insight* were developed, in part, through reflection on the mistakes of economists that led to the Great Depression and of efforts on his own part to develop a theory of macroeconomics that would avoid such pitfalls in the future.[13]

As already noted, *Laudato Si'* is the major contribution Pope Francis makes to reflecting on the *ad extra* mission of the church. He identifies the challenge of care for our natural environment as a key sign of the times today. Several Lonergan scholars have been exploring the relevance of his notion of emergent probability for ecological ethics.[14] In fact, Lonergan's comments in his article "Healing and Creating in History" have a particular relevance for the ecological awareness of today:

> When survival requires a system that does not exist, then the need for creating is manifest. While it can take a series of disasters to convince people of the need for creating, still the long, hard, uphill climb is the creative process itself.[15]

In ways that are not fully explained in this book, Lonergan's thought can help Christian theology engage in the "long, hard, uphill climb" that will be required of theology in future decades. Consequently, the Canadian philosopher-theologian can help the church undertake the task for which Pope Francis calls in *Evangelii Gaudium*:

> Sometimes I wonder if there are people in today's world who are really concerned about generating processes of people-building, as opposed to obtaining immediate results which yield easy, quick short-term political gains, but do not enhance human fullness. History will perhaps judge the latter with the criterion set forth by Romano Guardini: "The only measure for properly evaluating an age is to ask to what extent it fosters the development and attainment of a full and authentically meaningful human existence, in accordance with the peculiar character and the capacities of that age." (no. 224)

Notes

FOREWORD

1. See Bernard Lonergan, "The Supernatural Order," in *Early Latin Theology*, Collected Works of Bernard Lonergan, vol. 19, ed. Robert M. Doran and H. Daniel Monsour, trans. Michael G. Shields (Toronto: University of Toronto Press, 2011), 229–53.

2. Robert M. Doran, *Theology and the Dialectics of History* (Toronto: University of Toronto Press, 1990).

3. See "Report on Notes for 'De Systemate et Historia,'" in *Early Works on Theological Method 2*, Collected Works of Bernard Lonergan, vol. 23, ed. Robert M. Doran and H. Daniel Monsour, trans. Michael G. Shields (Toronto: University of Toronto Press, 2013), 339.

4. Bernard Lonergan, "The Method of Theology," in *Early Works on Theological Method 2*, 403.

5. See Daniel Berrigan, "Letter to the Jesuits," in *America Is Hard to Find* (New York: Doubleday, 1972), 36–37.

INTRODUCTION

1. John Thavis, "Cardinal Kasper: Pope Francis Has Launched 'New Phase' on Vatican II," April 11, 2013, http://www.johnthavis.com/cardinal-kasper-pope-francis-has-launched-new-phase-on-vatican-ii #.W-5CNodKg2x; See also Walter Kasper, *Pope Francis' Revolution of Tenderness and Love* (Mahwah, NJ: Paulist Press, 2015), 7, 12; "*Amoris Laetitia*, Bruch oder Aufbruch?" *Stimmen der Zeit*, November 2016, 723–32, at 724.

2. See Massimo Faggioli, *Vatican II: The Battle for Meaning* (Mahwah, NJ: Paulist Press, 2012).

3. Speaking of the differences between Pope Francis and Pope Benedict XVI, Kasper states, "It is a program for the century in which differences are evident—differences not in the truths of faith, but certainly in style, in methodological starting-point and in emphases." Kasper, *Pope Francis' Revolution of Tenderness and Love*, 10.

4. Our Lonergan group at the Gregorian maintains a Facebook page, "Lonergan alla Gregoriana."

I. THE QUESTION OF METHOD

1. These three categories converge with the analysis of Kasper; however, when discussing method, the cardinal places most stress on the inductive method of Francis, which is my second point. My biographical comments on Jorge Bergoglio rely especially on Austen Ivereigh, *The Great Reformer: Francis and the Making of a Radical Pope* (New York: Henry Holt and Company, 2014), and Massimo Borghesi, *Jorge Mario Bergoglio: Una biografia intellettuale* (Milan: Jaca Book, 2017).

2. When Pope Francis is asked, "What element of Ignatian spirituality helps you live your ministry?," he answers, "discernment," and adds, "Discernment is one of the things that worked inside St. Ignatius. For him it is an instrument of struggle in order to know the Lord and follow him more closely." Antonio Spadaro, ed., *A Big Heart Open to God* (New York: HarperCollins, 2013), 12.

3. Fr. Antonio Spadaro, "Interview with Pope Francis," September 2013. Available online at http://w2.vatican.va/content/francesco/en/speeches/2013/september/documents/papa-francesco_20130921_intervista-spadaro.html.

4. Spadaro, "Interview with Pope Francis."

5. For a study of the influence of Ignatian spirituality on the model of leadership followed by Pope Francis, see Chris Lowney, *Pope Francis, Why He Leads the Way He Leads: Lessons from the First Jesuit Pope* (Chicago: Loyola Press, 2013).

6. One such teacher of Bergoglio at the Colegio Máximo in Buenos Aires was Juan Carlos Scannone, SJ, who wrote a series of articles explaining dimensions of Bergoglio's thought after his former student was elected pope, e.g., "Pope Francis and the Theology of the People," *Theological Studies* 77, no. 1 (2016): 118–35. Scannone would later

become a colleague of Bergoglio when his former student spent six years as rector of the Colegio Máximo in Buenos Aires.

7. Pope Francis, Apostolic Constitution, *Veritatis Gaudium: On Ecclesiastical Universities and Faculties*, December 8, 2017, https://press .vatican.va/content/salastampa/en/bollettino/pubblico/2018/01/29/ 180129c.html.

8. Scannone, "Pope Francis and the Theology of the People," 127–30. See also Ivereigh, *The Great Reformer*, 140–43.

9. These quotations are taken from Pope Francis, *Evangelii Gaudium*, nos. 224–34. Scannone suggests that these four principles had already been established as central to his thought in speeches given when Bergoglio was Jesuit provincial during the 1970s (Scannone, "Pope Francis and the Theology of the People," 127–30. See also Ivereigh, *The Great Reformer*, 140–43).

10. Gustavo Gutiérrez, *A Theology of Liberation: History, Politics, and Salvation* (Maryknoll, NY: Orbis Books, 1988 [first published 1969]).

11. One such Marx-influenced theologian was Juan Louis Segundo, who was critical of the Argentine approach to theology. See Scannone, "Pope Francis and the Theology of the People."

12. Bernard Lonergan, *Insight: A Study of Human Understanding*, Collected Works of Bernard Lonergan, vol. 3, ed. Frederick E. Crowe and Robert M. Doran, 5th ed. (Toronto: University of Toronto Press, 1992).

13. John Courtney Murray, who was primary author of the Declaration on Human Freedom, *Dignitatis Humanae*, visited Lonergan at the Gregorian often during the council and is acknowledged as having been much influenced by him (see J. L. Hooper, *The Ethics of Discourse: The Social Philosophy of John Courtney Murray* [Washington, DC: Georgetown University Press, 1986]). This matter is discussed further in chapters 4 and 5 of this present work.

14. Lonergan, *Method in Theology*, Collected Works of Bernard Lonergan, vol. 12, ed. Robert M. Doran and John D. Dadosky (Toronto: University of Toronto Press, 2017 [first published 1972]).

15. See Frederick E. Crowe, *Lonergan* (Collegeville, MN: The Liturgical Press, 1992), chap. 1. See also William A. Mathews, *Lonergan's Quest: A Study of Desire in the Authoring of Insight* (Toronto: University of Toronto Press, 2005), chap. 1.

16. Bernard Lonergan, *Philosophical and Theological Papers, 1965–1980*, Collected Works of Bernard Lonergan, vol. 17, ed. Robert

C. Croken and Robert M. Doran (Toronto: University of Toronto Press, 2004), 256.

17. The lecturer at Heythrop who inspired Lonergan's thinking on a philosophy of history was Lewis Watt, SJ; see Crowe, *Lonergan*, 13; and Mathews, *Lonergan's Quest*, 33, 42–43.

18. In a letter to his provincial, Lonergan wrote of his desire to produce a philosophy "that will leave Hegel and Marx, in spite of the enormity of their achievement, in the shade." Commentators note that this somewhat arrogant statement was made in a private letter where the young man was following a tradition of communicating his innermost thoughts to his religious superior. Lonergan, "Letter to Fr. Keane," *Method: Journal of Lonergan Studies* 5, no. 2 (Fall 2014): 23–42, at 33. See also comment in Crowe, *Lonergan*, 27.

19. Frederick Crowe, *Christ and History* (Ottawa: Novalis/St. Paul University, 2005), 168.

20. Crowe, *Lonergan*, 27; see also Crowe, *Christ and History*, 37. William Mathews suggests that this decision came after an illness and considerable personal struggle, *Lonergan's Quest*, 185–90.

21. Lonergan, *Insight*, 22.

22. Regarding the supernatural quality of redemption in history, see Lonergan, *Insight*, chap. 20. For an explanation of notions of progress and decline, see *Insight*, chap. 7.

23. Lonergan, *Insight*, 263.

24. On "moral conversion" and "religious conversion," see Lonergan, *Method in Theology*, 226, 227.

25. Lonergan, *Method in Theology*, 3.

26. Lonergan, *Method in Theology*, 362.

27. Lonergan's appropriation of the *Spiritual Exercises of St. Ignatius* over time is carefully explored in Gordon Rixon, "Bernard Lonergan and Mysticism," *Theological Studies* 62, no. 3 (2001): 479–97.

28. Lonergan wrote this in a letter of recommendation for academic promotion for Harvey Egan, SJ, reproduced as "Bernard Lonergan to Thomas O'Malley," *Method: Journal of Lonergan Studies* 20, no. 1 (2002): 81–82.

29. Lonergan interview in *Caring about Meaning: Patterns in the Life of Bernard Lonergan*, ed. Pierrot Lambert et al. (Montreal: Thomas More Institute, 1982), 145.

30. See Rixon, "Bernard Lonergan and Mysticism," 483–88.

31. Crowe, *Christ and History*, 28–29.

32. Bernard Lonergan, *Existenz and Aggiornamento*, in *A Third Collection* (Mahwah, NJ: Paulist Press, 1985), 222–31, at 231.

33. The understanding that Pope Francis has of this second principle, concerning how to negotiate conflict, is in my opinion particularly deep. It is born of a lifetime of often painful experience. I suggest that, even at a level of general methodological theory, Lonergan studies can benefit from the insights of Pope Francis here. It helps illuminate issues such as Lonergan's thinking on the law of the cross, and, more generally, just how the forces of redemption need to interact with the forces of progress and decline.

2. HISTORICAL CONSCIOUSNESS

1. Lonergan offers an overview of the history of philosophy and Catholic theology in many of his later articles and interviews. His most comprehensive treatment is in "Questionnaire on Philosophy," in *Philosophical and Theological Papers, 1965–1980*, Collected Works of Bernard Lonergan, vol. 17, ed. Robert Croken and Robert M. Doran (Toronto: University of Toronto Press, 2004), 352–83. In this article Lonergan refers to three other sources that are especially significant for him: Yves Congar, *The History of Theology* (New York: Doubleday, 1968); Herbert Butterfield, *The Origins of Modern Science* (New York: First Free Press, 1965); and Alan Richardson, *History Sacred and Profane* (London: SCM Press, 1964). In this chapter, the limitations of space require me simply to offer an overview of Lonergan's thought on the history of philosophy, even though I am aware that some scholars would dispute aspects of Lonergan's view. Indeed, when not quoting Lonergan, I quote mostly those authorities, such as Congar, Butterfield, and Richardson, upon which he himself relied. It is beyond the scope of this chapter to illustrate that the insights of these authors can be supported by current research.

2. Bernard Lonergan, "Dimensions of Meaning," in *Collection*, Collected Works of Bernard Lonergan, vol. 4, ed. Frederick E. Crowe and Robert M. Doran (Toronto: University of Toronto Press, 1988), 232–45, at 235.

3. Karl Jaspers, *The Origin and Goal of History* (Oxford: Routledge, 2010). Lonergan makes frequent reference to Jaspers in a variety of works. He discusses the book just cited in *Phenomenology and Logic*, Collected Works of Bernard Lonergan, vol. 18, ed. Philip J. McShane

(Toronto: University of Toronto Press, 2001), 224–25, and employs a version of Jasper's analysis in his account of "Stages of Meaning," in *Method in Theology*, 82–95.

4. Jaspers, *The Origin and Goal of History*, 3.

5. Jaspers, *The Origin and Goal of History*, 3.

6. Jaspers, *The Origin and Goal of History*, 51–66. Lonergan also liked to cite the work of Eric Voegelin on the key characteristics of classical culture in ancient Greece and Rome. He employed Voegelin's argument that a "world-cultural humanity" today should rediscover and employ the capacity for mythmaking of primary peoples. See Lonergan, "Horizons and Transpositions," in *Philosophical and Theological Papers, 1965–1980*, 409–32, at 411–43. It should be noted that Lonergan's use of these authors was not uncritical. As explained later in this chapter, he believed that neither of these German historicists overcame the problem of philosophical idealism, and consequently, of relativism.

7. Matthew Lamb, "Lonergan's Transpositions of Augustine and Aquinas," in *The Importance of Insight: Essays in Honor of Michael Vertin*, ed. John J. Liptay and David S. Liptay (Toronto: University of Toronto Press, 2007), 12–13.

8. Bernard Lonergan, "The Origins of Christian Realism," in *A Second Collection*, Collected Works of Bernard Lonergan, vol. 13, ed. Robert M. Doran and John D. Dadosky, 2nd ed. (Toronto: University of Toronto Press, 2016), 202–20.

9. Lamb, "Lonergan's Transpositions of Augustine and Aquinas," 12–13.

10. A Lonergan-based account of much of content in this section is found in Kenneth R. Himes, "The Human Person in Contemporary Theology," in *Introduction to Christian Ethics: A Reader*, ed. Ronald. P. Hamer and Kenneth R. Himes (Mahwah, NJ: Paulist Press, 1989), 51–62. See also John O'Malley, "Reform, Historical Consciousness, and Vatican II's Aggiornamento," *Theological Studies* 32, no. 4 (1971): 573–601.

11. Herbert Butterfield, *The Origins of Modern Science*. See Lonergan, "Questionnaire on Philosophy," 353–54.

12. Butterfield, *The Origins of Modern Science*, 14.

13. Butterfield, *The Origins of Modern Science*, 353.

14. For a complementary account of historical consciousness, see John O'Malley, "Reform, Historical Consciousness, and Vatican II's Aggiornamento," 573–601.

15. Alan Richardson, *History Sacred and Profane*, 32–33. See Lonergan, "Questionnaire on Philosophy," 354.

16. Richardson suggests that one such prophetic voice included a French aristocrat of the eighteenth century, Montesquieu (*History Sacred and Profane*, 89–90). He also identifies the author of a history of England, Edmund Burke, of whom he states, "Burke recoils in aversion from the Rousseau-type anti-historical exaltation of 'conscience' which, discounting 'the virtue which is practicable,' confers infallibility upon the morality of the moment and pronounces absolution upon the excesses of revolutionary fanaticism. History in Burke's view involves an encounter of every generation in its turn with the eternal moral order: 'moral values are disclosed through the movement of Providence in the temporal process'" (*History Sacred and Profane*, 168).

17. Richardson, *History Sacred and Profane*, 175.

18. Richardson, *History Sacred and Profane*, 163.

19. Richardson, *History Sacred and Profane*, 165. See also a comment by John O'Malley on the nature of historical consciousness: "Contemporary philosophy of history is based upon one fundamental presupposition: history as a *human* phenomenon. By history is meant both past reality as it actually happened and the reconstruction or understanding of that reality as it takes place in the historian's mind and imagination. Contemporary philosophy of history labors to explore the implications of this fundamental presupposition" (O'Malley, "Reform, Historical Consciousness, and Vatican II's Aggiornamento," 596).

20. Lonergan introduces a discussion of the nature of bias in chaps. 6 and 7 of *Insight*. He suggests that bias can be present at each of the cognitional levels and describes dramatic bias (214–31), individual bias, group bias, and general bias (244–66).

21. In referring to questions of medieval philosophy, Lonergan liked to refer to the short work by Yves Congar, *The History of Theology*.

22. Mark D. Morelli, *On the Threshold of a Halfway House* (Boston: Lonergan Research Institute, 2007), traces how Lonergan's reading of Plato was influenced by an Oxford professor of the late nineteenth century, John A. Stewart, who opposed simplistic explanations of Plato's notion of eternal ideas. Lonergan understood Stewart to be explaining that, instead of being "things you can take a good look at," ideas were something closer to heuristic categories through which we arrive at an understanding of instances of proportionate being. By contrast, Lonergan suggests that a more simplistic notion of eternal ideas emerged in

most expressions of Neoplatonism. He expresses the suspicion that Augustine of Hippo inherited this bias in epistemology from the Neoplatonists.

23. Congar, *The History of Theology*, 74–75.

24. Congar, *The History of Theology*, 119–20.

25. Lonergan, *Verbum: Word and Idea in Aquinas*, Collected Words of Bernard Lonergan, vol. 2, The Robert Mollot Collection, ed. Frederick E. Crowe and Robert M. Doran (Toronto: University of Toronto Press, 1997), 39n126.

26. Lamb, "Lonergan's Transpositions of Augustine and Aquinas," 12–13. Lamb's comments are based on the major study Lonergan, *Verbum: Word and Idea in Aquinas*, Collected Works of Bernard Lonergan, vol. 2, ed. Frederick E. Crowe and Robert M. Doran (Toronto: University of Toronto Press, 1997).

27. This brief account of the history of philosophy does not allow me to indicate ways in which the Franciscan school had positive qualities that were lacking in Scholastics such as Aquinas. Lonergan scholars have stressed that these positive qualities included an appreciation of the role of symbol and the aesthetic in philosophical and theological reasoning. See Robert Doran, "Lonergan and Balthasar: Methodological Considerations," *Theological Studies* 58, no. 1 (1997): 61–84.

28. Lonergan engages in a dialectical critique of other philosophers through history in a variety of places. See "The Dialectic of Method in Metaphysics," in *Insight*, 426–54; "The Theory of Philosophical Differences," in *Topics in Education*, Collected Works of Bernard Lonergan, vol. 10, ed. Robert M. Doran and Frederick E. Crowe (Toronto: University of Toronto Press, 1993), 158–92; and "The Dialectic of Methods," (parts 1, 2, and 3), in *Method in Theology*, 238–48.

29. For discussions of Descartes see Lonergan, *Insight*, 413–14, 438, 439, 551–52. On how Lonergan explains intellectual conversion by contrasting it first with Kantian analysis and then with relativist analysis more generally, see Lonergan, *Insight*, 362–71. See also Giovanni Sala, *Lonergan and Kant: Five Essays on Human Knowledge*, ed. Robert M. Doran, trans. Joseph Spoerl (Toronto: University of Toronto Press, 1994).

30. Lonergan, *Method in Theology*, 200–201.

31. Louis Roy, "Overcoming Classicism and Relativism," in *The Hermeneutic of Reform and Renewal: Lonergan Workshop* 27, ed. Fred Lawrence (Boston: Boston College, 2017), 239–62.

32. Lonergan, "Horizons," in *Philosophical and Theological Papers, 1965–1980*, 10–29, at 13.

3. THE PROBLEM OF MODERNITY

1. "Intrinsic to the nature of healing, there is the extrinsic requirement of a concomitant creative process....The healing process, when unaccompanied by creating, is a soul without a body. Christianity developed and spread within the ancient empire of Rome. It possessed the spiritual power to heal what was unsound in that imperial domain. But it was unaccompanied by its natural component of creating...the Roman Empire decayed and disintegrated" (Bernard Lonergan, "Healing and Creating in History," in *A Third Collection* [Mahwah, NJ: Paulist Press, 1985], 100–109, at 107–8).

2. As with the previous chapter, a point of reference for Lonergan's analysis of the history of Catholic theology is "Questionnaire on Philosophy," in *Philosophical and Theological Papers, 1965–1980*, Collected Works of Bernard Lonergan, vol. 17, ed. Robert Croken and Robert M. Doran (Toronto: University of Toronto Press, 2004), 352–83, and especially the use made in that article of Yves Congar, *The History of Theology* (New York: Doubleday, 1968).

3. Joseph A. Komonchak, "Lonergan's Early Essays on the Redemption of History," in *Lonergan Workshop* 10, ed. Fred Lawrence (Atlanta: Scholars Press, 1994), 168.

4. Bernard Lonergan, "Theology in its New Context," in *A Second Collection*, Collected Works of Bernard Lonergan, vol. 13, ed. Robert M. Doran and John D. Dadosky, 2nd ed. (Toronto: University of Toronto Press, 2016), 48–59, at 49–50.

5. Congar, *The History of Theology*, 137–43.

6. Lonergan, "The Subject," in *A Second Collection*, 60–74, at 62.

7. Lonergan, "Belief: Today's Issue," in *A Second Collection*, 75–85, at 80–81.

8. Nicholas Atkin and Frank Tallett, *Priests, Prelates and People: A History of European Catholicism since 1750* (Oxford: Oxford University Press, 2003), 45. The first two chapters of this book serve as a helpful introduction to the Catholic Church during the eighteenth century: chap. 1, "Catholicism in Retrenchment"; and chap. 2, "Catholicism in Revolution."

9. John O'Malley, *What Happened at Vatican II* (Cambridge, MA: Belknap Press, 2008), 57–58.

10. O'Malley, *What Happened at Vatican II*, 58–59.

11. O'Malley, *What Happened at Vatican II*, 59–60; see also Atkin and Tallett, *Priests, Prelates and People*, 130–41.

12. O'Malley, *What Happened at Vatican II*, 57.

13. O'Malley, *What Happened at Vatican II*, 61, quoting Vatican I, *Paster Aeternus*, chap. 3, https://w2.vatican.va/content/pius-ix/la/documents/constitutio-dogmatica-pastor-aeternus-18-iulii-1870.html.

14. O'Malley, *What Happened at Vatican II*, 69–70, 86.

15. Atkin and Tallett, *Priests, Prelates and People*, 129.

16. O'Malley, *What Happened at Vatican II*, 88, asserts that since the publication of a book on the state of Catholic theology in 1954 by Roger Aubert, it became accepted that the new theological ideas were mostly coming from Northern Europe. The term *transalpine* was coined by the conservative Cardinal Siri during Vatican II to characterize the leaders of the majority in the council who were proposing a more progressive theology than his (114).

17. Atkin and Tallett, *Priests, Prelates and People*, 108–9.

18. Atkin and Tallett, *Priests, Prelates and People*, 109.

19. O'Malley, *What Happened at Vatican II*, 63.

20. O'Malley, *What Happened at Vatican II*, 71.

21. See O'Malley, *What Happened at Vatican II*, 67; and Alan Richardson, *History Sacred and Profane* (London: SCM Press, 1964), 45–47. One can note that criticisms of the historicity of the Bible were at least as offensive to Protestants as to Catholic thinkers, in the light of the Protestant teaching of "Scripture alone."

22. O'Malley, *What Happened at Vatican II*, 72.

23. O'Malley, *What Happened at Vatican II*, 74.

24. Cardinal Bea was involved in another expansion of Christian thinking. Like many other biblical scholars of the Old Testament, Protestant and Catholic, he came to recognize the importance of drawing on the understanding that Jews had of their own Scriptures. In consequence, he became aware of the sin of Christian antisemitism and the need to reform Catholic theology in this field.

25. The authority on the history of German theology in the 1700s and 1800s is Hünermann, who writes in German. An excellent summary of the account of Hünermann's analysis is offered by Grant Kaplan, "The Renewal of Ecclesiastical Studies: Chenu, Tübingen, and

Theological Method in *Optatam Totius*," *Theological Studies* 77, no. 3 (2016): 567–92.

26. Regarding the teamwork of the Tübingen Catholic faculty, Kaplan describes how, in dialoging with each other, they were motivated by "a notion of being unified by an organic conception of a living tradition" (Kaplan, "Renewal of Ecclesiastical Studies," 574).

27. Kaplan, "Renewal of Ecclesiastical Studies," 574. In fact, it is an oversimplification to suggest that innovative thinking on *ressourcement* occurred only in Tübingen. Joseph Carola points to additional stirrings of change at the same time represented by John Henry Newman, and, even in Rome, a *Scuola Romana* of theology in the Gregorian University that made increasing reference to the church fathers (Joseph Carola, "La metodologia patristica nella teologia preconciliare dell'Ottocento," *Gregorianum* 97, no. 3 [2016]: 605–17.) However, such initiatives did not influence the mainstream of theology, which became increasingly uniform in proposing manualist, neo-Scholastic theology.

28. Hünermann, quoted in Kaplan, "Renewal of Ecclesiastical Studies," 575. A *ressourcement* approach to theology was not completely absent from the Catholic scene in the later nineteenth century. John Henry Newman, an Anglican priest and Oxford professor, converted to the Catholic faith in 1845 through his study of the church fathers, and he became widely read in Catholic circles. Also, during the years 1844–66, Jacques-Paul Migne, a diocesan priest and publishing entrepreneur, published multivolume sets of the writings of the Latin and Greek church fathers. This became a valued resource for professors who were willing to read beyond the seminary manuals.

29. O'Malley, *What Happened at Vatican II*, 76–78.

30. Pope John Paul II gave an important speech on Galileo in 1992; see http://w2.vatican.va/content/john-paul-ii/it/speeches/1992/october/documents/hf_jp-ii_spe_19921031_accademia-scienze.html. Also, at a "Public Mass for Pardons" in 2000, he asked for forgiveness for the sins of church leaders during the first millennium and included an apology for the way the church had treated Galileo. See http://w2 .vatican.va/content/john-paul-ii/en/homilies/2000/documents/hf_jp-ii _hom_20000312_pardon.html.

31. I choose these two for two reasons: Chenu was about ten years older than most of the other theologians of *la nouvelle théologie* and acted as a father figure to some of them, such as Yves Congar, perhaps the most prominent *peritus* and also a thinker who grasped the significance of

Vatican II in terms of a shift to historical consciousness. Courtney Murray made explicit use of Lonergan and so had insights into questions of method that were often deeper than those of others. It is only for reasons of space that I omit a discussion of Karl Rahner, and his impressive analysis of Vatican II as inaugurating the era of a "world church" (Karl Rahner, "The Abiding Significance of the Second Vatican Council," in *Theological Investigations* [New York: Crossroads, 1981], 90–102).

32. A valuable account of Chenu's life and theology is offered in the proceedings of a conference, *Marie-Dominique Chenu: Moyen-age et modernité, Département de la recherce de l'Institut Catholique de Paris, Centre d'etudes du Saulchoir* (Paris: Cerf, 1997). I also draw on Grant Kaplan, "Renewal of Ecclesiastical Studies," who suggests that Chenu's insights into theological method in some respects anticipated Lonergan's *Method in Theology*. For further comment on Lonergan's enthusiasm for Chenu, see Louis Roy, "Overcoming Classicism and Relativism," *Lonergan Workshop* 27 (2013), 248–51.

33. Chenu, *Une ècole de théologie: Le Saulchoir*, ed. Giuseppe Alberigo (Paris: Cerf, 1985).

34. Chenu, *Une ècole de théologie: Le Saulchoir*, 141, cited in Kaplan, "Renewal of Ecclesiastical Studies," 581.

35. Chenu, "Une Constitution Pastoral de l'église," in *Peuple de Diu dans le monde* (Paris: Cerf, 1966), 11–34, at 18.

36. John Courtney Murray, "The Problem of Religious Freedom," sec. 3, para. 8. The literary legacy of Murray is largely in the form of articles. The Woodstock Theological Library at Georgetown University, USA, under the editorial direction of J. Leon Hooper, SJ, has placed online most of Murray's published works at http://www.library.georgetown.edu/woodstock/Murray. Each article is listed in terms of the year it was published and then in the order publication within that year. For example, the article just cited is listed as 1965h.

37. John Courtney Murray, "The Declaration on Religious Freedom" (1966c).

38. J. Leon Hooper, *The Ethics of Discourse: The Social Philosophy of John Courtney Murray* (Washington, DC: Georgetown University Press, 1986), 213.

39. Quoted in Hooper, *The Ethics of Discourse*, 103–4. Murray made this statement when involved in a public controversy with a Protestant author, R. M. MacIver, who publicly opposed his opinions in the 1930s.

40. John O'Malley, "Reform, Historical Consciousness, and Vatican II's *Aggiornamento*," *Theological Studies* 32, no. 4 (1971): 601.

4. VATICAN II AND THE CHURCH IN THE MODERN WORLD

1. Bernard Lonergan, "The Future of Christianity," *A Second Collection*, Collected Works of Bernard Lonergan, vol. 13, ed. Robert M. Doran and John D. Dadosky, 2nd ed. (Toronto: University of Toronto Press, 2016), 127–39, at 136.

2. Lonergan is not alone in describing Vatican II as involving a shift to historical consciousness, although he offers his own analysis of what historical consciousness should mean. Authors who speak explicitly about the shift to historical consciousness as key to interpreting Vatican II include John O'Malley, *What Happened at Vatican II* (Cambridge, MA: Belknap Press, 2008); and John O'Malley, "Reform, Historical Consciousness, and Vatican II's Aggiornamento," *Theological Studies* 32, no. 4 (1971): 573–601; Ormond Rush, *Still Interpreting Vatican II: Some Hermeneutic Principles* (Mahwah, NJ: Paulist Press, 2004), and contributing authors to the five-volume series, *History of Vatican II*, ed. Giuseppe Alberigo and Joseph A. Komonchak (Maryknoll, NY: Orbis Books/Leuven: Peeters, 1995, 2006).

3. See http://w2.vatican.va/content/john-xxiii/la/speeches/1962/documents/hf_j-xxiii_spe_19621011_opening-council.html.

4. Emphasis added.

5. In addition to O'Malley, "The First Period" (chap. 4), *What Happened at Vatican II*, 127–41, a resource for studying the debate on the document on revelation is Giuseppe Ruggieri, "The First Doctrinal Clash," in Alberigo and Komonchak, *The History of Vatican II*, 2:233–66.

6. In the first chapter of the draft document, a doctrine regarding a "two-source theory" was proposed where Scripture and Tradition are explicitly stated as having equal weight in revelation. Such a doctrine was even more aggressively anti-Protestant than anything declared in the Council of Trent (O'Malley, *What Happened at Vatican II*, 143).

7. O'Malley, *What Happened at Vatican II*, 150.

8. O'Malley, *What Happened at Vatican II*, 151.

9. Robert Rouquette writing in *Études*, quoted in O'Malley, *What Happened at Vatican II*, 152.

10. In addition to O'Malley, "The First Period," a resource for

studying the importance of the speech of Suenens on December 4 is found in Giuseppe Ruggieri, "Beyond an Ecclesiology of Polemics," in Alberigo and Komonchak, *The History of Vatican II*, 2:281–357, esp. at 343–44. Giovanni Turbanti, *Un concilio per il mondo moderno: La redazione della costituzione pastorale* "Gaudium et spes" *del Vaticano II* (Bologna: Il Mulino, 2000), has a particular interest in the debates that produced *Gaudium et Spes* but devotes a chapter to explaining the significance for the whole council of the speech of Suenens in the first period.

11. In early 1965, Pope Paul VI announced that Fr. Joseph Cardijn would be made a cardinal. In connection with this, he was ordained bishop by Cardinal Suenens and attended the final period of the council in this capacity. He made three speeches on the floor of the council, supporting the document on religious freedom as well as *Gaudium et Spes*.

12. Shortly after the council, Suenens published a book that captured the spirit of many of his interventions during it: Léon Joseph Suenens, *Coresponsibility in the Church* (New York: Herder and Herder, 1968).

13. O'Malley, *What Happened at Vatican II*, 157–58.

14. O'Malley, *What Happened at Vatican II*, 161. See also Jan Grootaers, "The Drama Continues between the Acts," and "The Ebb and Flow between the Two Seasons," in Alberigo and Komonchak, *The History of Vatican II*, 2:359–564.

15. In addition to O'Malley, "The First Period," a resource for studying the debate on the document on revelation is Giuseppe Ruggieri, "The First Doctrinal Clash," in Alberigo and Komonchak, *The History of Vatican II*, 2:233–66.

16. O'Malley, *What Happened at Vatican II*, 164.

17. Ruggeiri, "Beyond an Ecclesiology of Polemics," 344.

18. Biographers comment on the different but complementary gifts of the two popes. See Peter Hebblethwaite, *Pope John XXIII: Pope of the Council* (London: Chapman, 1984), esp. 199–284. See also Peter Hebblethwaite, *Paul VI: The First Modern Pope* (Mahwah, NJ: Paulist Press, 1993).

19. Examples of the gestures by which Pope Paul VI supported the dynamic of the council include the following: Trips to the Holy Land and India, made in 1964, supported the thinking about interreligious dialogue that would find expression in *Nostra Aetate*. A trip to the United Nations on October 4, 1965, was intimately related to the

passing of the Declaration on Religious Freedom two months later. The gesture of selling the papal tiara to donate the money to the poor was considered an act of support of *Gaudium et Spes*. So too was the publishing of the encyclical *Ecclesiam Suam*, in 1964, which stressed the importance of dialogue both *ad intra*, with the church, and *ad extra*, with the world.

20. Twenty years after Vatican II, a synod of bishops met to evaluate the reception of the council. They suggested that more needed to be done to promote familiarity with its documents. They added that the four constitutions should be studied as "providing the orientations according to which the remaining documents were to be interpreted" (O'Malley, *What Happened at Vatican II*, 3).

21. O'Malley, *What Happened at Vatican II*, 129–41; see also Mathijs Lamberigts, "The Liturgy Debate," in Alberigo and Komonchak, *The History of Vatican II*, 2:107–68.

22. An authoritative interpreter of *Dei Verbum* is Christophe Théobald; see "The Church under the Word of God," in Alberigo and Komonchak, *The History of Vatican II*, 5:275–357.

23. See Ronald D. Witherup, *Scripture*: Dei Verbum (Mahwah, NJ: Paulist Press, 2006).

24. This list with further elementary descriptions is offered in O'Malley, *What Happened at Vatican II*, 2–3.

25. O'Malley, *What Happened at Vatican II*, 2–3.

26. The terminology of the council majority and council minority emerged in October 1963. During the debates concerning the draft text of *Lumen Gentium* particularly heated differences emerged on the theme of how it described the relationship of collegiality between the pope and the "order of bishops as an apostolic body." An approximately equal number of speeches either strongly supported or strongly opposed the progressive formulation of this principle in a draft text. Members of the drafting commission for the document told the moderators of the council that they did not know what position to take as they redrafted the text. The moderators decided to take a straw vote on the matter. This occurred on October 30. Results of the vote revealed that a large majority favored the progressive interpretation found in the draft text (2,148 in favor; 336 opposed). One commentator describes this vote as "another turning point of the council," where the council majority became increasingly confident in not letting a small minority of council fathers exercise an inordinate control over proceedings (O'Malley, *What*

Happened at Vatican II, 184; see also 176–84). For brief biographical descriptions of prominent members of both the council majority and minority, see ibid., 108–114.

27. O'Malley, *What Happened at Vatican II*, 293. Concerning a tendency to depression in Montini, see Hebblethwaite, *Paul VI: The First Modern Pope*, 290–92.

28. See O'Malley's comment on Pope Paul VI: "He had a complex relationship to the assembly in St. Peter's. He sometimes acted as a council father like any other, sometimes as a promoter of the council's direction, sometimes as a brake to it, sometimes as an agent to promote consensus, sometimes as the arbiter of procedural conflicts…sometimes as rival to its authority" (O'Malley, *What Happened at Vatican II*, 294).

29. O'Malley, *What Happened at Vatican II*, 175–85.

30. O'Malley notes how one cardinal wrote to the pope of his pleasure with this "'most opportune' note of *'fundamental importance'*" (O'Malley, *What Happened at Vatican II*, 244–45).

31. See Luis Antonio Tagle, "The 'Black Week' of Vatican II (November 14–21, 1964)," in Alberigo and Komonchak, *The History of Vatican II*, 4:388–452.

32. O'Malley, *What Happened at Vatican II*, 252–53. "The decisions of Paul VI to arrogate to himself both the establishment of a collegial body at the level of the universal Church (the Synod of Bishops) and the treatment of some especially pressing problems (birth control and clerical celibacy), even though these were problems keenly felt not only within the assembly but throughout the whole of contemporary society, showed beyond a doubt that the conciliar stage was now left behind. This was confirmed by the placing, for the first time, of an elevated throne behind the table of the council of presidents, a throne reserved for the pope." See Giuseppe Alberigo, "The Conclusion of the Council and the Initial Reception," in Alberigo and Komonchak, *History of Vatican II*, 5:541–42.

33. O'Malley, *What Happened at Vatican II*, 311.

34. O'Malley notes that the spirit of positive engagement with the world is "found most typically in three of the most hotly contested texts—*Nostra Aetate, Dignitatis Humanae, and Gaudium et Spes*" (O'Malley, *What Happened at Vatican II*, 309).

35. John Courtney Murray, "The Problem of Religious Freedom."

36. On Murray's disagreement with "the French view" that influ-

enced *Dignitatis Humanae*, see John Courtney Murray, "This Matter of Religious Freedom," *America* 112 (January 9, 1965): 40–43. See also Leon Hooper, *The Ethics of Discourse*, 146–48. For a historical account of how Congar seemed to "waver" before the innovation of Murray's thought, see G. Miccoli, in Alberigo and Komonchak, *The History of Vatican II*, 4:544–45.

37. This issue had also been pressed by Cardinal Bea, the influential rector of the Pontifical Biblical Institute in Rome, who had been in dialogue for years with Jewish scholars in the study of the Old Testament. See O'Malley, *What Happened at Vatican II*, 114–17.

38. Alberigo and Komonchak, *The History of Vatican II*, 4:629. "There was a profound difference between the inductive method and the usual deductive method. With his call to read the 'signs of the times,' John XXIII had hoped that the Council in tackling problems would start not from eternal principles but from the consciousness that contemporary humanity had of its problems....Nonetheless, it was hard for many fathers to accept a cultural 'conversion' that they perceived as difficult and dangerous, whereas the familiar deductive method of Scholasticism seemed easy and safe." Ibid., 5:544–45.

39. A comprehensive account of the debates leading up to the passing of *Gaudium et Spes*, including a study of the private journals of many of the participants, is provided in Giovanni Turbanti, *Un concilio per il mondo moderno: La redazione della costituzione pastorale "Gaudium et spes" del Vaticano II* (Bologna: Il Mulino, 2000). Other sources include Norman Tanner, "The Church in the World (*Ecclesia ad Extra*)," in Alberigo and Komonchak, *The History of Vatican II*, 4:270–387; Gilles Routhier, "Finishing the Work Begun. The Trying Experience of the Fourth Period," in Alberigo and Komonchak, *The History of Vatican II*, 5:122–76. See also O'Malley, *What Happened at Vatican II*, 157–58, 162, 204–5, 249–50, 253–67.

40. Paul Gauthier, *Christ, the Church and the Poor*, trans. Edward Fitzgerald (Westminster, MD: The Newman Press, 1965).

41. Rohan Michael Curnow, *The Preferential Option for the Poor: A Short History and a Reading Based on the Thought of Bernard Lonergan* (Milwaukee: Marquette University Press, 2012), 28, 39. For a list of over fifty bishops and *periti* who attended, see 29n17.

42. Influence on *Gaudium et Spes* by the Group of the Church of the Poor is found in the explicit link between the social mission of the church and ecclesiology (*GS* 63–72), and in the comment on the

responsible development of creation as related to the coming reign of God (*GS* 39). See Curnow, *Preferential Option for the Poor*, 36–37. Influence on *Lumen Gentium* is also evident in the following references: differences between wealthy and poor nations of the world (*LG* 8); close links between earthly things and those that transcend the world (*LG* 76); and the justice and love of Christ toward the poor (*LG* 90). Giuseppe Alberigo claims that among several "resounding omissions" in the council, "the biggest of these has to do with commitment to the poor and with the poverty of the Church." See Alberigo, "The Transition to a New Age," in Alberigo and Komonchak, *The History of Vatican II*, 5:608 and n75, which includes an extensive comment on the Group of the Church of the Poor.

43. Gilles Routhier, "Finishing the Work Begun," 126, citing J. Prignon, a current commentator on council proceedings (Prignon papers, 1585, 3).

44. Joseph Ratzinger, "The Dignity of the Human Person," in *Commentary on the Documents of Vatican II*, ed. Herbert Vorgrimler, vol. 5, part 1, "The Pastoral Constitution on the Church in the Modern World" (New York: Herder and Herder, 1969), 120. See also Joseph Ratzinger, *Theological Highlights of Vatican II* (New York: Paulist Press, 1966; reprint, 2010), 147–71.

45. Routhier, "Finishing the Work Begun," 127.

46. Marie-Dominique Chenu, "Une Constitution Pastorale de l'église," in *Peuple de Die dans le monde* (Paris: Cerf, 1966).

47. Routhier, "Finishing the Work Begun," 130, including n327 on that page. See also Peter Hunnerman, who explains that among those who helped *Gaudium et Spes* get accepted, "One of the most important pioneers in this way of thinking was Marie-Dominique Chenu, O.P.," in "The Final Weeks of the Council," in Alberigo and Komonchak, *The History of Vatican II*, 5:390n45.

48. It is worth noting that Congar suggests that *Gaudium et Spes* represents a final break by the Catholic Church with "political Augustinianism," and that such a shift of thinking was analogous to that which the "Albertine-Thomist revolution" had effected in the thirteenth century. Congar quoted in Joseph A. Komonchak, "Augustine, Aquinas, or the Gospel *Sine Glossa*? Divisions over *Gaudium et Spes*," in *Unfinished Journey: The Church 40 Years after Vatican II; Essays for John Wilkens*, ed. Austen Ivereigh (New York: Continuum, 2003), 113.

49. Hunnerman, "The Final Weeks of the Council," 404–6, 422–29.

50. Alberigo, "Major Results, Shadows of Uncertainty," in Alberigo and Komonchak, *The History of Vatican II*, 4:624–25.

51. René M. Micallef, "Weapons Having Uncontainable Effects in Vatican II and in the Age of Cyberwarfare," *Gregorianum* 97, no. 3 (2016): 517–41. This article makes extensive reference to Turbanti, *Un concilio per il mondo moderno: La redazione della costituzione pastorale "Gaudium et spes" del Vaticano II*.

5. THE BATTLE FOR MEANING OF VATICAN II

1. Bernard Lonergan, "Dimensions of Meaning," in *Collection*, Collected Works of Bernard Lonergan, vol. 4, ed. Frederick E. Crowe and Robert M. Doran (Toronto: University of Toronto Press, 1988), 232–45, at 244–45.

2. The title for this chapter is taken from a book, Massimo Faggioli, *Vatican II: The Battle for Meaning* (Mahwah, NJ: Paulist Press, 2012). The notion of a battle for meaning expresses the reality of the polarization of left and right that Lonergan anticipated.

3. A resource for understanding Lonergan's attitude to postconciliar Catholic theology is a series of lectures he gave to an Anglican audience where he was asked to address this topic. See Lonergan, "The Larkin-Stuart Lectures at Trinity College, University of Toronto," in *Philosophical and Theological Papers 1965–1980*, The Robert Mollot Collection, Collected Works of Bernard Longergan, vol. 17, ed. Robert C. Croken and Robert M. Doran (Toronto: University of Toronto Press, 2004), 221–98. The titles of these lectures are "A New Pastoral Theology," "Variations in Fundamental Theology," "Sacralization and Secularization," and "The Scope of Renewal."

4. Lonergan, "Horizons and Transpositions," in *Philosophical and Theological Papers 1965–1980*, 427 and 410. See also a critique of the position of Piet Shoonenberg, who, he suggests, amounts to affirming that "Jesus was a person and a man and only a man" (Lonergan, "Christology Today: Methodological Reflections," in *A Third Collection* [Mahwah, NJ: Paulist Press, 1985], 95).

5. Lonergan, "The Scope of Renewal," 290–91.

6. It should be stressed that Lonergan's response to liberation theology was nuanced. He expresses respect for Gustavo Gutiérrez, the

founder of the movement, whom he met at a theology conference. He recounts how he shared some of his methodological concerns with the Latin American, especially about the superficial use of social science in the movement. Gutiérrez agreed with him and explained that a good part of the reason for this deficit was a lack of educational and financial resources on the part of Latin American theologians. He adds that Gutiérrez appealed for help from theologians from the developed North to assist Latin America in this respect. He then explains that this appeal influenced his decision to devote much of his energies in the 1970s to a study of economics. Cited in Fred Lawrence, "Editor's Introduction," in Bernard Lonergan, *Macroeconomic Dynamics*, Collected Works of Bernard Lonergan, vol. 15, ed. Fred Lawrence, Charles Hefling, and Patrick Byrne (Toronto: University of Toronto Press, 1999), xi.

7. Lonergan, "Theology and Praxis," in *A Third Collection*, 184–201.

8. Lonergan, *Method in Theology*, Collected Works of Bernard Lonergan, vol. 12, ed. Robert M. Doran and John D. Dadosky (Toronto: University of Toronto Press, 2017 [first published 1972]), 78. In other words, for Lonergan, an appropriate notion of praxis in theology notes that there are "basic theological questions whose solution depends on the personal development of the theologians" (Lonergan, "Theology and Praxis," 184).

9. CDF, 1984, "Instruction on Certain Aspects of Liberation Theology," accessed November 19, 2018, http://www.vatican.va/roman _curia/congregations/cfaith/documents/rc_con_cfaith_doc_19840806 _theology-liberation_en.html.

10. Lonergan, "The Larkin-Stuart Lectures at Trinity College," 221–98. See also n. 3 above.

11. Michael Paul Gallagher, "Lonergan as Therapy for Confused Cultures," in *Lonergan's Anthropology Revisited: The Next Fifty Years of Vatican II*, ed. Gerard Whelan (Rome: G&B Press, 2013), 231–44, at 237–38.

12. One can perceive an acknowledgment that a solid right was present in the 1970s in writings by Lonergan on two issues. First, he offers a criticism of the Aristotelian, nonmodern-scientific reasoning that is employed in the 1968 encyclical of Pope Paul VI on birth control, *Humanae Vitae* (Lonergan, Letter to Fr. Ora McManus, 1968, *Lonergan Studies Newsletter* 11, no. 1, 1990, Lonergan Research Institute, Toronto, accessed January 2018, http://www.lonerganresearch.org/site/assets/

files/1184/lsn_set_3_-_90-94.pdf). Second, he defends his approach to interpreting Aquinas over against criticisms from a postconciliar school of a Thomism inspired by Étienne Gilson. He suggests that these scholars fail to recognize that Thomism needs to be transposed so as to engage with historical consciousness (Lonergan, "Horizons and Transpositions," 427, 410).

13. Faggioli, *Vatican II: The Battle for Meaning,* 51.

14. Faggioli, *Vatican II: The Battle for Meaning,* 52.

15. Originally published as "*Communio*—a Programme," in *International Catholic Review* (the forerunner to *Communio: International Catholic Review*) 1 (January–February 1972): 3–12.

16. Von Balthasar, "*Communio*—a Programme," 3–12. Quoted in Faggioli, *Vatican II: The Battle for Meaning,* 52.

17. An important biography of Pope John Paul II is George Weigel, *Witness to Hope: The Biography of Pope John Paul II* (New York: HarperCollins, 1999).

18. See Weigel, "A Son of Freedom: Poland *Semper Fidelis*" (*Witness to Hope,* chap. 1). See also Rocco Buttiglione, *Karol Wojtyla: The Thought of the Man Who Would Become Pope John Paul II,* trans. Paolo Guietti and Francesca Murphy (Grand Rapids, MI: Eerdmans Publishing Company, 1997).

19. See Weigel, *Witness to Hope,* 38–43; 62–67; 87; 93–98; 119–21; 124–44.

20. Deborah Savage, *The Subjective Dimension of Human Work: The Conversion of the Acting Person According to Carol Wojtyla/John Paul II and Bernard Lonergan* (New York: Peter Lang, 2008), 247 (parenthesis added).

21. Louis Roy, "Between Classicism and Relativism," *The Lonergan Workshop* 27 (Boston: Boston College, 2013), 239–62, at 244–45.

22. James Corkery, *Joseph Ratzinger's Theological Ideas: Wise Cautions and Legitimate Hopes* (Mahwah, NJ: Paulist Press, 2009), 25. See also Thomas P. Rausch, *Pope Benedict XVI: An Introduction to His Theological Vision* (Mahwah, NJ: Paulist Press, 2009). In chap. 2, "Theological Vision," Rausch offers subsections, "The Platonic Heritage," "Augustine," "Bonaventure," and "Attitude to Modernity."

23. Corkery, *Joseph Ratzinger's Theological Ideas,* 21–22.

24. Corkery, *Joseph Ratzinger's Theological Ideas,* 23, quoting from Joseph Ratzinger, *Aus meinem Leben: Erinnerungen 1927–1977* (Munich: Wilhelm Heyne Verlag, 1998), 21–23. The English translation

of this book is *Milestones: Memoirs 1927–1977* (San Francisco: Ignatius Press, 1977).

25. David Gibson, quoted in Rausch, *Pope Benedict XVI*, 14.

26. Rausch, *Pope Benedict XVI*, 15–17.

27. Corkery, *Joseph Ratzinger's Theological Ideas*, 20.

28. Rausch, *Pope Benedict XVI*, 17–18.

29. The Kasper controversies of the 1960s is studied closely by James Corkery, *Joseph Ratzinger's Theological Ideas*, in chap. 5, "*Questiones Disputatae*: With Walter Kasper and Gustavo Gutiérrez," 70–74.

30. Corkery, *Joseph Ratzinger's Theological Ideas*, 70.

31. Ratzinger, *Introduction to Christianity* (New York: The Seabury Press, 1969, original German 1968), 155, quoted in Corkery, *Joseph Ratzinger's Theological Ideas*, 70.

32. Corkery traces how Ratzinger articulates a robust defense of his position in his exchange of articles with Kasper in the late 1960s. Corkery sides with Kasper in this debate: "Ratzinger is not so convincing, having failed to provide an adequate refutation of Kasper's challenges of latent idealism during the course of their exchange" (Corkery, *Joseph Ratzinger's Theological Ideas*, 74). Elsewhere, Corkery criticizes the inherent pessimism of Ratzinger and Ratzinger's tendency to undervalue the goodness of creation, while becoming a "detective of sin" (ibid., 26–27).

33. See Weigel, "Losing Twice: The Communist Occupation of Poland," in *Witness to Hope*, 75–77.

34. See Weigel, "From the Underground, The Third Reich vs. the Kingdom of Truth," and "Losing Twice: The Communist Occupation of Poland," in *Witness to Hope*, 75–77.

35. Weigel outlines how Wojtyla began increasingly to travel outside Poland once he had been made a cardinal and developed some negative opinions about what he witnessed (*Witness to Hope*, 206–26).

36. Rausch, *Pope Benedict XVI*, 21.

37. Rausch, *Pope Benedict XVI*, 18.

38. See Weigel's account of the first months of the papacy of John Paul II, culminating in the publication of *Redemptor Hominis* (*Witness to Hope*, 259–90).

39. There were two events that prepared the way for the synod of 1985. The first was the publishing of a new *Code of Canon Law* in 1983. This had been promised at the end of Vatican II but had been delayed. Commentators noted that, under the influence of Pope John Paul II, it

tended to emphasize an ecclesiology of *communio*, understood in a von Balthasarian mode. One commentator suggests that the *Code* represented an "ambiguous" ecclesiology that lay somewhere between a preconciliar approach of regarding the church as a "perfect society" and "the more theological ecclesiology of *communio*." Eugenio Corecco, "Aspects of the Reception of Vatican II in the Code of Canon Law," in *The Reception of Vatican II*, ed. Giuseppe Alberigo, Jean-Pierre Joshua, and Joseph A. Komonchak (Washington, DC: Catholic University of America Press, 1987), 295. Quoted in Faggioli, *Vatican II: The Battle for Meaning*, 86. A second precursor was the publishing of a book-length interview with the prefect of the CDF, called *The Ratzinger Report*. Some commentators suggested that this book represented the beginning of a campaign to influence the outcome of the forthcoming synod. See *The Ratzinger Report*, ed. Vittorio Messori (San Francisco: Ignatius Press, 1985).

40. Avery Dulles, "The Extraordinary Synod of 1985," in *The Reshaping of Catholicism: Current Challenges in the Theology of Church* (San Francisco: Harper & Row, 1988), 184–206.

41. See Faggioli, *Vatican II: The Battle for Meaning*, 88–89.

42. Dulles, *The Reshaping of Catholicism*, 191–92.

43. Dulles, *The Reshaping of Catholicism*, 190.

44. Mandroli, quoted in Faggioli, *Vatican II: The Battle for Meaning*, 86.

45. Faggioli, *Vatican II: The Battle for Meaning*, 87. This opinion about the ideological use of the ecclesiology of *communio* is echoed in Bradford E. Hinze, "The Prophetic People of God Eclipsed," in *Prophetic Obedience: Ecclesiology for a Dialogical Church* (Maryknoll, NY: Orbis Books, 2016), 37–72; and Neil Ormerod, "A (Non-*Communio*) Trinitarian Ecclesiology: Grounded in Grace, Lived in Faith, Hope and Charity," *Theological Studies* 76, no. 3 (2015): 448–67.

46. Gilles Routhier quoted in Faggioli, *Vatican II: The Battle for Meaning*, 87. Furthermore, some Thomists expressed discontent about this unprecedentedly rapid shift to a theology inspired by von Balthasar and standing within a Bonaventurian tradition. See Fergus Kerr, "After Vatican II," in *Twentieth Century Catholic Theologians: From Neo-Scholasticism to Nuptial Mysticism* (Oxford: Blackwell Publishing, 2007), 203–22.

47. Congregation for the Doctrine of the Faith issues a letter entitled "Letter to the Bishops of the Catholic Church on Some Aspects of the Church Understood as Communion" (1992, no. 9), cited in Kilian

McDonnell, "The Ratzinger/Kasper Debate: The Universal Church and the Local Churches," *Theological Studies* 63, no. 2 (June 2002): 227–50, at 228.

48. See McDonnell, "The Ratzinger/Kasper Debate," 227–250.

49. *Acta Apostolicae Sedis* 90 (1998): 641–58; *Origins* 28 (July 30, 1998): 152–58. The publication of Kasper's critical comments about the *moto proprio* were made newsworthy by the fact that, in the same year, 1999, he was appointed by Pope John Paul II to be secretary of the Pontifical Council for Promoting Christian Unity. However, there was reason to believe that, subsequently, Cardinal Kasper was not in an inner circle of decision-making in the Vatican during the pontificates of John Paul II or Benedict XVI.

50. McDonnell conducts a careful analysis of the debate between Kasper and Ratzinger of 1999. He states that difficulties arise in evaluating the different arguments because of "category shifts within the conversation." He suggests that, in a certain sense, the two authors are basing themselves on different philosophical presuppositions and so sometimes misinterpret what the other means. He explains, "Kasper's fear is that Ratzinger's universal church is a logical construct, an abstraction, existing apart from the historical reality. Ratzinger's fear is that Kasper's emphasis on the empirical reduces ecclesiology to sociology" (McDonnell, "The Ratzinger/Kasper Debate," 247). I suggest that what McDonnell calls "category shifts" are the result of Ratzinger adopting a Platonist, classicist position and Kasper adopting one closer to interiorly differentiated conscious. As a result, what McDonnell notices is an example of what John Courtney Murray described in terms of "our minds are not meeting—in the sense I mean that they are not even clashing" (quoted in J. L. Hooper, *The Ethics of Discourse: The Social Philosophy of John Courtney Murray* [Washington, DC: Georgetown University Press, 1986]), 103–4.

51. In *Redemptoris Missio*, Pope John Paul II spoke of three forms of evangelization. The first is the preaching of the word of God to those who had never heard it before; the second is catechetical instruction for practicing Catholics; he then explains, "Thirdly, there is an intermediate situation, particularly in countries with ancient Christian roots, and occasionally in the younger Churches as well, where entire groups of the baptized have lost a living sense of the faith, or even no longer consider themselves members of the Church, and live a life far removed from Christ and his Gospel. In this case what is needed is a 'new evangeliza-

tion' or a 're-evangelization'" (Pope John Paul II, *Redemptoris Missio*, no. 33, http://w2.vatican.va/content/john-paul-ii/en/encyclicals/docu ments/hf_jp-ii_enc_07121990_redemptoris-missio.html).

52. An analysis of the significance of the Synod of Bishops of 1985 and its relationship to key themes of the pontificate of Popes John Paul II and Benedict XVI is offered by a friend and theological advisor to Pope Francis, Carlos María Galli, "El 'retorno' del Pueblo de Dios misionero. Un concepto-símbolo de la eclesiología del Concilio a Francisco," in *La Eclesiologia del Concilio Vaticano II*, ed. V. R. Azcuy, J. C. Camano, and C. M. Galli (Buenos Aires: Agape Libros, 2016). Galli suggests that Pope Francis has restored an emphasis on an ecclesiology of the people of God and no longer stresses either the theme of New Evangelization or the priority of communicating the contents of the *Catechism of the Catholic Church*.

53. Pope Benedict XVI, "*Porta Fidei*: For the Indiction of the Year of Faith," Apostolic Letter, "Motu Proprio Data," October 11, 2011, no. 2, http://w2.vatican.va/content/benedict-xvi/en/motu_proprio/docu ments/hf_ben-xvi_motu-proprio_20111011_porta-fidei.html.

54. Pope Benedict XVI, "*Porta Fidei*," nos. 2–3. For a further analysis of statements of Pope Benedict as classicist, especially regarding an interpretation of Vatican II, see Louis Roy, "Overcoming Classicism and Relativism," 244–52.

6. VATICAN II AND LATIN AMERICA

1. Avery Dulles, "The Reception of Vatican II at the Extraordinary Synod of 1985," in *The Reception of Vatican II*, ed. Giuseppe Alberigo and Joseph A. Komonchak, trans. Matthew J. O'Connell (Washington, DC: The Catholic University of America Press, 1987), 349–63, at 354.

2. Walter Kasper, *Pope Francis' Revolution of Tenderness and Love* (Mahwah, NJ: Paulist Press, 2015), 16.

3. Resources for an account of romanticism and its impact on Argentina include the following: Rafael Luciani, *Pope Francis and the Theology of the People*, trans. Philip Berryman (Maryknoll, NY: Orbis Books, 2017); Austen Ivereigh, *The Great Reformer: Francis and the Making of a Radical Pope* (New York: Henry Holt and Company, 2014); Rogelio Garcia Mateo, *Religiòn y razon: En el Krausismo y en la Generaciòn del 98* (Madrid: Biblioteca Nueva, 2015); Viki A. Spencer, *Herd-*

er's Political Thought: A Study of Language, Culture, and Community
(Toronto: University of Toronto Press, 2012).

4. Kasper, *Pope Francis' Revolution of Tenderness and Love*, 18.

5. Spencer, *Herder's Political Thought*, 413, quoting Johann Gott-fried von Herder, "Letters for the Advancement of Humanity (1793–97), Tenth Collection." Commentators note that, one hundred years later, philosophers would employ romantic notions of *Volk* to develop a nationalistic ideology under von Bismark and Hitler that would be racist and totalitarian. However, they stress that Herder refused to iden-tify the *volk* with any one state and explicitly rejected the notions of imperial conquest that can be associated with nationalism. In fact, he remained something of an impractical thinker, regarding all the bureau-cratic structures of the modern state as rationalistic evils that subordi-nate and suffocate the true spirit of the people. See Spencer, *Herder's Political Thought*, 81–82, 145.

6. A careful study of the phenomenon of "Krausismo" in the Spanish-speaking world is provided by Rogelio Garcia Mateo in *Religiòn y razon*. This book traces a paradox: Krausismo took on anti-Catholic characteristics in Spain but became closely allied with Catholic culture in Latin America.

7. Kasper, *Pope Francis' Revolution of Tenderness and Love*, 17; Ivereigh, *The Great Reformer*, 25–30, 77, 80.

8. See Gerd-Reiner Horn in "Left Catholicism in Western Europe: A Brief Survey," in *The Transformation of the Christian Churches in Western Europe: 1945–2000*, ed. Leo Kenis, Jaak Billet, and Patrick Pasture (Leuven: Leuven University Press, 2010), 77–95.

9. Horn, "Left Catholicism in Western Europe," 89. Horn also notes that Marie-Dominique Chenu functioned as a "'spiritual father' of the 'first generation' of European Left Catholicism" (ibid., 87–88). Horn's comments are verified in autobiographical comments offered by Gustavo Gutiérrez , in "The Church and the Poor: A Latin American Perspective," in Alberigo and Komonchak, *The Reception of Vatican II*, 171–93. See also Nicholas Atkin and Frank Tallett, "Catholicism Revised: 1945–2002," in *Priests, Prelates and People: A History of European Catholicism since 1750* (Oxford: Oxford University Press, 2003), 265–321.

10. Rohan Michael Curnow, *The Preferential Option for the Poor: A Short History and a Reading Based on the Thought of Bernard Loner-gan* (Milwaukee: Marquette University Press, 2012), 26–39.

11. Curnow, *The Preferential Option for the Poor*, 39.

12. Kasper, *Pope Francis' Revolution of Tenderness and Love*, 16. Kasper's insight into the distinctiveness of Argentine theology is expressed by Juan Carlos Scannone, "Pope Francis and the Theology of the People," *Theological Studies* 77, no. 1 (2016): 118–35, and by numerous works in Spanish on the topic of a theology of the people. An important intellectual biography of Pope Francis has not been translated into English at the time of writing, Massimo Borghesi, *Jorge Maria Bergoglio, Una Biografia Intellettuale: Dialettica e Mistica* (Milano: Jaca Book, 2017). Other resources for this section include Clodovis Boff and Leonardo Boff, *Introducing Liberation Theology* (Maryknoll, NY: Orbis Books, 1987); Gustavo Gutiérrez, *Theology of Liberation* (Maryknoll, NY: Orbis Books, 1973); "The Church and the Poor: A Latin American Perspective," in Alberigo and Komonchak, *The Reception of Vatican II*, 171–93; Arthur F. McGovern, *Liberation Theology and Its Critics: Towards an Assessment* (Maryknoll, NY: Orbis Books, 1990); Donal Dorr, *Option for the Poor: A Hundred Years of Catholic Social Teaching* (Dublin: Gill and Macmillan, 1992); Todd Hartch, *The Rebirth of Latin American Christianity* (Oxford: Oxford University Press, 2014).

13. Câmara is a figure of continuity through the stages of emergence of liberation theology. In the 1940s and 1950s, he studied in Belgium and made a close study of the life of Joseph Cardijn and the method of See-Judge-Act. Later achievements included helping to establish a movement of "Basic Christian Communities" across Brazil; helping to set up the Brazilian National Conference of Bishops in 1952; playing an active role in the Group of the Church of the Poor in Vatican II (as archbishop of Olinda e Recife in northeast Brazil); and in promoting the new notion of liberation theology at the CELAM conference at Medellín in 1968. See McGovern, *Liberation Theology and Its Critics*, 1–22, 200; Scot Mainwaring, *The Catholic Church and Politics in Brazil, 1916–1985* (Stanford, CA: Stanford University Press, 1986), 43–78.

14. For an exploration of the question "What are the epistemological consequences of a Church of the Poor?," see Clemens Sedmak, *A Church of the Poor: Pope Francis and the Transformation of Orthodoxy* (Maryknoll, NY: Orbis Books, 2016), xv.

15. Paragraphs 1 and 2, "The Church in the Present-day Transformation of Latin America in the Light of the Council," concluding document of Medellín, accessed November 20, 2018, http://www.geraldschlabach.net/medellin-1968-excerpts/. See also Alfred Hennelly, "Second General Conference of Latin American Bishops," in

Liberation Theology: A Documentary History (Maryknoll, NY: Orbis Books, 1990), 89–120, http://www.povertystudies.org/TeachingPages/EDS_PDFs4WEB/Medellin%20Document-%20Poverty%20of%20the%20Church.pdf.

16. Gutiérrez, *Theology of Liberation*. The survey of events offered in this paragraph draws mostly on Boff and Boff, *Introducing Liberation Theology*, 68–70.

17. Gauthier, *Christ, the Church, and the Poor*, 69, cited in Curnow, *Preferential Option for the Poor*, 28. See also Gutiérrez, "The Church and the Poor," 183–87.

18. Vladimir Lenin, *Imperialism the Highest Stage of Capitalism* (London: Penguin Books, 2010).

19. An important figure in promoting the relevance of dependency theory for analyzing Latin America at this time was Raul Prebisch, who was director of the United Nations Economic Commission on Latin America. See McGovern, *Liberation Theology and Its Critics*, 117–20; Luciani, *Pope Francis and the Theology of the People*, 6–28.

20. Jon Sobrino, *Christology at the Crossroads: A Latin American Approach* (Maryknoll, NY: Orbis Books, 1978); Leonardo Boff, *Jesus Christ Liberator: A Critical Christology for Our Time* (Maryknoll, NY: Orbis Books, 1978). For a wider discussion of these and similar liberation theologians, see Boff and Boff, *Introducing Liberation Theology*, 68–72; McGovern, *Liberation Theology and Its Critics*, 62–82.

21. Kasper comments on the thought of Gera and the "theology of the people" of Argentina in "Historical-Theological Classification—Argentine and European Roots," in *Pope Francis' Revolution of Tenderness and Love*, 15–21. A variety of other sources have also emerged that explain for English-speaking audiences the content and nature of the theology of the people of Argentina. These are often offered as part of biographical studies of Pope Francis (e.g., Rafael Luciani, *Pope Francis and the Theology of the People*; Austen Ivereigh, *The Great Reformer: Francis and the Making of a Radical Pope* [London: Allen & Unwin, 2014]; Allan Figueroa Deck, *Francis, Bishop of Rome: The Gospel for the Third Millennium*; Massimo Faggioli, *Pope Francis: Tradition in Transition* [Mahwah, NJ: Paulist Press, 2013]). Also significant is an article by Juan Carlos Scannone, "Pope Francis and the Theology of the People," *Theological Studies* 77, no. 1 (2016): 118–35, who has written extensively on this topic in Spanish. An article of importance by Scannone in Italian is "Lucio Gera: Un teologo del popolo," *La Civiltà Cattolica*, 3954 (March 21, 2015), 539–50.

22. Hartch, *The Rebirth of Latin American Christianity*, 63; Kasper, "Historical-Theological Classification—Argentine and European Roots," 16; Luciani, *Pope Francis and the Theology of the People*, 1–9.

23. Ivereigh, *The Great Reformer*, 111.

24. Scannone, "Pope Francis and the Theology of the People," 119–20. The theology of Rafael Tello is outlined by Allan Figueroa Deck in *Francis, Bishop of Rome: The Gospel for the Third Millennium* (Mahwah, NJ: Paulist Press, 2016). See also Luciani, *Pope Francis and the Theology of the People*.

25. Scannone, "Pope Francis and the Theology of the People," 119–20; Kasper, "Historical-Theological Classification—Argentine and European Roots," 15–21; Ivereigh, *The Great Reformer*, 5–9, 77, 80; see also an analysis of the "San Miguel" document produced by COEPAL as its submission to the Argentine bishops in 1972, Luciani, *Pope Francis and the Theology of the People*, 71–73.

26. Juan Louis Segundo, *The Liberation of Theology* (Maryknoll, NY: Orbis Books, 1976), 196–200. See Scannone, "Pope Francis and the Theology of the People," 124.

27. Ivereigh, *The Great Reformer*, 112.

28. See Deck, "Raphael Tello and the Faithful People of God," in *Francis, Bishop of Rome*; see also Ivereigh, *The Great Reformer*, 111. Unlike Gera, Tello had family roots in northern Argentina, where there is a strong presence of indigenous peoples. He was deeply impressed by the value of the culture of these peoples and this influenced his theology.

29. On this matter, Tello interprets Aristotle in the same way as Lonergan. In *Insight*, Lonergan explains how the notion of insight outlined by Aristotle is superior to that of Plato and helps to avoid a perceptualist appeal to universal ideas in the act of knowing. Lonergan states that it is Aquinas who adds to Aristotle a distinct level of cognition where one affirms the truth or falsity of an insight.

30. See Deck, *Francis, Bishop of Rome*, 49, 54.

31. Deck, *Francis, Bishop of Rome*, 48. Tello's interest in indigenous people of northern Argentina led him to acknowledge how they were compelled to migrate to cities in the south. This led him to study the dynamics of culture in the Argentine slums (cf. ibid., 50).

32. The phrase "true Church of the poor" was used by Leonardo Boff. In 1985, Boff would be censured by the CDF for proposing ideas concerning the structure of the church that were so extreme as to "endanger the sound doctrine of the faith." Congregation for the Doctrine of

the Faith, "Notification on the Book, *Church, Charism and Power*, by Father Leonardo Boff O.F.M.," March 11, 1985, http://www.vatican .va/roman_curia/congregations/cfaith/documents/rc_con_cfaith_doc _19850311_notif-boff_en.html. Another issue of concern by some bishops was a movement of "Christians for Socialism" that emerged in Chile after the overthrow of President Alliende by a military junta in 1973. See Curnow, *Preferential Option for the Poor*, 49; McGovern, *Liberation Theology and Its Critics*, 47–50.

33. Scannone traces how one Argentine bishop, Eduardo Francisco Pironio, had a role in alerting Pope Paul VI to the value of the theology that was emerging in Argentina. Pironio had served as a *peritus* in Vatican II and had served as secretary general of CELAM from 1967 to 1972. Pironio had been an active participant in Medellín but had become increasingly convinced of helping liberation theology mature along lines being drawn by Argentine theologians. Commentators suggest that Pironio contributed ideas to the apostolic exhortation *Evangelii Nuntiandi* (1975) and note that Pope Paul VI called Pironio to work in Rome during the year this letter was published. See Scannone, "Pope Francis and the Theology of the People," 123; Luciani, *Pope Francis and the Theology of the People*, 73–77.

34. *Puebla Final Document*, 1134.

35. Luciani, *Pope Francis and the Theology of the People*, 78.

36. CDF document of 1984: "Instruction on Certain Aspects of the 'Theology of Liberation'" (no. IX, 3–5) quoted in Curnow, *The Preferential Option for the Poor*, 59. The document adds further comment on the use of a logic of class conflict: "as a consequence, faith, hope, and charity are given a new content: they become 'fidelity to history,' 'confidence in the future,' and 'Option for the Poor.' This is tantamount to saying they have been emptied of their theological reality." See http://www.vatican.va/roman_curia/congregations/cfaith/documents/rc_con _cfaith_doc_19840806_theology-liberation_en.html.

37. Scannone reports that Gutiérrez had described non-Argentine liberation theologians as adopting a "socio-economic mediation," whereas those of Argentina adopted one of "socio-cultural mediation" and adds that Gutiérrez had remained respectful of the Argentine option. See Scannone, "Pope Francis and the Theology of the People," 124.

38. Gustavo Gutiérrez, "Introduction to the Revised Edition: Expanding the View," in *A Theology of Liberation: History, Politics, and*

Salvation, trans. Caridad Inda and John Eagleson (Maryknoll, NY: Orbis Books, 1988), xxv–xxviii.

39. In 1979, Pope John Paul II appointed Trujillo as archbishop of Medellín, in 1983 he raised him to be the youngest member of the college of cardinals, and in 1990 he called him to Rome to become prefect of the Pontifical Council for the Family. From this position, Trujillo played a key role in the Pontifical Commission for Latin America, which took a directive role in guiding the affairs of CELAM. Pope John Paul also appointed another Colombian and a prominent critic of CELAM, Archbishop Dario Castrillon Hoyos, to be its president (Ivereigh, *The Great Reformer*, 235).

40. Ivereigh, *The Great Reformer*, 235.

41. Ivereigh, *The Great Reformer*, 235.

42. Ivereigh, *The Great Reformer*, 236.

43. This is an analysis of events at Santo Domingo by both Juan Carlos Scannone and Dr. Guzmán Carriquiry Lecour, vice president of the Pontifical Commission for Latin America, who had attended the General Assembly. At a conference held in Rome and organized jointly by La Civiltà Cattolica and the Pontifical Gregorian University, March 27–28, 2014, "Le radici di Papa Francesco. Un anno di Pontificato," both commented on this matter. Carriquiry, a long-term friend of Pope Francis, offered an apology for the behavior of officials of the Pontifical Commission for Latin America at Santo Domingo and assured participants that the self-understanding of the role of the Commission by its officials had now changed.

44. CDF document of 1984: "Instruction on Certain Aspects of the 'Theology of Liberation'" (no. IX, 3 5) quoted in Curnow, *The Preferential Option for the Poor*, 59.

45. Curnow, *The Preferential Option for the Poor*, 61.

46. Pope John Paul II, *Solicitudo Rei Socialis*, no. 42, quoted in Curnow, *The Preferential Option for the Poor*, 63.

47. Curnow, *The Preferential Option for the Poor*, 63.

48. Curnow, *The Preferential Option for the Poor*, 64.

49. Curnow, *The Preferential Option for the Poor*, 66–67.

50. In fact, Scannone adds that these meetings served also as a helpful occasion of encounter between the Latin American theologians themselves. He describes how decisions by thinkers such as Gutiérrez to abandon the use of dependency theory for social analysis led to a new openness to the Argentine approach to liberation theology. He adds

that members of the faculty of theology at the University of Louvain heard about the private meetings that had been occurring with Cardinal Ratzinger, and how the Argentine approach to liberation theology was becoming increasingly accepted. He notes that these stressed the novelty of this development in a book they produced: G. De Schrijver, ed., *Liberation Theologies on Shifting Grounds: A Clash of Socio-Economic and Socio-Cultural Paradigms* (Louvain: Leuven University Press and Peeters, 1998). See Scannone, "Pope Francis and the Theology of the People," 125.

7. BERGOGLIO'S THEOLOGICAL VISION

1. While many biographical commentaries on Pope Francis have been published in the first four years of his pontificate, one is widely regarded as being authoritative: Austen Ivereigh, *The Great Reformer: Francis and the Making of a Radical Pope* (New York: Henry Holt and Company, 2014). Two further works written by Latin Americans and translated into English are valuable: Elisabetta Piqué, *Pope Francis, Life and Revolution: A Biography of Jorge Bergoglio*, trans. Anna Mazzotti and Lydia Colin (Chicago: Loyola Press, 2014); and Rafael Luciani, *Pope Francis and the Theology of the People*, trans. Philip Berryman (Maryknoll, NY: Orbis Books, 2017). Also helpful is a study by an Italian academic, Massimo Borghesi, *Jorge Mario Bergoglio, Una Biografia Intellettuale: Dialettica e Mistica* (Milan: Jaca Book, 2017). In my biographical comments I have benefitted from private conversations with Argentine theologians who know Bergoglio well: my fellow Jesuits, Juan Carlos Scannone, and Miguel Yanez (former student of Bergoglio at Colegio Máximo, and a current professor at the Gregorian University), and Fr. Carlos Galli (a diocesan priest of Buenos Aires, a member of the International Theological Commission, and coauthor with Bergoglio of the Aparecida document, and an occasional lecturer at the Gregorian University).

2. A detailed account of Bergoglio's childhood is offered by Piqué, "The First Steps," in *Pope Francis, Life and Revolution*, 37–52. See also Paul Vallely, *Pope Francis: Untying the Knots* (London: Bloomsbury, 2013), 21–36.

3. Piqué, *Pope Francis, Life and Revolution*, 37–45.

4. Bergoglio describes how as an adolescent "I had a political

restlessness" prompting him to read widely, including Marxist literature. See Vallely, *Pope Francis*, 29.

5. Argentine political culture is outlined in greater detail in chap. 6.

6. Ivereigh, *The Great Reformer*, 30. Austen Ivereigh, although an Englishman, wrote a doctoral dissertation on "Catholicism and Politics in Argentina." Consequently, his ability to explain the political and ecclesial background of Pope Francis is exceptional. On the influence of Peronism on Bergoglio, see *The Great Reformer*, 25–30.

7. An indication of the Peronist tendencies in the Bergoglio family is that a cousin of Jorge was a colonel in the army. In 1956, when Perón had been ousted by a military dictatorship, this cousin became part of a plot to stage a countercoup that would allow Perón to return. The plot was discovered, and his cousin was executed, something that deeply affected Jorge's family (Ivereigh, *The Great Reformer*, 9–18, 71).

8. Ivereigh, *The Great Reformer*, 9–18, 71.

9. Piqué, *Pope Francis, Life and Revolution*, 46.

10. Piquè, *Pope Francis, Life and Revolution*, 49–50.

11. Piqué, *Pope Francis, Life and Revolution*, 50–51. This commitment was inspired by a Chilean Jesuit, Padre Hurtado, who died only a few years before Bergoglio arrived in the country. He organized a nationwide movement to help the homeless poor and was canonized in 2005.

12. In an address to Jesuits in Myanmar in 2017, Pope Francis speaks of the influence on him of Miguel Angel Fiorito, a Jesuit professor at the Colegio Máximo. This scholar was an expert on Pierre Favre, one of the first companions of St. Ignatius and a gifted interpreter of the *Spiritual Exercises*. One of the first actions of Pope Francis would be to declare Favre a saint. Pope Francis, "At the Crossroads of History: Conversations with the Jesuits of Myanmar and Bangladesh," *La Civiltà Cattolica*, English Edition, December 2017, 7. Available online at https://laciviltacattolica.com/wp-content/uploads/2017/12/LCC-E-book-December-2017.pdf.

13. Ivereigh, *The Great Reformer*, 72.

14. Ivereigh, *The Great Reformer*, 110–11, reporting on an autobiographical radio interview given by Cardinal Bergoglio in 2012.

15. The question of whether Bergoglio changed over time from being an "ultraconservative" to being more progressive has been a source of debate between biographers. Paul Vallely, in *Pope Francis*, sug-

gests that this was the case but is criticized on this point by Ivereigh. The latter suggests that Vallely fails to understand the role that a theology of the people played in the apostolic vision of Bergoglio throughout and that Vallely adopts, instead, a perspective informed by more Marxist-influenced interpreters of liberation theology. See Eamon Duffy, "Who Is the Pope?" *New York Times Review of Books*, February 19, 2015, http://www.nybooks.com/articles/2015/02/19/who-is-pope-francis/. In this debate, Ivereigh's argument is persuasive, but it is worth reading Vallely's interpretation, too (see Vallely, *Pope Francis*, 127–48).

16. Ivereigh, *The Great Reformer*, 71.

17. Ivereigh, *The Great Reformer*, 191–92.

18. The Thirty Second General Congregation of the Society of Jesus, 1974, Decree 4.

19. Strictly speaking, COEPAL ceased to exist in 1967 when it submitted its pastoral proposal to the Argentine bishops. However, members continued to meet in a semiformal manner and publish their thought. They would later become recognized as representing a distinct school of theology. See Juan Carlos Scannone, "Pope Francis and the Theology of the People," *Theological Studies* 77, no. 1 (2016): 119–25; see also Piqué, *Pope Francis, Life and Revolution*, 74–78; Luciani, *Pope Francis and the Theology and the People*, 1–36.

20. For example, in 1974, one of the CIAS community, Orlando Yorio, published an article where he suggested that socialism was the political expression of the gospel, and that socialists must, for practical reasons, create alliances with Marxists. He also praised members of the "armed forces," including the Montoneros movement, for seeking to "guarantee the reality of popular socialism." See Ivereigh, *The Great Reformer*, 114, quoting Orlando Yorio, "Reflexión crítica desde la teología," *Stromata* 29, nos. 1/2 (1973): 131–39.

21. See Ivereigh, *The Great Reformer*, 106; and Vallely, *Pope Francis*, 45.

22. Ivereigh, *The Great Reformer*, 196.

23. See Piqué, *Pope Francis, Life and Revolution*, 61–82.

24. Ivereigh, *The Great Reformer*, 115–16. On the roots of Bergoglio's thinking in a theology of the people, as well as European romantic thinkers, see Borghesi, "La Compagnia de Gesù come sintesi delle opposizioni," in *Jorge Mario Bergoglio, Una Biografia Intellettuale*, 79–103.

25. In an action that would be much criticized by left-wing critics, Bergoglio closed several communities in impoverished areas that

had been created by members of CIAS. He considered these to be more political than pastoral. The situation would become complicated when certain members of CIAS refused to move from these communities and were imprisoned and tortured by the military government. Bergoglio went to great lengths to have these people released but would later be accused as having been responsible for their suffering. For an account that adopts the perspective of Bergoglio's left-wing critics, see Vallely, "Jesuit Secrets" (chap. 3) and "What Really Happened in the Dirty War" (chap. 4), in *Pope Francis*, 37–94. By contrast, more persuasive is the analysis of events offered by Austen Ivereigh, *The Great Reformer*, 116–19, 143–51, 157–61. For a wider discussion of related matters, see Gustavo Morello, *The Catholic Church and Argentina's Dirty War* (Oxford: Oxford University Press, 2015).

26. Ivereigh, *The Great Reformer*, 171, 177.

27. Bergoglio's curriculum reform at the Colegio Máximo was characterized by the theology of the people (see Ivereigh, *The Great Reformer*, 140–42). While such an emphasis diverged from thinking on "faith and justice" by Jesuits at an international level, it converged with an increasing tendency among Jesuits to take up a theme that had been initiated by theologians in Africa: inculturation. In 1985, Bergoglio organized an international conference in the Colegio Máximo entitled "The Evangelization of Culture and the Inculturation of the Gospel" (see Luciani, *Pope Francis and the Theology of the People*, 81–85). Commentators have noted that, within African theology, a similar conflict sometimes occurred between theologians of liberation and theologians of inculturation. See John Parratt, *Reinventing Christianity: African Theology Today* (Grand Rapids, MI: Eerdmans, 1995), 1–24.

28. These four principles of pastoral decision-making are outlined in Pope Francis, *Evangelii Gaudium*, nos 224, 227, 232, 234. For a discussion of how they emerged in Bergoglio's thought during the 1970s, see Ivereigh, *The Great Reformer*, 142–43; and Scannone, "Pope Francis and the Theology of the People," 127–30.

29. Ivereigh, *The Great Reformer*, 195, see also 192–96; and Piqué, *Pope Francis, Life and Revolution*, 79–82. These authors offer an interpretation of events that are favorable to Bergoglio. For a perspective that articulates and agrees with the perspective of the left-wing critics of Bergoglio, see Vallely, *Pope Francis*, 90.

30. The reasons that Fr. Kolvenbach had for taking this step deserve further study. However, three seem evident. First, the theological

orientation of the leadership of the Society of Jesus during these years had more in common with members of CIAS than with proponents of a theology of the people. Second, it was unusual in the Society of Jesus for one man to exercise the kind of dominant influence on a province that Bergoglio had in Argentina. A third reason has to do with the political circumstances in Argentina. In 1983, rule by the military junta collapsed and was replaced by a democratically elected government. Fr. Kolvenbach judged that the time was right for a more hard-edged social critique to emerge among the Argentine Jesuits, along the lines offered by CIAS (see Piqué, "Toward the Exile" [chap. 7], in *Pope Francis, Life and Revolution*, 83–93).

31. The provincial superior who was appointed in 1986 began introducing controversial changes. These changes were unpopular with many Jesuits in the province, most of whom were young and had known Bergoglio either as provincial superior or rector of the Colegio Máximo. They expressed their displeasure by electing Bergoglio to travel to Rome as a representative of the province of Argentina for a "Procurators Congregation" held in Rome in 1987. Fr. Kolvenbach was reported to be not pleased by the election of Bergoglio, and this gesture of protest by Bergoglio's fellow province members had negligible effect. See Piqué, *Pope Francis, Life and Revolution*, 84–93; Ivereigh, *The Great Reformer*, 165–209; Vallely, *Pope Francis*, 57–60.

32. Pope Francis, interview with Antonio Spadaro, "Intervista a Papa Francesco," *La Civiltà Cattolica*, 3918 (year 164), September 19, 2013, 449–77, at 457–58 (republished as Antonio Spadaro, ed., *A Big Heart Open to God* [New York: HarperCollins, 2013]). While this statement includes a remarkable expression of psychological insight, it is also significant at a theological level. Bergoglio suggests that some of his opponents misunderstood him to be "ultraconservative." He implies that, despite his twelve years of implementing a vision based on a theology of the people, certain critics were so caught in a left-wing, rationalist horizon that they could not recognize how he was employing a method that differed from both options. His statement also implies that while his years of suffering prompted deepening at various levels, they did not cause him to change his theological outlook.

33. Bergoglio's devotion to Our Lady Untier of Knots derives from a visit he spent to a church in Germany in 1986, where he saw a painting of this image of the Blessed Mother. See Piqué, *Pope Francis, Life and Revolution*, 91–93; and Ivereigh, *The Great Reformer*, 197–201.

34. Borghesi offers a helpful account of Bergoglio's theological deepening during his Cordoba years. Borghesi suggests that, during his Cordoba years, Bergoglio deepened his understanding of one of his four dictums: "unity is more important than conflict." Borghesi, "La teoria dell'opposizione polare, Bergoglio e Romano Guardini," in *Jorge Mario Bergoglio, Una Biografia Intellettuale*, 197–98.

35. Piqué, *Pope Francis, Life and Revolution*, 96.

36. George Weigel describes how Pope John Paul II intervened in the governance of the Jesuits in 1981, imposing his own delegate as general superior, because of his concern about such left-wing tendencies (*Witness to Hope*, 353–55). See also Kevin Burke, "Introduction," in *Pedro Arrupe: Essential Writings* (Maryknoll, NY: Orbis Books, 2004).

37. See Piquè, "The Return to Buenos Aires," in *Pope Francis, Life and Revolution*, 95–103. See also Ivereigh, *The Great Reformer*, 220–21.

38. Ivereigh, *The Great Reformer*, 228.

39. Piqué, "A Different Sort of Archbishop," in *Pope Francis, Life and Revolution*, 105–24; Vallely, "The Bishop of the Slums," in *Pope Francis*, 95–126; and Ivereigh, *The Great Reformer*, 230–32.

40. Ivereigh, *The Great Reformer*, 232. See also Piqué, *Pope Francis, Life and Revolution*, 105–24.

41. Jorge Bergoglio, *Diálogos entre Juan Pablo II y Fidel Castro* (Buenos Aires: Cuidad, 1998).

42. Ivereigh, *The Great Reformer*, 238.

43. Archbishops recognized that a key opportunity for commentary on political affairs was the national feast day, May 25. Here, it was the custom for a *Te Deum* Mass to be celebrated by the archbishop of Buenos Aires that was attended by the president and his cabinet. Historically, these had been little more than formulaic events where representatives of church and state celebrated their joint importance in Argentine society. Under Archbishop Bergoglio, the homilies during these events became thinly veiled criticisms of current government policies. Commentators noted that so vehement were the homilies of Bergoglio that President Menem and his cabinet eventually stopped attending the *Te Deum* masses. Vallely, *Pope Francis*, 113; Ivereigh, *The Great Reformer*, 250.

44. On Bergoglio's interaction with the Kirchner governments, see Piqué, *Pope Francis, Life and Revolution*, 137–42; Vallely, *Pope Francis*, 113–20; Ivereigh, *The Great Reformer*, 265–68.

45. Ivereigh, *The Great Reformer*, 246–47.

46. Ivereigh, *The Great Reformer*, 217–18, 271.

47. Ivereigh, *The Great Reformer*, 311.

48. Ivereigh, *The Great Reformer*, 252. See also: "The Karlic-Bergoglio policy of critical distance from the government and the bishop's consistent denunciation of the neoliberal, borrow-and-spend policies that had brought on the crisis were part of the reason for the Church's popularity" (ibid., 268). For a wider discussion of Bergoglio's thinking on economics, see Borghesi, "Un Mondo Senza Legami: Il Primato Dell'Economia nell'era della Globalizzazione," in *Jorge Mario Bergoglio, Una Biografia Intellettuale*, 193–221; William Werpehowski, "The Social Vision of the Joy of the Gospel: Four Questions," in *Pope Francis and the Future of Catholicism: Evangelii Gaudium and the Papal Agenda*, ed. Gerard Mannion (Cambridge: Cambridge University Press, 2017), 125–42; Mary Doak, "Evangelization in an Economy of Death," in Mannion, *Pope Francis and the Future of Catholicism*, 179–202.

49. See Piquè, "Clerical and Political Adversaries," in *Pope Francis, Life and Revolution*, 125–42.

50. Ivereigh, *The Great Reformer*, 231, 342.

51. See a sociological analysis of the relevance of Pope Francis for institutional reform in the church in Rocco D'Ambrosio, *Will Pope Francis Pull It Off? The Challenge of Church Reform* (Collegeville, MN: Liturgical Press, 2016).

52. Bergoglio always distinguished between problems he was having with Vatican officials and his opinion of the pope. At a time of conflict, during the pontificate of Benedict XVI, one commentator stresses that Archbishop Bergoglio continued to hold Cardinal Ratzinger in high regard. See Victor Manuel Fernández, "Bergoglio a Secas," *Vida Pastoral*, "El Programa de un Pontificado," Edition 318, June 2013, http://www.sanpablo.com.ar/vidapastoral/revista.php?edicion=318. See further discussion below.

53. Piqué, *Pope Francis, Life and Revolution*, 126 (parentheses added). Piqué adds that she was contacted by an Argentine "bishop of the conservative anti-Bergoglio group" and threatened with having her permanent accreditation to the Vatican Press office rescinded because she was writing of the existence of a conservative anti-Bergoglio group among the bishops (ibid., 130)!

54. Piqué, *Pope Francis, Life and Revolution*, 131.

55. Fernández (my translation from the Spanish), quoted partially in Piqué, *Pope Francis, Life and Revolution*, 132.

8. POPE FRANCIS AND THEOLOGICAL METHOD

1. See Massimo Borghesi, "Chiesa e Modernità: Methol Ferré e il Risorgimento Cattolico in America Latina," in *Jorge Mario Bergoglio: Una biografia intellettuale* (Milan: Jaca Book, 2017), 155–92. See also Austen Ivereigh, *The Great Reformer: Francis and the Making of a Radical Pope* (New York: Henry Holt and Company, 2014), 106, 185, 220, 233–38, 285, 296, 301, 347. Finally, Methol Ferré gave a book-length interview before his death in 2009, in which he speaks about his friendship with Cardinal Bergoglio. Alver Metalli, ed., *El Papa y el filósofo* (Buenos Aires: Editorial Biblos, 2013).

2. Ivereigh, *The Great Reformer*, 234.

3. See Borghesi, *Jorge Mario Bergoglio, Una Biografia Intellettuale*, 162–71; and Ivereigh, *The Great Reformer*, 234–35.

4. Borghesi, "L'ateismo libertino e la critica della società opulenta," in *Jorge Mario Bergoglio, Una Biografia Intellettuale*, 184–92.

5. Ivereigh, *The Great Reformer*, 234.

6. Ivereigh, *The Great Reformer*, 230–37.

7. Ivereigh, *The Great Reformer*, 296.

8. Ivereigh, *The Great Reformer*, 257–60.

9. The appointment of Bergoglio to this role had occurred suddenly when the previously elected rapporteur, Cardinal Dolan of New York, had to return home suddenly after the bombing of the Twin Towers, September 11, 2001.

10. Ivereigh, *The Great Reformer*, 258–65.

11. Ivereigh, *The Great Reformer*, 284. The proceedings of the conclave that elected Pope Benedict XVI are supposed to be confidential, but commentators agree that leaks to newspapers resulted in the emergence of an accurate account of what happened.

12. Ivereigh, *The Great Reformer*, 288.

13. Elisabetta Piqué, *Pope Francis, Life and Revolution: A Biography of Jorge Bergoglio*, trans. Anna Mazzotti and Lydia Colin (Chicago: Loyola Press, 2014), 127–29; Ivereigh, *The Great Reformer*, 284. See also 294–301.

14. For an account of Bergoglio's activities at Aparecida, see Piqué, *Pope Francis, Life and Revolution*, 134–37.

15. Ivereigh, *The Great Reformer*, 299, quoting an interview with Fernández published in the journal *Clarin*, October 27, 2013.

16. See Robert Pelton, "Medellín and Puebla, Dead or Alive?" and Jose Marins, "Base Communities, a Return to Inductive Methodology" in Robert S. Pelton, ed., *Aparecida: Quo Vadis?* (Scranton, PA: Scranton University Press, 2008); also Carlos María Galli, "El 'retorno' del Pueblo de Dios misionero. Un concepto-símbolo de la eclesiología del Concilio a Francisco," in *La Eclesiologia del Concilio Vaticano II*, ed. V. R. Azcuy, J. C. Camano, and C. M. Galli (Buenos Aires: Agape Libros, 2016).

17. CELAM, *Aparecida Final Document*, 19. Available online at http://directoriocatolico.blogspot.it/2013/07/pdf-documento-docu ment-aparecida-celam.html.

18. *Aparecida Final Document*, 85, 87, 125, 471–74. Kevin W. Irwin, *A Commentary on* Laudato Si': *Examining the Background, Contributions, Implementation, and Future of Pope Francis's Encyclical* (Mahwah, NJ: Paulist Press, 2016), 37–39, documents the references to ecological themes in the Aparecida document in a discussion of how the ecological awareness of Pope Francis was formed.

19. *Aparecida Final Document*, 398.

20. *Aparecida Final Document*, 479.

21. *Aparecida Final Document*, 509–11.

22. *Aparecida Final Document*, 14.

23. Ivereigh, *The Great Reformer*, 300.

24. *Aparecida Final Document*, 258–65.

25. *Aparecida Final Document*, 36. In fact, several non-Argentine liberation theologians of the generation of the 1960s and 1970s expressed gratitude for this delicate turn of phrase in Aparecida. Prominent among these was Gustavo Gutiérrez, who accepted some self-criticism and accepted that his ideas had evolved over the course of the decades since the 1970s (Pelton, *Aparecida: Quo Vadis?*, 71–92).

26. Ivereigh, *The Great Reformer*, 300.

27. See Massimo Faggioli, *Pope Francis: Tradition in Transition* (Mahwah, NJ: Paulist Press, 2013), 22–28, 44–46, 63–64.

28. Before and during the conclave of 2013, the San Gallen group, mentioned in the previous chapter, moved into action again. Representatives of the group made sure to inform Bergoglio that they were proposing that cardinals vote for him. This time, the work of the group was made easier by a generalized conviction among cardinals that a major reform of the curia was needed. See Faggioli, *Pope Francis: Tra-*

dition in Transition, 1–8. See also the memoirs of an English cardinal who helped communicate the perspective of the San Gallen group to cardinals of Africa and Asia: Cardinal Cormac Murphy O'Connor, *An English Spring: Memoirs* (London: Bloomsbury, 2015).

29. Ivereigh, *The Great Reformer*, 365.

30. Piqué, "Deep-Seated Changes" (chap. 14), in *Pope Francis, Life and Revolution.*

31. Massimo Faggioli, *Pope Francis: Tradition in Transition*, 47. Another important analysis of the significance of Pope Francis for ecclesiology is *La Riforma a le riforme nella Chiesa*, ed. Antonio Spadaro and Carlos María Galli (Rome: Queriniana, 2016).

32. In an article, "Pope Francis and the Eight Cardinal Advisors," James Corkery, SJ, points to parallels between the practice of a Jesuit provincial having a group of consultors like this and the governance style of Pope Francis. *Thinking Faith*, September 30, 2013, http://www .thinkingfaith.org/articles/20130930_1.htm.

33. Strictly speaking, Pope Francis also produced an encyclical *Lumen Fidei* on the theme of the Christian faith. However, he acknowledged that this had been almost entirely written by Pope Benedict XVI. It completed a set of encyclicals that had also treated the other theological virtues: *Deus Caritas Est* (on charity) and *Spes Salvi* (on hope).

34. See Gerard Mannion, "Pope Francis's Agenda for the Church— *Evangelii Gaudium* as Papal Manifesto," in *Pope Francis and the Future of Catholicism*, 1–19. What is distinctive about Pope Francis is his theological method, and this book focuses the agenda of Pope Francis under three related areas: ecclesiological dimensions, the social justice agenda, and dialogical and global agenda (12).

35. Pope Francis, address to the bishops of Brazil, Rio de Janeiro, July 27, 2013, http://w2.vatican.va/content/francesco/en/speeches/ 2013/july/documents/papa-francesco_20130727_gmg-episcopato -brasile.html. One commentator goes so far as to suggest that the address of the pope to the World Youth Day audience at Rio de Janeiro represents also a kind of manifesto for the Francis papacy and deserves to be of magisterial importance equivalent to an encyclical. Gianfranco Brunelli, "L'enciclica di Rio," quoted in Faggioli, *Pope Francis: Tradition in Transition*, 48.

36. Carlos Maria Galli, "La Riforma missionaria della chiesa secondo Francesco: L'ecclesiologia del Popolo di Dio evangelizzatore," in *La Riforma e le riforme nella chiesa*, ed. Antonio Spadaro and Carlos Galli

(Rome: Quereniana, 2016), 37–65, at 48–49 (my translation from the Italian).

37. Carlos María Galli, "El 'retorno' del Pueblo de Dios misionero. Un concepto-símbolo de la eclesiología del Concilio a Francisco."

38. Allan Figueroa Deck, *Francis, Bishop of Rome: The Gospel for the Third Millennium* (Mahwah, NJ: Paulist Press, 2015); Kevin Irwin, *A Commentary on* Laudato Si', 37–39.

39. Joe Ware, "COP21: *Laudato Si'* a Major Talking Point at Climate Change Talks in Paris," *The Tablet*, December 6, 2015, http://www.thetablet.co.uk/news/2885/cop21-laudato-si-a-major-talking-point-at-climate-change-talks-in-paris.

40. Irwin offers a careful analysis of the encyclical document. See Kevin Irwin, "Contributions" (chap. 2), in *A Commentary on* Laudato Si'. See also René Micallef, "*Laudato Si'* e la sua metodologia: Un critico ascolto delle scienze empiriche?" in *Laudato Si': Linee di lettura interdisciplinari per la cura della casa comune* (G&B Press, 2017), 13–48.

41. Regarding the scientific accuracy of *Laudato Si'*, see Celia Dean Drummond, "*Laudato Si'* and the Natural Sciences, Possibilities and Limits," *Theological Studies* 77, no. 2 (June 2016): 392–415.

42. Michael Northcott offers an overview of the debates between biocentric and "moderately anthropocentric" arguments within ecological ethics in *The Environment and Christian Ethics* (Cambridge: Cambridge University Press, 1996). Essentially, the term *biocentrism* is associated with the thought of Robert Lanza, "A New Theory of the Universe: Biocentrism Builds on Quantum Physics by Putting Life into the Question," *Science*, Spring 2007. However, the term can also describe a wider set of arguments sometimes called "ecocentric." An example is the "deep ecology movement": cf. A. Naess, "The Shallow and the Deep, Long-Range Ecology Movement," *Inquiry* 16 (1973): 95–100. A prominent current critic of biocentrism is the physicist D. L. Krauss, "Exclusive: Response to Robert Lanza's Essay," accessed July 2018, https://usatoday30.usatoday.com/tech/science/2007-03-09-lanza-response_N.htm. Broader expressions of moderate anthropocentrism in secular debate include John Arthur Passmore, *Man's Responsibility for Nature* (New York: Scribner, 1974); William Grey, "Anthropocentrism and Deep Ecology," *Australasian Journal of Philosophy* 71, no. 4 (1993): 463–75; Mortimer J. Adler, *The Difference of Man and the Difference It Makes* (New York: Fordham University Press, 1993). A Lonergan-based engagement with the ecological ethics debate

is found in Cynthia Crysdale and Neil Ormerod, *Creator God, Evolving World* (Minneapolis: Fortress Press, 2013).

43.   Pope Francis concludes the encyclical with a similarly sacramental insight: "We take charge of this home which has been entrusted to us, knowing that all the good which exists here will be taken up into the heavenly feast. In union with all creatures, we journey through this land seeking God" (no. 244). Irwin stresses the value of the sacramental vision of *Laudato Si'* (Irwin, *A Commentary on* Laudato Si', viii).

44.   Neil Ormerod and Christina Vanin link the "moderate anthropocentrism" of Pope Francis to the thought of Bernard Lonergan in "Ecological Conversion: What Does It Mean?" *Theological Studies* 77, no. 2 (June 2016): 328–52.

45.   It should be noted that a concern for the environment—especially that of the Amazon basin—is expressed in the Aparecida document, of which Bergoglio was the primary author. The fact that he was deeply impressed by the importance of this issue is testified to by his convoking the Synod of Bishops of the Pan-Amazon region, scheduled for October 2019.

46.   Robert M. Doran, *Theology and the Dialectics of History* (Toronto: University of Toronto Press, 1990), 6. Doran adds, "Moments of genuine philosophy, so rare in history and even in the lives of those gifted with them…[that they] cannot be sustained or incrementally realized without what Christian theology has called grace; and so theology, by objectifying as best it can the ever elusive mystery of divine grace, functions foundationally in the understanding of the human" (ibid., 7).

9. THE TEST OF A PAPACY

1.   The lecture that Walter Kasper gave to the consistory of cardinals in February 2014 was leaked to the press. It is available online at http://chiesa.espresso.repubblica.it/articolo/1350729bdc4.html?eng =y (accessed November 21, 2018).

2.   Pope Francis, Opening Address to the Extraordinary General Assembly of the Synod of the Bishops on the Family, October 29, 2014, accessed July 25, 2018, http://w2.vatican.va/content/francesco/en/speeches/2014/october/documents/papa-francesco_20141006_padri-sinodali.html.

3.   Thomas Reese, "How the Synod Process Is Different under Pope Francis," *National Catholic Reporter*, October 17, 2014, accessed

January 2018, https://www.ncronline.org/blogs/faith-and-justice/how-synod-process-different-under-pope-francis.

4. Shortly before the 2015 synod, a group of thirteen cardinals wrote a letter to the pope protesting about the organization of the synod and requesting greater control over it. This letter, initially private, was leaked to the press. Francis was not pleased with this letter and struck a more admonishing note in his opening address to the synod of 2015 than he had with the previous synod. He stated, "The Synod is not a parliament in which to reach a consensus or a common accord by taking recourse to negotiation, to deal-making, or to compromise: indeed, the only method of the Synod is to open oneself up to the Holy Spirit with apostolic courage, with evangelical humility and confident, trusting prayer." Pope Francis, Opening Address to the General Assembly of the Ordinary Synod of the Bishops on October 5, 2015, accessed November 21, 2018, http://w2.vatican.va/content/francesco/en/speeches/2015/october/documents/papa-francesco_20151005_padri-sinodali.html.

5. *Amoris Laetitia* has begun to stimulate a wide range of comment in moral theology circles. See, e.g., James T. Bretzke, "In Good Conscience: What *Amoris Laetitia* Can Teach Us about Responsible Decision Making," *America*, April 8, 2016. Available online under the title "There Are Few, if Any, Simple 'Recipes' for What Following a Formed and Informed Conscience Looks Like" at http://americamagazine.org/issue/article/good-conscience (accessed November 21, 2018); and Conor M. Kelly, "The Role of the Moral Theologian in the Church: A Proposal in Light of *Amoris Laetitia*," *Theological Studies* 77, no. 4 (2016): 922–48.

6. This argument about being creatures and not omnipotent echoes *Laudato Si'*, nos. 1, 124, 244.

7. The fact that Schönborn would offer enthusiastic support for the exhortation surprised some. Joseph Ratzinger had directed his doctoral dissertation and Pope John Paul II had appointed him as general editor of *The Catechism of the Catholic Church*.

8. See also "Conversazione con il cardinale Schönborn su *Amoris Laetitia*," interview with Antonio Spadaro, SJ, *La Civiltà Cattolica* 3986, vol. 3 (July 23, 2016): 130–52.

9. Significantly, on April 16, 2016, Pope Francis gave an interview to journalists on the return flight from visiting migrants on the island of Lesbos, a Greek island in the northern Aegean Sea. A journalist from the *Wall Street Journal* asked him "whether or not there has been any change in the discipline concerning reception of the sacraments by

the divorced and remarried." The pope answered, "I could say 'yes' and leave it at that. But that would be too brief a response. I recommend that all of you read the presentation made by Cardinal Schönborn, a great theologian. He is a member of the Congregation for the Doctrine of the Faith and he knows the Church's teaching very well. Your question will find its answer in that presentation."

10. The *Acta Apostolica Sedis* for 2016 is published on the Vatican website. The document of the Argentine bishops and the response of Pope Francis is posted on pages 1071–72 and is available online at http://www.vatican.va/archive/aas/documents/2016/acta-ottobre2016 .pdf (accessed November 21, 2018).

11. Comments that are largely negative about *Amoris Laetitia* include the following: in April 2016, two voices in Germany offer a public rebuke to the pope: Robert Spaemann, a philosopher and friend of Pope Benedict and Bishop Athanasius Schneider; in June, Austrian philosopher and friend of Pope John Paul II, Josef Seifert; in August, a signed letter by forty-five theologians sent to the dean of the College of Cardinals; in September, four cardinals submit a "dubia" letter to Pope Francis, Raymond Burke, Walter Brandmüller, Joachim Meisner, and Carlo Caffarra; in November, the dubia letter is released to the public; in December, former members of the International Theological Commission, Germain Grisez and John Finnis, publish an article; in December and in the early months of 2017, various cardinals and bishops make statements in support of the dubia letter.

12. Walter Kasper, "*Amoris Laetitia*, Bruch oder Aufbruch?" *Stimmen der Seit*, November 2016, 723–32 (I quote from this article offering my own English translation); Stephan Goertz and Caroline Witting, eds., *Amoris Laetitia: Wendepunkt für die Moraltheologie?* (Frieburg im Breisgau, Germany: Verlag Herder, 2016).

13. John Finnis and Germain Grisez, "The Misuse of *Amoris Laetitia* to Support Errors against the Catholic Faith: A Letter to the Supreme Pontiff Francis, to All Bishops in Communion with Him, and to the Rest of the Christian Faithful," accessed November 21, 2018, http://www.twotlj.org/OW-MisuseAL.pdf. John Finnis is a professor of philosophy at Oxford. He was a member of the International Theological Commission, 1986–91, as well as the Pontifical Academy for Life, until he was removed from this role by Pope Francis in 2016. Grisez, from French Canada, is widely considered to have influenced the encyclical of John Paul II on moral theology, *Veritatis Splendor*. Like Finnis, he was

a member of the Pontifical Academy for Life until he was let go by Pope Francis.

14. Remarkably, Finnis and Grisez also speak directly to the bishops of the world, recommending that, if Pope Francis should fail to act against the eight erroneous readings of *Amoris Laetitia*, "in fulfilling your responsibility to the whole church," the bishops should "join us in our request to Pope Francis and yourselves condemn the eight positions dealt with above." In effect, Finnis and Grisez call for a polite rebellion against the pope by an alliance of the bishops of the world! Finnis and Grisez, "The Misuse of *Amoris Laetitia*," 1.

15. Finnis and Grisez, "The Misuse of *Amoris Laetitia*," 2.

16. For a study of moral reasoning that resembles the approach of Lonergan and engages with both John Finnis and Germain Grisez, see Mark Graham, *Josef Fuchs on Natural Law* (Washington, DC: Georgetown University Press, 2002). See also John Thomas Noonan: *A Church that Can and Cannot Change: The Development of Catholic Moral Thinking* (South Bend, IN: University of Notre Dame Press, 2005); Albert Jonsen, Stephen Toulmin et al., *The Abuse of Casuistry: A History of Moral Reasoning* (Los Angeles: University of California Press, 1988).

17. Walter Kasper, "*Amoris Laetitia*, Bruch oder Aufbruch?" *Stimmen der Seit*, November 2016, 723–32 (English translation of the quotations from this article are the author's).

18. Kasper, "*Amoris Laetitia*, Bruch oder Aufbruch?," 724.

19. Kasper, "*Amoris Laetitia*, Bruch oder Aufbruch?," 725–26.

20. Kasper, "*Amoris Laetitia*, Bruch oder Aufbruch?," 725.

21. Kasper also points to other themes in Thomas that support the same approach as that of treating doctrine as a final cause: the difference between speculative and practical reason, and the virtue of prudence. (Kasper, "*Amoris Laetitia*, Bruch oder Aufbruch?," section, "Reflections on Thomas Aquinas," 725–29.)

22. On the issue of diverse readings of Aquinas, including "incommensurable interpretations," see Fergus Kerr, *After Aquinas: Versions of Thomism* (Oxford: Blackwell Publishing, 2002).

23. Lonergan entered deeply into the question of how to interpret Aquinas. He explains that he underwent an "eleven-year apprenticeship to Thomas Aquinas," before being ready to write *Insight* (he used the term in a letter to Frederick Crowe in 1980, quoted in Frederick E. Crowe, *Lonergan* [Collegeville, MN: The Liturgical Press, 1992], 6). This apprenticeship culminated in Lonergan publishing *Verbum: Word*

and Idea in Thomas Aquinas, Collected Works of Bernard Lonergan, vol. 2, ed. Frederick Crowe and Robert M. Doran (Toronto: University of Toronto Press, 1997). In this work, he criticizes perceptualist readings of the medieval doctor. However, he also suggests that Aquinas is only implicitly intellectually converted, and that the modern philosopher needs to make this step explicit. This insight would prompt him to write *Insight: A Study in Human Understanding*. In the years after writing *Method in Theology*, he wrote frequently of the need for theology today to "transpose" the thought of Aquinas; see Lonergan, "The Future of Thomism," in *A Second Collection*, Collected Works of Bernard Lonergan, vol. 13, ed. Robert M. Doran and John D. Dadosky, 2nd ed. (Toronto: University of Toronto Press, 2016), 43–54, and "Horizons and Transpositions" in *Philosophical and Theological Papers, 1965–1980*, Collected Works of Bernard Lonergan, vol. 17, ed. Robert C. Croken and Robert M. Doran (Toronto: University of Toronto Press, 2004), 409–32.

24. Lonergan, "Sacralization and Secularization," in *Philosophical and Theological Papers, 1965–1980*, 280.

CONCLUSION: BEYOND THE PONTIFICATE OF FRANCIS

1. From an article by Walter Kasper appearing in *L'Osservatore Romano* April 11, 2013, quoted in Dennis M. Doyle, "Pope Francis's New Vision for the Church as Expressed in *Evangelii Gaudium*," in *Pope Francis and the Future of Catholicism: Evangelii Gaudium and the Papal Agenda*, ed. Gerard Mannion (Cambridge: Cambridge University Press, 2017), 35–36.

2. Robert M. Doran, *Theology and the Dialectics of History* (Toronto: University of Toronto Press, 1990), 8.

3. Doran, *What Is Systematic Theology?* (Toronto: University of Toronto Press, 2005), 200. See also *Theology and the Dialectics of History*, 422–23.

4. John Courtney Murray, "Information and the Church: The Function of the Catholic Press within the Catholic Church," quoted in J. L. Hooper, *The Ethics of Discourse: The Social Philosophy of John Courtney Murray* (Washington, DC: Georgetown University Press, 1986), 181–82. The bluntness of Murray's expression is much criticized

by Hooper, who, by the way, does not share Murray's enthusiasm for Lonergan (Hooper, *Ethics of Discourse*, chap. 6).

5. John Courtney Murray, "Freedom, Authority, Community," *America*, 115 (December 3, 1966), 734–41. See also Hooper, *Ethics of Discourse*, 183–86.

6. John Courtney Murray, "Freedom, Authority, Community," 734. See also Lonergan's explanation of community in terms of constitutive meaning (*Method in Theology*, Collected Works of Bernard Lonergan, vol. 12, ed. Robert M. Doran and John D. Dadosky [Toronto: University of Toronto Press, 2017 {first published 1972}], 76–78). Murray implies that unless laypeople feel they have been authentically consulted before bishops make decisions, there will emerge problems at the level of reception of doctrine.

7. The term *reconciled diversity* is often used in ecumenical circles; see "Vigil of Pentecost and Ecumenical Prayer with Pope Francis," June 3, 2017, accessed November 22, 2018, https://press.vatican.va/content/salastampa/en/bollettino/pubblico/2017/06/03/170603g.html. See also Catherine E. Clifford, "Lonergan's Contribution to Ecumenism," *Theological Studies* 63, no. 3 (2002): 521–38.

8. Pope Francis, *Laudato Si'*. These five areas of dialogue form the subheadings of chap. 6.

9. Lonergan speaks of proportionate being as all that we are capable of knowing by direct acts of insight and judgment. He contrasts this with transcendent being (God), the existence of which we can only deduce by analogy with references to our acts of knowledge of contingent, proportionate, being. See *Insight: A Study of Human Understanding*, Collected Works of Bernard Lonergan, vol. 3, ed. Frederick E. Crowe and Robert M. Doran, 5th ed. (Toronto: University of Toronto Press, 1992), "The Notion of Being" (chap. 12), and "General Transcendent Knowledge" (chap. 19).

10. Lonergan, *Insight*, introduction, 22.

11. On general empirical method, see *Insight*, "Heuristic Structures of Empirical Method" (chap. 2) and "The Complementarity of Classical and Statistical Investigations" (chap. 4). On the application of generalized empirical method to a heuristic study of human history, see "Common Sense as Object" (chap. 7) and "Special Transcendent Knowledge" (chap. 20), especially discussions of "The Heuristic Structure of the Solution," 718–24, 740–52. On helping curb the "totalitarian ambitions" of academics, see *Method in Theology*, "Functional Specialization" (chap. 5), 131. In

this later book, Lonergan relates a notion of emergent probability to the use of functional specialties. While his focus is primarily the use of these in theology, he states that functional specialties can be used in each of the social sciences.

12. Lonergan, *Healing and Creating in History, A Third Collection* (Mahwah, NJ: Paulist Press, 1985), 100–109, at 107.

13. See Michael Shute, *Lonergan's Discovery of the Science of Economics* (Toronto: University of Toronto Press, 2010).

14. See Ann Marie Dalton, *A Theology for the Earth: Contributions of Thomas Berry and Bernard Lonergan* (Ottawa: University of Ottawa Press, 1999); Cynthia Crysdale and Neil Ormerod, *Creator God Evolving World* (Minneapolis: Fortress Press, 2013).

15. Lonergan, *Healing and Creating in History*, 108.

Index

Abelard, 30

Acta Apostolica Sedis, 153

Ad extra mission of church, 57, 60, 64–66, 69, 79, 87, 141, 146, 164–67

Ad Gentes Divinitus (on missionary activity), 61

Ad intra mission of church, 56–57, 60, 79, 146, 163–64

Aeterni Patris, 47, 49

Affectivity, 13

Aggiornamento, 52–53

Amoris Laetitia: *ad intra* mission of church and, 146, 163; contents, 148–52; controversy provoked by, 152–53; criticism of, 154–56; defense of, 156–59; Finnis and, 154–56; Francis and, 135, 145–54; Grisez and, 154–56; impact of, 153; inductive method in, 149–52; issues addressed in, 146; Kasper and, 156–59; overview, 146; publication of, 148; reception of, 152–53;

See-Judge-Act process in, 149–52; Synods of Bishops and, 147–48

Amoris Laetitia: A Leap forward for Moral Theology?, 153

Ancient Greece, 21

Aparecida CELAM meeting and document (2007), 87, 107–8, 131–34, 136–37, 141, 147

Apostolicam Actuositatem (on the apostolate of the laity), 61

Apostolica Sollicitudo, 63

Apostolos Suos (On the Theological and Juridical Nature of Episcopal Conferences), 85

Aquinas, Thomas, 8, 22–23, 30, 36, 45, 47, 49, 68, 100

Argentine Jesuits, 113–14

Aristotelian philosophy, 23, 40

Aristotle, 36, 100, 144

Arrupe, Pedro, 114

Augustine of Hippo, 22, 80

Augustinian school, 84

Baldisseri, Lorenzo, 147
Baptism, 139
Bea, Augustine, 45, 56
Beauduin, Dom Lambert, 45
Being, notion of, 29
Benedictines, 42–43
Benedict XVI, Pope: *Evangelii
Gaudium* and, 136; Francis's
shift in style from, 1;
liberation theology and,
106–7; preferential option for
the poor and, 107; resignation
of, 134–35; right and, solid,
72, 74–75; Vatican II and, 72,
86–89
Bergoglio, Jorge: adolescence
of, 109–10; Aparecida
CELAM meeting and, 107–
8, 131–34, 141; birth of, 108;
centralization of church and,
124–25; childhood of, 109;
at Colegio Máximo,
111–12, 116; Cordoba years
of, 116–17; Cuba visit by,
119; culture of encounter
and, 117; deductive method
and, 125; economic recession
in Argentina and, 120–22;
family of, 109; Fernández and,
124; Ferré and, 126–29, 131;
God's plan and, 115; inductive
method and, 3; international
profile of, 129–31; Jesuits in
Argentina and, 113–16;
Jesuit training of, 108,
111–12; John Paul II and,
118–19, 123; Kirchner
governments and, 120–
22; local concerns of, 126;

mandates of as pope, 135;
Marxism and, 113–14,
119–20, 125; Menem and,
118–20; neoliberalism and,
117–22, 125; ordainment
of, 3, 16; papal election of,
129, 135; Peronism and,
109–10; *Proyecto de pais*
(country project) and, 121–22;
ressourcement theology and,
112; reversal of policies of,
116–17; *Spiritual Exercises of
St. Ignatius* and, 15, 111–12,
114–15; theological identity
of, 108–12, 125; Vatican
curia's politics and opposition
to, 122–26, 130–31; Vatican II
and, 3–4, 89; "Vatileaks" and,
134–35. *See also* Francis,
Pope
Bernard of Clairvaux, 30
Bias of perceptualism: decline in
the second stage of meaning
and, 29–31; historical
consciousness and, 28–33;
Lonergan's view of, 28–29,
74–75; in modern philosophy,
31–32; in postmodern
philosophy, 32–33; resistance
to modernity and, 36
Bible, 43–44, 60, 97–98
Biblicum, 44
Black week (*la settimana
nera*), 63
Boff, Leonardo, 98
Bonaventure, 30, 81
Buddhism, 65
Butterfield, Herbert, 24–25,
36, 48